Fifth Dimensional Operations:

Space-Time-Cyber Dimensionality in Conflict and War

Fifth Dimensional Operations:

Space-Time-Cyber Dimensionality in Conflict and War—

A Terrorism Research Center Book

ROBERT J. BUNKER AND
CHARLES "SID" HEAL, EDITORS

FIFTH DIMENSIONAL OPERATIONS:
SPACE-TIME-CYBER DIMENSIONALITY IN CONFLICT AND WAR—
A TERRORISM RESEARCH CENTER BOOK

iUniverse books may be ordered through booksellers or by contacting:

iUniverse LLC
1663 Liberty Drive
Bloomington, IN 47403
www.iuniverse.com
1-800-Authors (1-800-288-4677)

ISBN: 978-1-4917-3872-6 (sc)
ISBN: 978-1-4917-3873-3 (e)

Printed in the United States of America.

iUniverse rev. date: 07/01/2014

Also by Robert J. Bunker

Non-State Threats and Future Wars (editor)
Networks, Terrorism and Global Insurgency (editor)
Criminal-States and Criminal-Soldiers (editor)
Narcos Over the Border: Gangs, Cartels and Mercenaries (editor)
Red Teams and Counterterrorism Training (with Steven Sloan)
Mexico's Criminal Insurgency (primary author; with John P. Sullivan)
Criminal Insurgencies in Mexico and the Americas: The Gangs and Cartels Wage War (editor)
Mexican Cartel Essays and Notes: Strategic, Operational, and Tactical (primary author)
Body Cavity Bombers: The New Martyrs (primary author; with Chris Flaherty)
Studies in Gangs and Cartels (with John P. Sullivan)

Also by Charles "Sid" Heal

Sound Doctrine: A Tactical Primer
An Illustrated Guide to Tactical Diagramming: How to Determine Floor Plans from Outside Architectural Features
Field Command

About the Terrorism Research Center

The Terrorism Research Center (TRC) is non-profit think tank focused on investigating and researching global terrorism issues through multi-disciplinary collaboration amongst a group of international experts. Originally founded as a commercial entity in 1996, the TRC was an independent institute dedicated to the research of terrorism, information warfare and security, critical infrastructure protection, homeland security, and other issues of low-intensity political violence and gray-area phenomena. Over the course of 15 years, the TRC conducted research, analysis, and training on a wide range of counterterrorism and homeland security issues.

******

First established on April 19, 1996, the year anniversary of the Oklahoma City terrorist bombing, the TRC operated for 15 years as a commercial entity providing research, analysis, and training on issues of terrorism and international security.

The three original co-founders, Matthew Devost, Brian Houghton, and Neal Pollard, are reconstituting a new board of directors, comprised of researchers, first responders and academic and professional experts. "The TRC had an incredible legacy as a commercial company," says Matthew Devost. "We believe there is still a strong need to continue the research and collaboration on such critical topics in the public's best interest."

From 1996 through 2010, the TRC contributed to international counterterrorism and homeland security initiatives such as Project Responder and the Responder Knowledge Base, Terrorism Early Warning Groups, Project Pediatric Preparedness, Global Fusion Center, and the "Mirror Image" training program. These long-standing programs leveraged an international network of specialists from government, industry, and academia. Reconstituting TRC as a non-profit will help establish the next generation of programs, research, and training to combat the emerging international security issues.

"Thousands of researchers utilized the TRC knowledge base on a daily basis, says Brian Houghton. "Our intent is to open the dialog, provide valuable counterterrorism resources, and advance the latest thinking in counterterrorism for the public good."

"We want to put the 15-year legacy and goodwill of TRC to continuing benefit for the public, rather than focus on a specific business model," says Neal Pollard. "TRC was founded in the wake of the 1995 Oklahoma City bombing and made its most significant contributions to the nation and the world after the attacks of September 11, 2001. Now that the War on Terrorism has evolved and the United States is entering a new era of transnational threats, the TRC will maintain its familiar role as the vanguard of next-generation research into these emerging threats."

For more information visit www.terrorism.org

Contents

Introduction:
Fifth Dimensional Operations

Robert J. Bunker

The origins of this book can be traced back as early as June 1995 when I was reporting for *Military Review*, a U.S. Army Command and General Staff College journal, on an information warfare conference being held in Los Angeles, California. One of the themes presented was on data fusion which allowed for "...taking points or information concerning three-dimensional space and 'fusing the data' to image a target" [1]. I vividly remember being greatly excited with a pixel and periscope example during one of the presentations. If enough pixels (points) were identified in a scan across the waves in the ocean, the periscope of an opposing force's submarine could be identified—that which had been invisible became unmasked.

While those seated around me were most definitely not as elated as I was, a flash of insight immediately struck me—invisible, stealth masked forces could become uncloaked, acquired, and killed before retreating back from whence they came. Some sort of dimensional dynamic or boundary had to be in play between those forces that were invisible and those that were visible. This was of great significance for me because I had never been able to theoretically account for the presence of a terrorist, whom I considered to be an invisible criminal-soldier, on the modern battlefield—our definitions of battlespace were insufficient. Derived from the data fusion approach, facial recognition technology for instance, could pull a terrorist—an invisible force—out of the defensive dimension in which he or she resided in relative immunity from attack. This would take place by fusing the pixels of a known face via surveillance scans and picking the terrorist out of a much larger crowd of people in which he or she blended in. This new insight empowered me to begin to develop advanced—later 5th dimensional—battlespace constructs and concepts off and on now for almost twenty years.

This research was quickly incorporated into the older and more strategic vision of Fourth Epoch War theory that analyzed the shifts in human civilization in Western history from the Classical to the Medieval to the Modern and then into the Post-Modern epochs. This theory had earlier been developed in 1987 and then specifically refined in order to support U.S. national security efforts by myself and T. Lindsay Moore, one of my mentors and dissertation chair, who is also contributing to this book project. Sid Heal, my co-editor on this project, then joined me in these endeavors ever since my research presentations to him at the Emergency Operations Bureau, LA County Sheriff's Department and then, per his request, to the entire I Marine Expeditionary Force (I MEF), I Marine Air-Ground Task Force (MAGTF) Augmentation Command Element (I MACE) in March and April 1996, respectively. Additionally, if this book's long pedigree could not get anymore extensive, the writings on this subject of John Sullivan, who I first met at the April 1996 I MACE briefing are also highlighted in this book.

The reason that I mention the initial context and pedigree behind this book project is to provide the reader with an appreciation of how long some of the scholars and practitioners involved in 5th dimensional analysis have been thinking and experimenting with the constructs contained in this work. Along with this old guard of researchers, a more recent strata of contributors to this endeavor have emerged—Adam Elkus, initially an Occidental College undergraduate protégé of Dr. Sullivan; Lois Clark McCoy with the National Institute for Search and Rescue (NISUR), and Lois (Pilant) Grossman, then working with the National Institute of Justice (NIJ), both of whom had been exposed to these concepts by Sid Heal; Daniel Musa at the University of Southern California and Khirin Bunker at University of California Riverside who have served as research assistants to Robert Bunker; and Greta Andrusyszyn with the Army War College Library who had recently finished a cyberspace bibliography project and had met Robert Bunker in Carlisle at that military educational institution.

The involvement of Dr. Flaherty, on the other hand, came from a more oblique route. He had earlier worked on body cavity bomber research with Robert Bunker who then learned of Flaherty's much earlier 'defence work on nonlinearity, decentralised units, and rhizome manoeuvre.' Both of the editors of this book agree that his very creative research, especially on the rhizome tactic of entering through walls and ceilings—which ignored the traditional conventions of 3rd and 4th dimensional urban space—was independently drifting

2

towards 5th dimensional capabilities while yet devoid of the construct. For that reason, he was invited to join this project as a contributor with a couple of his earlier articles related to such dimensionality reprinted in this work.

With this background information and legacy in mind, this research project, *Fifth Dimensional Operations: Space-Time-Cyber Dimensionality in Conflict and War—A Terrorism Research Center Book*, is composed of this introduction, fourteen sections, a postscript, a symbol key and glossary, three appendices, and the biographies of the editors and the contributors. The work itself covers 5th dimensional writings on conflict and war beginning in 1996 through the Spring of 2014. This provides for an historical overview portraying the maturation of the theories and constructs related to it and their proposed, and in some instances actual, application in special policing, counter-terrorism, and military venues. The first sections of this book, through 1999, portray my developing ideas on this subject matter. From 2002 on, a number of scholars, professionals, and even some university research assistants, weigh in with new viewpoints and interpretations of fifth dimensional conflict and war. Of these individuals, the most significant contribution to this body of work by far has come from my co-editor Sid Heal who wrote Sections 6, 9, and 12 and the Postscript. He has been taking the constructs that I had initially developed and has been refining them and then utilizing them to train law enforcement and military personnel for many years now.

From a pure theoretical perspective, Section 8 by John Sullivan and Adam Elkus and part of Section 14 and Appendix 1 by T. Lindsay Moore must also be singled out as important contributions and commentary on 5th dimensional theory. Additionally, some of the pre-5th dimensional research of Chris Flaherty republished in this work also has great theoretical merit— rhizome manoeuvre via a hole punched through the ceiling of a barricaded room definitely has a 'dimensional bubble' sense of affinity to it. In these later sections, a number of my newer theoretical essays on this subject matter are also evident. Section 4 by Lois (Pilant) Grossman and Section 7 by Lois Clark McCoy on the other hand provide more descriptive contributions to this topical matter—essentially engaging in the important function of explaining the tactical benefits of 5th

dimensional ideas to practitioner audiences. Further, Appendix II by Khirin Bunker provides an overview of how modern military dimensionality definitions have evolved and Appendix III by Greta Andrusyszyn, Daniel Musa, and myself provide a cyberspace and dimensionality reference listing.

The target audience of this book project is U.S. military, law enforcement, and governmental personnel willing to explore 'out-of-the-box' thinking on dimensionality in conflict and war. While the work is full of space-time and cyber constructs and examples, it has an applied theory focus and is ultimately meant to stimulate creativity in order to further the development of new TTPs (tactics, techniques, and procedures) and CONOPS (concepts of operations) that can be applied by special policing, counter-terrorism, and military personnel. In this way, 5th dimensional principles can be developed and tested from the bottom up by U.S. forces and governmental bodies from the tactical to the operational and then eventually incorporated into the strategic and policy levels. This vision is not only shared by the co-editors and the contributors to this book but also by the Terrorism Research Center (TRC) which has graciously allowed us to publish this work under its auspices.

End Notes

[1]. Robert J. Bunker, "Information Warfare Conference." *Military Review.* July-August 1995, Vol. 75. No. 4: 102-103. (Report on "Information Warfare," Technical Marketing Society of America (TMSA) Conference, Los Angeles, CA., 5-6 June 1995.)

Section 1:
Advanced Battlespace and Cybermaneuver Concepts: Implications for Force XXI

Robert J. Bunker

Originally published in
Parameters, Autumn 1996: 108-120.

Force XXI has proven to be an ambitious and farsighted Army vision of future warfighting and a tribute to now retired Chief of Staff General Gordon R. Sullivan. Because it is an institutional attempt at US Army reform, however, the changes being promoted are at times more evolutionary than revolutionary. Force XXI organizations—at brigade, division, and ultimately corps levels—will represent a synthesis of conventional military hardware with integrated digital communications. This experimental force will exist within and dominate the battlefield defined by the range of human senses; it is essentially the force and the concept of the battlefield with which the United States defeated Iraq in 1991.

This article argues that the traditional perception of the battlefield reveals the limiting assumptions upon which Force XXI is built, that it is constrained by its three dimensions, and that it is most likely outmoded. Paradoxically, it is the rise of non-Western warfare and the proliferation of advanced weaponry that together have made current "spatial concepts" of the modern battlefield obsolete.[1] To be an effective military force into the 21st century, the US Army should start now to redefine the battlefield so that new operational concepts can evolve and produce the doctrine and materiel requirements that will lead to meaningful restructuring of all components of the land force. Without a new conceptual model, Force XXI will fail to take full advantage of the potential inherent in new and emerging technology, no matter how successful it is in developing technology appliqués for its existing fleets of tanks, infantry fighting vehicles, artillery systems, and aircraft.

Modern Battlespace

The Army's Field Manual (FM) 100-5, *Operations* (June 1993), defines the modern battlefield, or battlespace as it is called, as follows:

> Battle space is a physical volume that expands or contracts in relation to the ability to acquire and engage the enemy.[2]

> Components [are] determined by the maximum capabilities of a unit to acquire and dominate the enemy; [it] includes areas beyond the AO [area of operations]; it varies over time according to how the commander positions his assets.[3]

The above passages share a common liability: they ignore the electromagnetic spectrum.[4] Department of the Army Pamphlet (DA Pam) 525-5, *Force XXI Operations*, a visionary document published in 1994 by the Army's Training and Doctrine Command (TRADOC), better defines battlespace:

> Components of this space are determined by the maximum capabilities of friendly and enemy forces to acquire and dominate each other by fires and maneuver and in the electromagnetic spectrum.[5]

Current Army thought holds that battlespace is composed of separate, discrete physical and electromagnetic dimensions, each of which must be controlled if friendly operations are to be successful. Recent naval doctrinal publications share that perception.[6] Military forces are said to operate in the physical dimension, which represents the world in which humans and their machines move and fight. The boundaries of this specific "three dimensional battlespace" are, for the purposes of this article, defined by the limitations of human-sensing capabilities. Conversely, information warfare is said to be conducted within the electromagnetic realm where there are no physical military forces.[7]

The Army's outmoded definition of battlespace has proven adequate for maneuver warfare in the three dimensional physical battlespace. Armored spearheads and amphibious thrusts seek to defeat opposing forces by exploiting weaknesses and vulnerabilities. Maneuver warfare with its encirclements, flanking operations, and disruption of the enemy's command and control processes works well within the constraints of a physical dimension where military forces and the human senses operate. It has, in fact, come to represent the dominant Western mode of warfare.

The concept of extended battlespace developed in Force XXI operations enlarges this concept of the physical three dimensional battlefield with an increase in depth, breadth, and height, but in no way fundamentally alters it. In fact, the attribute of extended battlespace that comes closest to challenging the linear assumptions that underpin current doctrine is the concept of the "empty battlefield." This concept, loosely described as the dispersal of forces for survival purposes, is significant because it most clearly depicts the breakdown of some of the fundamental assumptions—and hence principles—of warfare dominated for several centuries by Western philosophies.[8]

Future Battlespace

The reason for this breakdown of our Western mode of warfare is twofold. First, nontraditional adversaries and forms of conflict have evolved in the recent past that challenge the assumptions that underpin maneuver warfare. Various "gray area phenomena," including terrorists, narcocartels, and forces based on clan and ethnic affiliations bring to conflict characteristics that are asymmetrical to conventional Western forms of warfare.[9] And since safety for such forces may be achieved by staying off of the conventional battlefield, they have no option but to leave the three dimensional battlespace acknowledged in US doctrine and disappear in accord with the maxim "if you can't see a force you can't kill it."

Examples of this form of disappearance include the use of underground tunnel networks at Cu Chi and the integration of the Vietcong among the populace in Vietnam, the civilian clothing of a terrorist, and the blending of snipers into unarmed Somali mobs. Since these forces have left the human-sensing dimension in which maneuver warfare dominates, maneuver based doctrine is insufficient when applied against them. Second, the breakdown in maneuver warfare can also be seen in the advent of advanced target detection and precision guided munitions.[10] Any military force, even those fielded by the West, which exists within the dimension of the human senses can now be acquired and killed. Since maneuver warfare doctrine was based on a synthesis of decades old technology and ideas, it is not surprising that the advanced technologies now emerging negate the presumed benefits that justified this earlier synthesis. The only solution to this dilemma again requires leaving the human-sensing dimension and disappearing—or seeming to do so. The stealth fighter and the submarine both rely on this tactic as their primary form of defense.

Stealth capability has not yet been an applicable technical option for land based and amphibious forces, so tactical and operational innovations have been developed by way of compensation. This has resulted in Western military forces increasingly turning their attention toward the development of advanced maneuver warfare concepts. Nonlinear operational concepts based on the absence of front lines or any recognizable rear area have been developing in Russia for a number of years and are extensively described in various publications.[11] Similar concepts existed in the mid-to-late 1980s in TRADOC's *Army 21 Interim Operational Concept*, with its references to islands of conflict and deliberate non-contiguity on the battlefield.[12]

The value of stealth capability has, however, been recognized; it was given a priority one requirement in the May 1994 ARPA *Report of the Senior Working Group on Military Operations Other Than War (OOTW)*. Termed "Invisible Soldier Image Avoidance and Signature Reduction," it called for a capability that would "make the individual soldier invisible, day or night, to the whole range of battlefield sensors across the electromagnetic spectrum."[13] As one outcome of this recognized need we may expect the United States to develop and use either active or metamorphic camouflage systems for defensive purposes.

Advanced Battlespace Concepts

As noted earlier, the implementation of Force XXI will likely be severely compromised unless an advanced definition of battlespace is created to support it. I propose that it should be based upon two spatial concepts—humanspace and cyberspace—and two spatial transcendents—stealth and data fusion (see Figure 1).[14]

Criteria	Definition
Humanspace	That aspect of battlespace composed of the traditional physical dimension of the human senses in which humans and their machines move and fight; the killing ground of future war.
Cyberspace	That aspect of battlespace composed of the electromagnetic spectrum and the non-human sensing dimension in which stealth-masked forces seek refuge from attack.
Stealth	The application of sensory defeating procedures and technologies which allow military forces to enter cyberspace.
Data fusion	The application of adaptive information processes to stealth-masked forces for target detection, identification, and location.

Figure 1. Advanced Battlespace Concepts

Humanspace represents the traditional physical dimension of the human senses within which military forces operate. This spatial concept has already been defined in *Force XXI Operations*, omitting the electromagnetic aspect. Cyberspace, on the other hand, represents not only the electromagnetic spectrum, but also that dimension in which military forces seek refuge for defensive purposes. Forces that enter this dimension are removed from the human-sensing based battlefield and are thus invulnerable to attack; at the same time, they retain the capacity to attack military forces that exist in humanspace. Any military force that has the capability of entering this non human-sensing dimension, be it Western or non-Western, must now be considered, respectively, either a highly advanced asset or a direct threat. Since emerging forms of non-Western warfare and advanced technology applications appear to possess many of the same operational characteristics, this is not an unreasonable characterization.[15]

As an outcome of the development of the concepts of humanspace and cyberspace, a more precise definition of battlespace dominance in the 21st century may also be required. Cyberspace may be considered dominant over humanspace. For this reason, the goal of the Army in future war, beyond that of securing assigned politico-military objectives, will be that of total cyberspace dominance—not just digital battlespace dominance.[16] Army forces may ultimately look toward cyberspace as a place of refuge from attack while denying that refuge and capability to opposing forces.

The means of entering this refuge will be based upon the application of stealth technology and processes.[17] In hindsight, it can be said that when Mao Zedong referred to guerrillas as fish in a sea of surrounding population he was inadvertently stating early principles of what we would now term stealth and cyberspace.[18] Advanced weaponry, beyond that of the submarine, bomber (B2), and fighter (F117), is now being configured for the very purpose of exploiting the recognized defensive potential stealth offers. Follow on programs to the 21st Century Land Warrior project seek to incorporate chameleon-like camouflage composed of biomaterials into the modular Soldier Integrated Protection Ensemble (SIPE) system.[19] Cruise missile successors to the canceled AGM137A TriService Standoff Attack Missile (TSSAM), as well as the recently unveiled Army RAH66 Comanche scout/light attack helicopter, are also now stealth-based.

The counter to stealth-masked forces will be based upon the spatial transcendent of data fusion.[20] Just as stealth allows a military force to leave humanspace and enter cyberspace, data fusion will negate the protection stealth provides. Data fusion describes the concept of using information gathered across the electromagnetic spectrum to locate stealth-masked military forces in space and time.[21] In future operations, opposing forces that appear invisible to conventional means of detection and identification will be identifiable via superior data fusion systems and procedures so that they can be immediately neutralized or destroyed. The urgency here acknowledges that each of the opposing forces will be operating within its own data acquisition and information processing cycles. [22] Differences in response times measured in seconds will separate the quick and the dead.

Based upon this tension between stealth and data fusion, the "human-sensing dimensional barrier" separating humanspace and cyberspace will represent a dynamic and contested frontier, a transdimensional forward edge of the battle area (FEBA) between opposing forces.[23] As a result, new spatial premises of offense and defense may develop based on two basic formulas. Whenever individuals, organizations, and materiel can avoid or counter efforts at data fusion, those entities can be said to be operating in cyberspace. Conversely, when efforts to counter data fusion fail, the entities will be considered to be operating within humanspace, vulnerable to attacks by an adversary, whether a stealthy cruise missile or a sniper heretofore concealed in the midst of a crowd. The two concepts can be expressed as follows:

Defensive Premise: Stealth $>$ Data Fusion $=$ Cyberspace
Offensive Premise: Stealth $\leq$ Data Fusion $=$ Humanspace

These spatial premises of advanced battlespace can be viewed in Figure 2, which portrays a three dimensional volume of battlespace bisected by a human-sensing fourth dimensional barrier. (Were time to be included in this concept of battlespace, it would represent a fifth dimensional attribute.) The figure is misleading-humanspace and cyberspace actually coexist in a given volume of battlespace—but it will have to suffice until conventions for expressing these concepts have become commonplace. Because stealth masked forces are inherently "invisible" to normal military forces, they can maneuver with relative impunity in cyberspace. Hence, the "battlefield" addressed in this essay, and portrayed crudely in Figure 2, appears to have twice the potential volume of the battlespace currently defined in FM 100-5 and being applied to develop Force XXI theory.

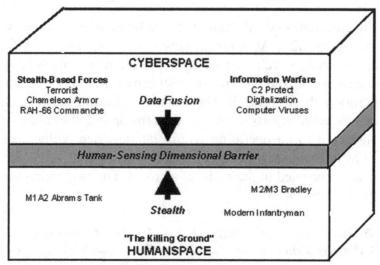

Figure 2. Spatial Premises of Advanced Battlespace

Army forces will rely upon the "maneuver force protection" envisioned in *Force XXI Operations* to extend their ability to conduct operations.[24] Within a few decades, however, non stealth-masked Army forces will have become highly vulnerable—even with the development of high technology proactive armor and point defense systems.[25] For this reason, the initial digitalization of Army mechanized and armor forces which rely upon maneuver as the basis of their operational art, while a bold move, can still only be viewed as an incremental step into future warfare.

This redefinition of battlespace suggests that our traditional concepts of maneuver warfare may be made obsolete because forces that conduct maneuver warfare operate in humanspace, and humanspace represents the killing ground of future war. One can only speculate when—or if—this style of warfighting might be replaced by dispersed land forces engaging in cybermaneuver as a complement to precision strike operations conducted by stealth-cloaked missiles and aircraft.[26]

Cybermaneuver Concepts

With this redefinition of the battlefield based upon principles of dual dimensional space, early concepts of cybermaneuver may now find their way into future editions of *Force XXI Operations*. The potential need for the development of such a new form of doctrine was recognized in 1992 by John Arquilla and David Ronfeldt in a RAND paper entitled *Cyberwar is Coming!*[27]

For an example of what cybermaneuver warfare may look like, consider two opposing helicopters in a meeting engagement. Initially, each helicopter will rely upon stealth technologies to keep itself off the other's battlefield. Both will be using data fusion and information cycle processing technologies in an effort to acquire, identify, and engage the other. One belligerent will momentarily gain the initiative by using data fusion to force the other out of cyberspace and into humanspace. Finally, the "uncloaked" helicopter will be engaged by the other, whose intent will be to neutralize or destroy it before it can take offensive action itself or escape back into a "cyberspace" mode of operation by using countermeasures to defeat data fusion activities. Early, primitive applications of this concept include the firing of flares by aircraft to confuse heat-seeking missiles, or technology applied to helicopters to mask their infrared signature for the same purpose.

Similar concepts of battlespace underlay the functional basis of countersniper systems. Snipers, it can be argued, use cyberspace as their principle form of defense. They deftly stalk their intended targets by using disciplined body motions and breathing control to reach a suitable firing position without detection. After neutralizing their intended target, they fade back into cyberspace and either vanish forever or wait minutes, maybe hours, before momentarily letting their presence again be known with another kill. The danger of snipers for Army forces deployed overseas is growing in proportion to increasing urbanization.[28] That insurgents operating in these environments are likely to be dispersed among innocent noncombatants and have access to precision guided munitions (PGMs) is a more ominous concern.[29]

To deal with the sniper threat, a new defensive system called Lifeguard has been developed at the US Lawrence Livermore National Laboratories. Based on state-of-the-art commercial technologies, it can locate the point of origin of a bullet in flight within hundredths of a second. While Lifeguard is unable to return fire, a combat version with this capability, known as Deadeye, is under development.[30] In essence, this countersniper system, like the helicopter used in the first example, takes a cyberspace based force, in this instance a sniper, and strips it of its invulnerability to attack by bringing it into humanspace by means of data fusion. A sniper faced with this new technology has a range of choices, none of which is particularly appealing: decline to fire his weapon, target the countersniper system initially in hopes of disabling it (first the sniper must locate it, of course), or be equipped with innovative means for circumventing such technology.

These two examples bring up the most significant challenge that will probably face forces operating in cyberspace. Whenever they actively acquire an adversary in cyberspace, thereby moving it into humanspace, even if only for a few seconds, they will likely betray their own position in space and time. At that point, both the attacker and the intended victim can be engaged directly by other killing forces, be engaged by other allied forces via shared informational awareness, or launch strikes against opposing forces in humanspace. This window of vulnerability will likely be one of the primary features of the sort of information dominance that must be readily available to Force XXI and denied to opposition forces.[31]

As a result of technology evolution, future Army commanders may view the battlefield by means of real time holographic displays. All friendly forces can be made to appear on these displays; technically sophisticated opposition forces will appear and disappear from these displays as they are acquired and escape detection, literally "popping" out of and back into cyberspace. Forces in such a scenario would probably become quickly intermingled, resulting in a blurring of our traditional concepts of front lines and the tactical, operational, and strategic continuum.[32] In fact, older military forces and those forces of less advanced national and non-national entities which exist and function in humanspace can expect to be engaged simultaneously across the physical continuum by precision fires in the opening stages of a conflict.[33] The concept of safe rear areas would conceivably no longer exist because the entire human-sensing dimension would indeed become the battlefield. Within this context, safety would be gained only by means of the "cyberspace shifting" of forces and other national security assets outside the boundaries of traditional humanspace.

Such a perspective on the future battlefield reinforces the need for digital interoperability standards, the seamless tracking and engagement of enemy targets, and a future Army force structure primarily configured around stealth-based forces.[34] Based on these perceptions, a failure to explore cybermaneuver as an emerging warfighting style potentially risks setting up the Force XXI Army for a catastrophe much like that which befell France in the spring of 1940 when it eschewed both the new German operational art which had developed and the expanded concept of the battlefield underlying it.

Conclusion

The concepts developed in this essay represent an initial attempt to give substance to the meaning of "asymmetry" in force-on-force relationships. It has been proposed that advanced forces gain an asymmetrical battlefield advantage over traditional forces by means of techniques and processes such as cloaking, blending into civilian populations, concealment, and deception—all of which allow them to avoid detection by entering a realm which is frequently called cyberspace. At the same time, traditional forces, which remain in humanspace, are subject to detection and attack by these now stealthy systems. Current and emerging precision strike capabilities support this perception. When one force can attack another force and in the process not be attacked in return, a clear battlefield advantage exists.

Our traditional concepts of three dimensional battlespace are unable to explain such a military revolution because increases in the physical dimensions of a battlefield cannot account for it. Rather, a new concept of range is required, one that is defined by a "human-sensing dimensional barrier" which separates humanspace from cyberspace. Given this perceptual lens, a terrorist in civilian garb who is standing five meters from a US soldier and whom the US soldier views as a noncombatant is at a much greater battlefield range from that soldier than a hostile tank that is visible 1,000 meters away—and yet is potentially far more dangerous to the soldier than is the tank. To counter such forces, we will most likely be required to rely upon principles of data fusion which can provide us with the capability to bring such cloaked entities out into the open where they can be neutralized or destroyed. A number of implications can be derived from the development of such a technically advanced battlespace that bear directly on the Army's conduct of war in the future:

- The US Army should explore the development of cybermaneuver doctrine in support of Force XXI. It is proposed that such doctrine could better exploit the advanced battlespace which is developing than more traditionally based warfighting concepts such as maneuver or maneuver force protection as described in FM 100-5 and DA Pam 525-5 respectively. Cybermaneuver doctrine would be a natural complement to maturing precision strike concepts which are focused upon the neutralization or destruction of opposing humanspace residing forces. Implicit in this doctrine would be the development of a capability to defeat opposing stealth-masked forces.

- Lighter forces may possess more of a defensive advantage than heavier forces because lighter forces can more easily seek the defensive advantages that cyberspace offers. This could mean that defense would no longer be measured by such traditional concepts as heavier armor or even speed, but rather by the ability of a force to make itself "invisible" to detection.

- A further blurring of the distinction between soldier and civilian may likely result. War in the Western world has been conducted from the time of Frederick the Great by armies wearing distinctive uniforms which have distinguished combatants from noncombatants and one opposing army from another. Our modern camouflaged battledress uniforms are based upon this evolutionary pattern of uniform development. These uniforms are not worn by many soldiers representing non-Western cultures because behavioral norms and ethical systems to which these soldiers subscribe allow them to discard the symbols of the soldier in order to obtain the defensive benefits that cyberspace provides. We may expect this trend to intensify as American dominance of the humanspace battlefield increases.

- The perceptual abilities of US soldiers will likely be enhanced to provide them with "extrahumansensing capabilities" which will allow them to peer into cyberspace for the purposes of identifying threat forces. Two methods may be employed. The first is by technical means such as the Land Warrior program, which provides night vision capability. The second is by better exploiting the organic capabilities of our troops by training them to be aware of the different smells, habits, and behaviors of warriors in specific cultures or ethnic groups with which we may find ourselves in conflict.

- If our traditional concept of front lines-linearity-becomes blurred because of the effects of the "human-sensing dimensional barrier" separating cyberspace from humanspace, we may expect that the tactical, operational, and strategic continuum as we now understand it will be reexamined and possibly redefined. The three dimensional quality of that traditional continuum cannot be expected to define the reality of a fourth dimensional battlespace where rear areas and flanks may no longer exist, and where what was in earlier times known as the "Zone of the Interior" (the continental United States) is part of the region of conflict.

Implications such as these could prove difficult for an Army victorious in the Gulf War to consider, much less accept, because they challenge both the core of its doctrinal sensibilities and its traditional force structure preferences. Yet the value of informed challenges was recognized by General Sullivan, writing as Chief of Staff, along with Lieutenant Colonel Anthony M. Coroalles:

> Ideas that have the potential to overturn long established, bureaucratically entrenched methods of operation are not welcomed by the average man. When the paradigm shifts, most cannot grasp the full potential of new ideas. New technologies and processes can frighten those who are comfortable with the routines established to accommodate the old technologies. Furthermore, vested interests within the organization and within its bureaucracy—usually

for what to them are good and logical reasons—will resist ideas that threaten the status quo. Bureaucracies flourish on procedures instituted to ensure efficiency. Innovation is the enemy of efficiency because it threatens established procedures. This is a mindset that we cannot afford in Force XXI. While military professionals must hold the security of the nation as something with which they dare not gamble, they cannot afford to discourage the kind of imagination and innovation that is needed to meet the varied challenges that will arise in the 21st century.[35]

To be a relevant military force in the next century, the Army must learn to adapt itself like an entrepreneurial organization to the social, political, economic, and military changes which are now upon us. While Army traditions based upon individual integrity, honor, and service to country must be retained, those based on discredited perceptions of the battlefield and of warfighting itself will be left where they belong—in the twilight of the 20th century.

End Notes

The advanced concepts contained within this essay represent an attribute of Fourth Epoch War theory. For dissemination purposes, I have refrained from linking them to the larger theoretical paradigm within which they exist. This essay was initially prepared for US Army TRADOC as NSSP Report 95-2. National Security Studies program, California State University, San Bernardino, July 1995. It was presented at US Army TECOM "Visions of Future Conflict— Test Technology Drivers" TTS '96 Symposium at Johns Hopkins University, Applied Physics Laboratory, 4 June 1996. I wish to thank Professor Douglas C. Lovelace, Jr., Charles F. Swett, Lieutenant Colonel Matthew Begert, USMC, CWO5 Charles "Sid" Heal, USMCR, and Dr. T. Lindsay Moore for their comments on an earlier draft of this paper, and the US Army Command and General Staff College for its research support.

[1]. For background on the rise of non-Western and advanced technology warfare, see Robert J. Bunker, "The Transition to Fourth Epoch War," *Marine Corps Gazette*, September 1994, pp. 20-32.

[2]. US Army, Field Manual 100-5, *Operations* (Washington: Department of the Army, June 1993), p. 6-12.

[3]. Ibid., p. Glossary-1.

[4]. Ibid., p. 224. Mention of EW against enemy C^2 is as a capability that contributes to the effectiveness of combined arms operations.

[5]. US Army, Pamphlet 525-5, *Force XXI Operations* (Fort Monroe, Va.: US Army Training and Doctrine Command, 1 August 1994), p. Glossary-1. It should be noted that this pamphlet has defined the general tenets upon which the next version of FM 100-5 will be based. Of equal interest is the separation of the electromagnetic spectrum from the realm where engagements occur. It is among the premises of this article that engagements will occur with increasing frequency within the electromagnetic sphere, and that the conventional three-dimensional battlespace will become a killing ground for those forces that cannot use fourth dimensional assets to conceal themselves from attack.

[6]. Naval Doctrine Command, NDP-1, *Naval Warfare* (Washington: GPO, 1994), p. 72.

[7]. Discrete from the "bioelectric realm" of minds where psychological operations are waged. Some question also exists if a "computer virus" shouldn't be considered a new form of military force.

[8]. DA Pam 525-5, *Force XXI Operations*, p. 29.

[9]. Concern has been raised over my use of the term "non-Western warfare" because of its ethnocentric implications and the collapsing together of all forms of warfare other than that waged by the West. I would argue that Western civilization as we define it wages war collectively in a similar manner. Further, this civilization has dominated much of the global system since the 16th century. Non-Western warfare is an attempt by non-Western cultures to break this monopoly on warfare. Categorizing all forms of nonWestern warfare as one general type is indeed inaccurate since the various forms of nonnation forces, security forces, and armies that exist in the world today will wage war differently. However, until a concept similar to that of "non-Western warfare" replaces the flawed operations other than war (OOTW) concept, I see little utility in exploring the true

variations in non-Western modes of warfare. See Robert J. Bunker, "Rethinking OOTW," *Military Review,* 75 (November-December 1995), 34-41.

[10]. For a synopsis of ARDEC's smart munitions strategic plan, see Scott R. Gourley. "Smart Munitions," *Army,* July 1995, pp. 41-44. For other articles of interest see Glenn W. Goodman, Jr., "Fire and Forget: Terminally Guided Antitank Submunitions Reach Fruition," *Armed Forces Journal,* August 1994, pp. 36, 39; Robert Holzer, "U.S. Navy Study Promotes Precision Munitions," *Defense News,* 27 February 5 March 1995, p. 30; Pat Cooper, "USAF Considers Smaller, More Lethal Bombs," *Defense News,* 2723 April 1995, p. 6; Glen W. Goodman, Jr., "Fired, Forgotten, and Finished," *Armed Forces Journal,* December 1995, pp. 36, 38-39.

[11]. See principally the writings of Mary C. Fitzgerald: "The Soviet Image of Future War: 'Through the Prism of the Persian Gulf,'" *Comparative Strategy,* 10 (October-December 1991), 393-435; "Russia's New Military Doctrine," *Naval War College Review,* 46 (Spring 1993), 24-44; "The Russian Military's Strategy for 'Sixth Generation' Warfare," *Orbis,* 38 (Summer 1994), 457-76; "The Russian Image of Future War," *Comparative Strategy,* 13 (April-June 1994), 167-80.

[12]. US Army, *Army 21, A Concept for the Future: Umbrella Concept* (Fort Monroe, Va.: US Army Training and Doctrine Command, December 1988).

[13]. Advanced Research Projects Agency, *Report of the Senior Working Group on Military Operations Other Than War (OOTW),* May 1994, p. 24. Available on the Internet.

[14]. This will require a paradigm shift in our view of the battlefield and the military's place in it. For an example of what this type of shift will mean, see Alan G. R. Smith, *Science and Society in the Sixteenth and Seventeenth Centuries* (Norwich, Conn.: Harcourt Brace Jovanovich, 1972), pp. 9-27.

[15]. Western concepts of information warfare are mimicked by terrorism; high-technology stealth coatings for our aircraft are mimicked by soldiers wearing civilian clothing or hiding out in mobs of women and children; precision strike weaponry is mimicked by driving a vehicle laden with explosives into a military installation.

[16]. It is assumed digital battlespace dominance would represent mastery of the electromagnetic spectrum and the physical battlefield. This form of battlespace dominance is inferior to cyberspace dominance because one's military forces would remain within the human-sensing battlefield (i.e., humanspace).

[17]. Stealth has been written about extensively in military publications but no attempt has been made to link it directly to a fundamentally new concept of battlespace. For background on this subject, see James H. Patton, Jr., "Stealth Is a Zero-Sum Game: A Submariner's View of the Advanced Tactical Fighter," *Airpower Journal*, 5 (Spring 1991), 4-17; and "Stealth, Sea Control, and Air Superiority," *Airpower Journal*, 7 (Spring 1993), 52-62; John W. McGillvray, Jr., "Stealth Technology in Surface Warships," *Naval War College Review*, 47 (Winter 1994), 28-39; James Heitz Jackson, "Stealth: Potential vs. the Purse," *Defence Yearbook, 1992* (London: Brassey's, 1992), pp. 261-69.

[18]. Not only do fish live in the sea-its great volume protects them from detection. See Mao Tse Tung, *On Guerrilla Warfare*, trans. Samuel B. Griffith (New York: Praeger, 1961), pp. 92-93.

[19]. For background on SIPE, refer to the series of articles written over the last six years in *Army RD&A*. For a current perspective, see John G. Roos, "The 21st Century Land Warrior: The Army Becomes the Dominant Gene in Soldier Evolution," *Armed Forces Journal*, February 1995, pp. 1823; Mark Hewish and Rupert Pengelley, "New Age Soldiering," *International Defense Review*, 27 (January 1994), 26-33; "Land Warrior program consolidated," *Washington Update*, AUSA Institute of Land Warfare, Washington, May 1996, p. 2.

[20]. My use of the term data fusion and the concepts behind it have been simplified. My understanding of data fusion derives from presentations given by Edward Waltz, "Image and Spatial Data Fusion-Combining Data to Understand the Battlefield," and Dr. James Llinas, "Fusion in Information Warfare," at the TMSA Information Warfare Conference held in Los Angeles 5-6 June 1995. For more on this subject, see SPACECAST 2020, "Leveraging the Infosphere: Surveillance and Reconnaissance in 2020," *Airpower Journal*, 9 (Summer 1995), 8-25; Marvin G. Metcalf. "Acoustics on the 21st Century Battlefield," *Joint Force Quarterly*, No. 10 (Winter 1995-96), 44-47.

[21]. Facial and subdermal recognition technologies have immense potential in combating insurgency and terrorism as well as in law enforcement. For on the spot identification of known suspects in Haiti, see Gordon R. Sullivan, "A Vision for the Future," *Military Review*, 75 (May-June 1995), 8.

[22]. Better known as the OODA (Observe-Orient-Decide-Act) loop. See John R. Boyd, *Lecture on A Discourse on Winning and Losing* (Maxwell AFB, Ala.: August 1987).

[23]. It is proposed that this informational barrier is composed of either "noise" or "static" to the human senses and to lesser forms of technology. When a military force takes refuge in cyberspace, it becomes lost in the surrounding medium-human, organic, electromagnetic, et al.—and as a result is not subject to detection or target acquisition.

[24]. DA Pam 525-5, *Force XXI Operations*, p. 3-10.

[25]. "Advanced Armor Keeps New Ordnance at Bay," *National Defense*, 79 (May-June 1995), 16-17; "US Army to Test AFV Self-defense Suite," *International Defense Review*, 28 (June 1995), 12.

[26]. Attrition warfare is also becoming obsolete. See Memorandum for Vice Chairman, Joint Chiefs of Staff, Under Secretaries of Defense, Director, Net Assessment, "Terms of Reference for Strategic Studies Group I," Memo from The Deputy Secretary of Defense, 6 September 1995; "Kellogg: We don't play attrition warfare anymore," *AUSA News*, July 1996, pp. 11-12.

[27]. John Arquilla and David Ronfeldt, *Cyberwar is Coming!* (Santa Monica: RAND, P7791, 1992), p. 7; see also "The Transition to Fourth Epoch War," p. 29.

[28]. Jennifer Morrison Taw and Bruce Hoffman, *The Urbanization of Insurgency: The Potential Challenge to U.S. Army Operations* (Santa Monica: RAND, MR-398, 1994), pp. 1-45.

[29]. Marvin B. Schaffer, *Concerns About Terrorists with PGMs* (Santa Monica: RAND, P-7774, 1992), pp. 1-8.

[30]. Scott R. Gourley, "The sniper's latest nightmare," *International Defense Review*, 28 (April 1995), 66.

[31]. The other aspect of cyberspace, that which represents the information infrastructure of our society, represents another feature to be dominated. Robert L. Ayers, Chief, Information Warfare Division, Defense Information Systems Agency, "DISA and Information

Warfare," at the TMSA Information Warfare Conference, Los Angeles, 5-6 June 1995.

[32]. See the concept of simultaneity. DA Pam 525-5, *Force XXI Operations*, p. 29.

[33]. For the initial airspace offensive, see the interview with Defense Minister Pavel Grachev, "General Grachev on the Army and on the Soldier," *Argumenty i fakty*, February 1993, pp. 12, quoted in "The Russian Military's Strategy For 'Sixth Generation' Warfare," p. 2.

[34]. The Composite Armored Vehicle Advanced Technology Demonstrator (CAVATD) which seeks to reduce vehicular weight and active and passive signatures is viewed as a step in the right direction. Rupert Pengelley, "Towards the Plastic Tank," *International Defense Review*, 28 (July 1995), 61.

[35]. Gordon R. Sullivan and Anthony M. Coroalles, *The Army in the Information Age* (Carlisle Barracks, Pa.: US Army War College, Strategic Studies Institute, 31 March 1995), pp. 18-19.

Section 2:
Five-Dimensional (Cyber) Warfighting: Can the Army After Next Be Defeated Through Complex Concepts and Technologies?

Robert J. Bunker

Originally published by
Strategic Studies Institute, U.S. Army War College, 1998.

With the end of the Cold War, U.S. national security perceptions concerning "Who is the threat?" have been thrown into free fall along with those governmental and military institutions meant to contend with it. Resulting from the spreading chaos and ambiguity in the nation-state system, which stem from the simultaneous processes of fragmentation and regionalization, a new question now needs to be asked—"What is the threat?"

Increasingly, national security experts have argued that gray area phenomena, "...where control has shifted from legitimate governments to new half-political, half-criminal powers," will become the dominant threat.[1] Such entities flourish in the growing failed-state operational environment where a condition of "not war–not crime" prevails and nation-state forces operating within it find themselves facing a severe capability gap.[2] These entities disregard Western based "laws of war" and "rules of engagement" and are not concerned about such conventions as "legitimacy" or "public opinion."

Of further significance is the recognition that we are beginning the transition from the modern to the post-modern epoch in Western civilization. Past periods of transition such as this have historically witnessed the two collinear trends of the blurring of crime and war, along with shifts in social classes, economic modes, and motive sources which ultimately result in the fall of one civilization and its replacement by another more advanced one.[3] During the earlier shift from the medieval to the modern epoch, three new forms of social and political organization developed—dynastic- (proto nation-) states, city-states, and city-leagues—as competitors to the then dominant feudal structure,[4] in tandem with the domination of the battlefield by the non-state soldier. Ultimately the early nation-state form and its mercenary armies won out over both these competitors and the preexisting civilization based upon Church, empire, and fief.

As the shift to the post-modern epoch becomes more pronounced, we can expect similar competitors to the nation-state form and our modern civilization to emerge along with the accompanying non-state soldier. One such projected warmaking entity, "Black," and its advanced means of waging war will be discussed in this paper. It is based upon an organizational structure far different than the classical hierarchy to which we are accustomed. Rather, it is nonlinear in function, composed of informational paths analogous to webs and nets, and basic units characterized as nodes and free-floating cells.[5] Such an organizational structure allows for the greater exploitation of post- mechanical energy sources, advanced technologies, and new warfighting concepts which will come to dominate what we will term "war" in the decades to come.

Warfighting Scenario

The future isn't what it use to be!
—Blue Sports Figure

The military forces of Black (BlackFor) will be engaged in a land warfare conflict with the army of Blue (BlueFor), which represents the Army After Next (AAN) in the 2020-2025 time frame. The basis of this engagement results from Black's sustained terrorist campaign directed against Blue's homeland. Black is a major military competitor who is hostile to the cultural and strategic interests of the United States and its allies.[6] This competitor is not a nation-state. For that reason its existence is in variance with "the orthodox position within the Army and the Department of Defense [which] holds that the strategic environment of 2020 will be much like that of 1997."[7]

This competitor represents a new warmaking entity which can be considered both non- and post-Western in orientation. Its criminal and warmaking functions are intertwined as is its decisionmaking structure which is more networked than hierarchical.

25

Black's geographic boundaries may or may not be contiguous, not all of its territories may be delineated, and some may reside within zones currently occupied by failed states.[8] The common feature of Black's transnational territories is that they will likely include heavily urbanized coastal zones containing sprawling slums. (See Table 1.)

	1950	1990	2015
"Million Cities"	50	270	516
"Megacities" [pop. > 8 million]	Worldwide: 2 Developing World: 0	Worldwide: 21 Developing World: 16	Worldwide: 33 Developing World: 27

Reprinted from Marine Corps Combat Development Command, "A Concept for Future Military Operations on Urbanized Terrain," *Marine Corps Gazette*, Insert, Vol. 81, No. 10, October 1997, p. A-1.

Table 1. Trends in Urbanization.

Black is in competition with the Westphalian nation-state form, and its potential regional successor(s), over the world's future social and political organization.[9] By American standards, this new "network- or cyber-state" is both illegitimate and criminal. Black is highly entrepreneurial in nature, not ethically constrained in its conduct of war, and relies heavily on the "new warrior class" for its military recruits.[10] More than one military scholar has referred to this entity as a "confederation of high-tech criminals and barbarians."

The decisive American military victory in the Gulf War in 1991 and its ensuing Revolution in Military Affairs (RMA) have not been lost on the senior leadership of Black. Having successfully built upon the Force XXI and Army XXI programs, BlueFor is viewed as the world's dominant land power force. Black leader have long considered any symmetrical attempt at taking on BlueFor to be suicidal.[11] Conventional Black forces which would move in the "n-by-n" mile battlespace box dominated by BlueFor and its sister services would be sensed, fixed in time and space, and destroyed or neutralized by precision guided strikes and fires.[12]

As an outcome, Black leaders have had no alternative but to accept that BlueFor cannot now nor can they in the future ever be defeated on the battlefield as it is currently defined. This conclusion persists despite those asymmetric responses to BlueFor's firepower and information dominance discovered at the FY 97 Leavenworth

Games.[13] To concede that BlueFor was the dominant land power force would forever marginalize BlackFor, something which the leadership of Black would never accept. Instead, its leaders looked to the new complex concepts and technologies which were developing to overcome BlueFor battlefield dominance. Ultimately, they allowed BlackFor to redefine the battlefield to its own advantage and purposefully restructure its military forces around new concepts of operation (CONOPS). These new CONOPS are known as five-dimensional (cyber) warfighting.

Scientific Assumptions

It is better to ask the right questions and get the wrong answers than to ask the wrong questions and get the right answers.
—Black Chief Science Advisor

To understand the assumptions behind five-dimensional warfighting, a short overview of the influence of science on the evolution of technology and warfare is required. This provides Black leadership with a baseline of change allowing it to forecast the "...major long-term shifts rather than small, incremental, linear steps derived directly from current events."[14]

Black's basic assumption is that battlespace as it is currently defined, represents a three-dimensional box modified by the dimension of time (the fourth-dimension).[15] BlueFor is said to "rule the cube." Western history suggests that battlespace was not always four-dimensional. In fact, the medieval battlefield was three-dimensional in nature—composed of two spatial dimensions and a temporal one. This was the case because science in the Middle Ages was very backward by modern standards.[16]

The art of medieval warfighting represented an extension of this primitive science. It was conducted by armored noblemen on horseback wielding lance and sword supported by their retainers. Stone-walled castles provided an all but impenetrable vertical defense against armies lacking the proper equipment and logistical stamina to overcome high walls or conduct a long-term siege. Still, these scientific and warfighting views were adequate for the needs of a three-dimensionally based civilization founded on animal motive sources. As long as similar "armies" with like technologies and operational concepts fought each other on the battlefields of Europe, medieval civilization flourished.

The lesson learned by Black is that this earlier civilization eventually came crashing down at the hands of those who employed advanced warfighting methods.[17] The firearm and cannon, which exploited four-dimensional space for warfighting purposes, were weapons against which the knight and the castle were defenseless. Further, they provided a standoff capability which allowed the user to remain "off the battlefield" of the earlier weapons system and fortification form. This change from medieval to modern battlespace can be viewed in Figure 1.[18] It provides a comparison between the knight and the new threat force based upon the mercenary.

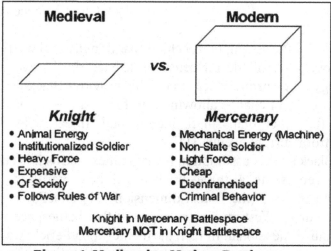

Figure 1. Medieval to Modern Battlespace.

Medieval civilization gave way to modern civilization founded on mechanical motive sources. This 500-year-old civilization of which Blue is the dominant state is, like its predecessor, based on its own level of science. In this instance, it is derived from four-dimensional thinking based upon Newtonian physics, linear dynamics, proportionality, synchronized processes, and reductionist principles. BlueFor warfighting techniques, while built upon highly refined mechanical forces (the Army XXI legacy), represent an extension of these centuries-old scientific principles.

Black's leadership was well aware that numerous scholars had argued that the world was in a transition between modern and post-modern civilization. Their own "renaissance state" was evidence of that fact with its emergent post-mechanical energy sources, webbed informational structure, knowledge based economy, and progressive views toward organ harvesting and cloning, drug use, sexual consent, neural implants, and bio-engineering. Shifts in scientific perceptions based on quantum physics, nonlinear dynamics, and chaos and complexity theory further supported those perceptions. Using the shift from three-dimensional to four-dimensional warfighting as a baseline, Black's leadership projected that a similar transition was underway.[19] If BlackFor could fully capitalize on this opportunity, it could make a quantum leap in military capability over BlueFor and defeat it. Black could then begin to establish its five-dimensionally-based civilization as the successor to the dimensionally inferior one belonging to the West.

Complex Concepts and Technologies

While we based our military reorganization on change equivalent to the 1920s and 1930s, they looked to change on the scale of the Dark Ages and the Renaissance.
—BlueFor Commander

Numerous forms of complex concepts and innovative technologies are emerging which challenge Newtonian views of war.[20] They can be found in such Blue works as the National Research Council's 1992-93 *STAR 21: Strategic Technologies for the Army of the Twenty-First Century* books, Brian Nichipourk and Carl Builder's 1995 *Information Technologies and the Future of Land Warfare*, and John Arquilla and David Ronfeldt's 1996 *The Advent of Netwar.*[21] For Black's purposes, a few of the lesser explored forms will be examined to help facilitate its development of five-dimensional warfighting capabilities: advanced battlespace concepts, advanced non-lethal weapons, chaos and complexity theory, and robotics platforms and machine soldiers.[22]

Advanced Battlespace. The basic theoretical outline of advanced, or five-dimensional, battlespace was provided in a BlueFor War College journal article.[23] It will suffice to say that it fuses the traditional three-dimensional battlespace cube (i.e., humanspace) and time (a fourth dimensional attribute) with the addition of a fifth-dimensional battlespace overlay which exists beyond the range of human senses (i.e., cyberspace). (See Figure 2.)

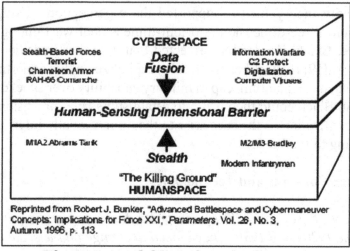

Figure 2. Spatial Premises of Advanced Battlespace.

The basic utility of this advanced form of battlespace is that it allows the physical limitations of four-dimensional space to be overcome for warfighting purposes. The cyber-dimension thus allows the potential for the barriers of time and space to be literally dissolved.[24] The massive warfighting advantage this represents can begin to be understood by concepts of spatial warping and dimensional shifting.[25] Spatial warping overcomes the limitations of physical range for both defensive and offensive purposes. Both spatial contraction and expansion principles can be used to warp four-dimensional space (see Figure 3). Spatial contraction takes two distant points in time and space and brings them together. This principle provides the underlying basis of telemedicine. A military doctor separated by thousands of kilometers from a wounded Blue soldier is able to directly interact with that soldier and, if need be, conduct surgery. Spatial expansion takes two immediate points in time and space and distances them from one another. The principle can be understood by thinking about a Black warrior in civilian garb. This combatant can be standing five meters from a Blue soldier but, for all intents and purposes, could be standing thousands of kilometers away because he or she has exited four-dimensional battlespace via stealth-masking.

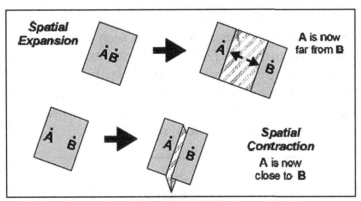

Figure 3. Spatial Warping of Modern Battlespace.

Dimensional shifting overcomes the limitations of physical structures for defensive and offensive purposes. In this case, range and time are not the considerations, but four-dimensionality itself. Body and vehicular armor and hardened hangers, underground bunkers, and command posts stop the penetrative and blast effects of physical projectiles from causing damage. Their effectiveness can be calculated by modern scientific formulas based upon thickness and density. While a flak jacket may stop a grenade fragment, it will do little against a 7.62mm rifle round. On the other hand, bullets and other projectiles are limited by the laws of ballistics and high velocity impact mechanics to that damage they can inflict to physical structures. Against the frontal armor of a Blue M1A2 Abrams, a conventionally fired small caliber round, like the aforementioned 7.62mm, would have no effect because of its lack of penetrative capability.

A weapon with dimensionally shifted capabilities can overcome traditional defenses such as vehicular armor by passing through its physical seams and even its molecular bonds unimpeded.

(See Figure 4.) By traveling through the structural matrix of the armor, it is thus able to avoid its defensive physical properties. On the other hand, a dimensionally shifted defense could be created by projecting a force shield around a physical object. This invisible field would not be able to affect a conventional projectile passing through it, however, that is not the intent. The field would be configured to dampen or negate dimensionally shifted attacks and those conventional weapons whose bonds and relationships based upon international systems and subsystems, such as electronic fuzing, can be influenced. An example of such field generation can be seen with the Shortstop system deployed to Bosnia.[26] While weapons with dimensional shifting, and in some cases spatial warping, capabilities would appear to be the stuff of science fiction, they are not. Some can already be purchased on the international arms market or be constructed from electronics parts sold at commercial retailers.[27]

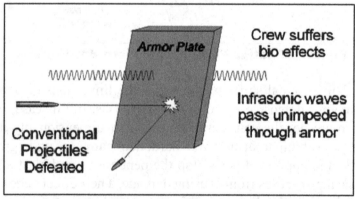

**Figure 4. Dimensionally Shifted Attack
through Vehicular Armor.**

Advanced Non-Lethal Weapons. Since the 1960s, over 600 documents have been published on non-lethal weapons.[28] Most of these weapons operate conventionally. Examples include flash-bang and sting-ball grenades, batons, net-guns, caltrops, sticky and aqueous foams, rubber and wooden bullets, ring-airfoil and sponge projectiles, and riot-control agents. Based upon past experience with these lower tier weapons in Somalia, one Blue military officer stated:

> Non-lethal weapons do not provide a new element
> of national power, as some have suggested. They are
> merely an extension of military force to fill the gap
> between warnings and deadly force.[29]

While technically correct regarding the weapons actually employed in Somalia, this generalization applied to all non-lethal weapons would be inaccurate. An upper tier of these weapons also exists which includes electromagnetic and directed energy weapons such as radio frequency weapons (RFW), high power microwave (HPM), lasers, optical munitions, acoustics, and bio-deteriorating organisms, vortexes, and computer programs. These advanced weapons are at odds with the Blue conventional military paradigm based on four-dimensional thinking. They don't shoot physical projectiles or rely upon penetration, fragmentation, or blast effects to achieve their results. In many applications they are not intended to even kill people or destroy objects but disable or disrupt them instead. Further, their elevated energy power sources and force projection mechanism requirements are, for the most part, post-mechanical in nature. Because of the alien characteristics of these weapons, the potential they offer is often misunderstood by Blue military officers and the institutions to which they belong:

> ...The last thing the military needs at this point is
> a family of weapons that has only limited tactical
> use in operations other than war and offers no clear
> advantage over other nonlethal methods.[30]

For five-dimensional warfighting requirements, however, advanced non-lethal weapons are integral. Their utility in offering tailored politico-military force to the situation at hand has already been widely recognized. This allows a military unit to selectively engage up and down the force continuum as required. Still, it could be argued that gaining this new capability may represent more of a linear progression of modern force application, than a qualitative breakthrough in warfighting. As a result, the truly revolutionary aspect of these weapons may be their ability to operate in and influence five-dimensional battlespace and the synergy that capability offers with the application of tailored force.[31]

The warfighting advantages they possess can be expressed by their ability to engage in dimensionally shifted attacks. The most basic form of such an attack is bypassing a physical defense such as tank armor. An acoustic weapon based on infra-sound can travel great distances and easily penetrate most buildings and vehicles. The long wavelengths of such a very low frequency sound can create biophysical effects in a tank's crew ranging from nausea, loss of bowels, disorientation, vomiting, potential internal organ damage or even death.[32] Another method of attack would be to fire a conventional round containing a pulsed electromagnetic warhead against a tank's armor. The warhead would detonate against the tank releasing a high energy burst of short duration which would energize it and thereby fry all of its electrical components. Low frequency electromagnetic field generators and warheads will also be critical for BlackFor as they will allow destruction of BlueFor electronics which are protected against electromagnetic pulse (EMP), conventional RFWs and HPM.[33]

Another form of dimensionally shifted attack appears to offer the ability for bond/relationship targeting. The space between two points or a grouping of points is attacked rather than the points themselves. This target set can range from the bonds holding molecules together, to the space between human synapses, to an air gap of an engine, to electromagnetic pathways between communication nodes. One weapon example would be liquid metal embrittlement (LME) agents. Such agents alter the molecular structure of base metals or alloys.[34] A successful LME strike against the support columns of a bridge would conceivably make the structure collapse under its own weight. Another example would be the employment of cheap "acetylene Molotov cocktails" or rocket propelled grenades in urban terrain against armored fighting vehicles (AFVs). A one pound device would create an acetylene gas bubble seven feet in diameter which would be sucked into the air intake of a diesel engine that would cause the fuel in each cylinder to ignite prematurely, with enough force to break piston rods.[35] Further, the targeting of gaps is particularly evident in HPM and high power millimeter wave (HPMMW) weapons. Gaps and seams serve as the pathway by which intense electromagnetic (EM) fields enter into the interior and components of the target.

As an outcome of the dimensionally shifted nature of these weapons, the problem of environmental degradation is also overcome. Many of these weapons are devoid of physical and chemical elements or utilize ones which do not generate collateral damage to the environment, as in the case of lead depleted uranium-based projectiles or conventional explosives. In a world where environmental security is at times becoming a dominant consideration, the value of such weaponry characteristics cannot be under- stated.

The spatial warping characteristic of upper tier non-lethal weapons can be readily viewed by using the example of a laser beam. Based upon the principle of spatial contraction, which seeks to take two points in time and space and collapse them together, this beam travels between the two points at 186,000 miles per second. For all intents and purposes, it instantaneously leaves the muzzle of the shooter's weapon and reaches the designated target. The physical range, be it in meters or even kilometers, has no bearing on this compressed "time window" because the human senses operate outside of it.[36] Further, because light travels at absolute velocity there can be no advanced warning of an attack.

The physics involved are far different than those of a conventional kinetic-kill round whose speed in thousands of feet per second results in a time of flight which may, depending on the physical range, end up making it miss the target or, as in the case of a wire-guided anti-tank round, get the firer killed while waiting for the munition to impact it. This time differential advantage, gained from spatial warping, may ultimately provide post-mechanical forces the ability to respond to conventional attacks with anti-lethal means if their stealth-masking has been compromised. It also suggests that emerging scientific forms need to be explored to better understand the non- linear potential that five-dimensional warfighting offers.

Chaos and Complexity Theory. One such form of scientific inquiry appears to offer great utility in this regard. Since the mid-to-late 1980s, a growing body of Blue literature based on chaos and complexity theory has developed.[37] Terms such as spontaneous self-organization, adaptation, and upheavals at the edge of chaos have been used to describe this new science.[38] Much of the momentum behind it has been generated by the Santa Fe Institute with its internationally known staff and fellows.

The basis of this evolving science is post-Newtonian in orientation. This means:

> ...the arrangement of nature—life and its complications, such as warfare—is nonlinear. It defines activities in which inputs and outputs are not proportional; where phenomena are unpredictable, but within bounds, self-organizing; where unpredictability frustrates planning; where solution as self-organization defeats control; and where a premium is placed on holistic, intuitive processes. It rewards those who excel in the calculus of bounds as the variable of management and command.[39]

It is at variance with Newtonian concepts based on four-dimensional perceptions: proportionality, reductionist processes, and the absolute nature of space and time central to Newtonian thinking. These views have already found an ally with Blue's Marine Corps. Since 1994, this service has adopted ideas related to nonlinear dynamics and complexity theory as implicit assumptions underlying their maneuver warfare doctrine. In the 1997 edition of MCDP-1 *Warfighting*, these ideas are evident.[40] In addition, an argument has been made that recent air power concepts based on the Five Ring model, OODA loop, and parallel warfare rely upon ideas intrinsic to complexity.[41] These ideas have also caught the attention of Blue's National Defense University which co-sponsored a symposium on *Complexity, Global Politics and National Security* in November 1996 with the RAND Corporation.[42]

A few five-dimensional warfighting applications of this theory can already be recognized for their utility. The first two represent maneuver-based and target-based operational approaches which strive for the same outcome—the disruption of an opponent.

Synergistic Attack. This is an attack based on the nonlinear premise that a certain amount of input can provide a disproportionate amount of output. This represents the basic underlying assumption of maneuver warfare conducted by BlueFor's sister service the Marine Corps. In essence, "Rather than pursuing the cumulative destruction of every component in the enemy arsenal, the goal is to attack the enemy 'system'—to incapacitate the enemy systematically. Enemy components may remain untouched but cannot function as part of a cohesive whole."[43]

This form of attack relies upon properly conducted attacks in time and space against enemy weaknesses, their physical and moral bonds/relationships, to create an increasingly deteriorating situation rather than mass materiel (e.g., four-dimensional) destruction based on attrition. It is considered inherently risky because of the four-dimensional exposure of attacking units with their open flanks but deemed worth the price of failure for the warfighting advantages gained.

Cross-System Effects. System targeting based on linkages between points, rather than the points themselves, offers a means to provide cross-system effects such as cascading breakdowns. Engineering techniques known as nodal analyses offer the ability to understand the impact of destroying certain nodes within a network. For military purposes, adaptive networks, such as an opponent's economy or command and control structure, could thus be targeted and either disrupted or brought down. Because this is a targeting approach to warfighting, Blue Air Force officers have taken the lead in developing it.[44]

It should also be noted that terrorist groups and local warlords recognized earlier the utility of disruption against Blue interests by targeting the bonds/relationships underpinning the Clausewitzian trinity of its society.[45] Similar operational concepts have thus already been developed and utilized by non-state warmaking groups:

> In a 'failed-state' scenario where Western forces are
> up against non-national groups, these groups are
> successfully utilizing [five-] dimensional battlespace
> against them. For defensive purposes they are using
> idea-generated cyberspace so as not to be acquired
> and killed or neutralized. For offensive purposes,
> they are using technology-generated cyberspace

against the West. Via real-time media broadcasts and, more recently, websites, they are allowed to bring 'the people' of the Westphalian nation-state to the physical battlefield so that they can be subjected to its horrors . . . these groups rely upon an alternative target set focused upon breaking the bonds/ relationships which hold 'the people,' 'the government,' and the military of the Westphalian nation-state together. The primary means of attacking this target set is by those criminal activities which we in the West term 'acts of terrorism.'[46]

Two other applications offer additional potentials for warfighting advantage.

Command by Influence. Blue forces have long been recognized to be at an immense disadvantage when operating against non-traditional opponents in restrictive terrain such as mountains, jungles, and cities. Their plans and actions are both transparent and predictable, while those of opposing forces remain shrouded in darkness. Command-by-influence offers a means to provide a networked military unit the ability to fight toward a common outcome. It is created by providing a commander's mental visualization (i.e., intent and/or concept of operations) to his subordinates who can then use their local situational awareness to shape their actions toward the common goal. This symbolic imagery process represents a system of controlled chaos. [47] It offers immense advantages over linear command-and-control because of its increased information flows and adaptive quality stemming from a unit's ability to fight toward a shared image.

Phase Weaponry. A matter state exists between solid and fluid structures known as a "phase transition." In dynamical systems, the condition between order and chaos is known as "complexity." Similar patterns appear to apply toward cellular automata classes and computation.[48] Based on these analogies, an advanced weaponry state between matter (i.e., solid projectiles) and energy (i.e., electro-magnetic wavelengths) could reasonably be expected to exist. Such a "phase state," found in the void between humanspace and cyberspace, complements the previously stated need for a dimensionally shifted defense. Possibly an early form now exists in the Blue's Navy Research Lab's "Agile Mirror" effort which seeks to generate a dense ionized plasma gas sphere, whose surface looks like metal, as an advanced radar sensing capability for ships and aircraft.[49]

Since it retains some physical properties it might be not only able to defeat five-dimensional attacks but also four- dimensional ones based upon projectiles. It has already been recognized that plasma sheeting may allow protection against HPM and EMP and in addition may lead to stealth type effects by tailoring radar cross section (RCS) of the object being defended.

As a counter to this defense, "phase weaponry" would conceivably be developed which would alter its structure to pass through the "phase shielding" modulations it encounters. One delivery method could be based on a hollowed laser beam filled with an ionized substance whose frequency could be tuned as it senses the modulation of the shielding it comes in contact with.

Robotics Platforms and Machine Soldiers. Another set of complex technologies of utility to Black, derived from advances in computer science, expert systems, and artificial intelligence, miniaturization, and robotics, are manifested in military aerial platforms and teleoperated vehicles. Such platforms and vehicles are currently viewed as an adjunct to Blue conventional military forces. They have been traditionally employed for scouting, as in the case of remotely piloted vehicles (RPVs), and for bomb-disposal and minefield clearing. During the late 1980s, a congressional ban on placing weapons on unmanned systems was enacted because of their potential for killing noncombatants.[50] This effectively stopped the development of BlueFor machine soldiers.[51] However, from a computer science perspective, this ban has long been broken. The "if armed and tripwire triggered, then explode" logic of a land mine makes it a robot even if Western perceptions are oblivious to this fact.[52]

From a post-Western perspective, these technologies offer the means to knowingly create robot soldiers as allies of the new warrior class. Rather than expensive behemoths on the scale of a main battle tank, the machine soldiers BlackFor prefers are small, compact, and cheap. Once deployed in complex terrain, they do not require logistical support, get tired or sick, or become frightened from suppressive fires or encirclement while waiting for Blue forces to activate their sensors.[53] One example of a machine soldier is the static ground holding "$19.95 Military Robot." (See Figure 5.)

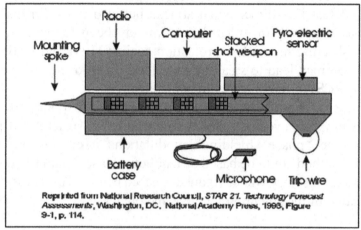

Figure 5. $19.95 Military Robot.

Another example is the biomorphic robot. This is a robot which resembles an insect with six legs, is the metric equivalent of half a foot to a foot long, and has a price range from twenty to a few thousand dollars, depending on its construction materials and level of programming sophistication. The most basic biomorphic robots can recharge using their solar cells, avoid perilous terrain, and fulfill some sort of simple mission. This makes them sophisticated enough to become silent hunter-killer systems in urban terrain. Given the mission of finding better ground, such as under a BlueFor tank or next to a Bluefor soldier, and then either detonating or activating their payload, they become deadly opponents. These robots could be allowed to wander independently or could be slaved to some sort of beacon or global positioning system (GPS) for a network centric zonal defense.[54]

A final form of machine soldier is the nano-robot or microelectromechanical system (MEMS). Alone such microscopic robots are insignificant but working together in hundreds or thousands, they could be employed as battlefield sensors or smart weapons.[55] They offer great potential as scouts for biomorphic robots or as a means to infiltrate and degrade BlueFor mechanical systems by means of the delivery of tiny electric shocks or LME agents.

To limit fratricide, identification friend-or-foe (IFF) implants can be worn by Black soldiers in regions where machine soldiers have been positioned or are freely moving. The smaller of these robots can be delivered by mortars or air-delivery systems, such as cruise missiles, to channel Blue forces into killing zones or to reinfest urban canyon terrain which Blue has painstakingly cleared and captured.[56] Sensor links can be provided to these robots to allow for BlackFor "telepresence" as required.

In addition to machine soldiers, BlackFor will employ unmanned aerial vehicles (UAVs) as both sensor and weapons platforms.[57] They can be used to fix BlueFor elements in time and space and breakup armor and infantry assaults by direct fires of advanced non-lethal weaponry. Further, they can be configured to directly contend with BlueFor attack helicopters by either going after their engines by means of radio frequency weapons, against their air intake system by means of cloggers, or targeting their blades and rotors using entanglers.

Other synthetic soldier options available to BlackFor, not discussed, include cyborgs, composed of animals or insects with computer implants, and plants, such as certain palms, whose fronds can serve as radio frequency antennas for advanced weaponry.

Five-Dimensional Warfighting

> *Don't do anything four-dimensionally that you can do five- dimensionally.*
> —BlackFor Commander

The basic strategy of the leadership of Black is to wage war against Blue in a post-Western manner just as a mercenary captain or dynastic prince waged war against a feudal lord in a post-medieval (e.g., early modern) manner. The change in battlespace involved can be viewed in Figure 6.[58] It provides a comparison between armor and mechanized forces fielded by BlueFor and terrorists and mercenaries fielded by BlackFor. The goal of BlackFor is to remain "off the battlefield" dominated by BlueFor. Not surprisingly, it is reminiscent of the knight vs. mercenary struggle portrayed earlier in Figure 1.

The overriding philosophy of Black is "small, fast, stealthy, ruthless, and cheap."[59] Because this is a post-Western approach to warfighting, it represents a "Clash of Civilizations" never imagined by Samuel Huntington or Blue's more traditionalist leaders.[60] To implement this form of warfighting against Blue, an "Order of Battle" has been created by Black. It is divided into AAN related and AAN directed actions. Pre-AAN related actions can be thought of as strategic level concerns. For this scenario's purposes, it is assumed that Black is carrying out a massive terrorist campaign against Blue's homeland and does not want to be linked to these attacks. This campaign could be based on any combination of physical and/or virtual forms of terrorist activity. Initially other entities, nation-states, or sub-national groups were set up to take the blame for these attacks.

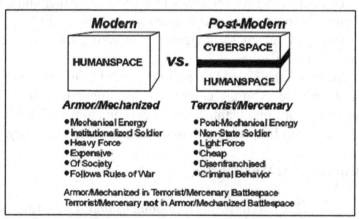

Figure 6. Modern to Post-Modern Battlespace.

AAN related actions take place after Black has been linked to the terrorist campaign. BlueFor and her sister services engage in standoff precision strikes against Black to stop the terrorist assault. This fails to deter Black. AAN directed actions are in response to a ground campaign in which BlueFor is sent in to physically invade Black's territories to stop these attacks and decisively defeat Black.

AAN Related Actions. When Blue finds out that it is fighting Black, Black will not easily allow Blue to locate its forces and assets because of the precision strike danger. Since Blue "rules the cube," Black will attempt to deny BlueFor and her sister services their four-dimensional standoff capability advantages via dimensional shifting of forces. At this time, Black will preemptively attack Blue's intelligence-gathering satellites via ballistic missiles or small ground based lasers.[61]

If Black forces and assets are located and precision struck by Blue, they will be placed in combinations of hard to hit, hardened sites, mixed with innocent civilians and hostages, and either under or next to foreign embassies or in other "ethically challenging sites" like prisoner or Red Cross camps. The potential exists to store Hazmat materials in some sites so that the vapors released could be used to cause a media event. Black will begin using real time media links, television and internet, to visually show the world the brutality of Blue's actions. At the same time, if Blue pilots or SOF operatives are captured, images of their mutilated bodies being dragged through the streets "in retaliation" to Blue actions will be fed to real time media links. The initiation of a global terrorism campaign against Blue assets, including its children in foreign schools and tourists, and internet based attacks to disrupt Blue's infrastructure, degrade its bonds between its people and government, and break up the arrival sequence of ground forces will also now take place. Black further has the option to physically, virtually, or dual-dimensionally threaten or attack third party states or entities, either allied or hostile to Blue, to complicate the conflict as Iraq did to Israel with its Scud missiles during the Gulf War.

AAN Directed Actions. When Blue brings in land warfare forces, Black will defend in complex terrain (urban, suburban, mountains, forests, jungles)[62] so it can fight from cyberspace and deny Blue its qualitative four-dimensional advantages. Further, such terrain as cities can swallow up immense numbers of soldiers and deny BlueFor much of its legacy armor and mechanized force advantages. No Black "soldiers" are to wear uniforms except those set up in complex killing zones as "bait" for BlueFor elements.

In the ground war, Black will be fighting under the following concepts of operation: stealthing and cyber-shielding, cybermaneuver, and bond/relationship targeting. These CONOPS as opposed to those from the Joint Vision 2010 Legacy can be viewed in Table 2.[63]

CONOPS	Blue: Four-Dimensionally Based	Black: Five-Dimensionally Based
Defense	Full-Dimensional Protection	Stealthing and Cybershielding
Movement	Dominant Maneuver	Cybershielding
Fires	Precision Engagement	Bond/Relationship Targeting

Table 2. Blue 2010 Legacy vs. Black CONOPS.

These joint Vision 2010 Legacy CONOPS have been modified by recent BlueFor lessons learned from AAN study results. These results based on surface-to-space continuum, split-based operations, interdependence, hybrid forces, and mature leaders leading cohesive units do not alter BlueFor's four-dimensional warfighting orientation. [64] The complex concept of interdependence is most significant for Black. Within it, "Time is [said to be] the enemy of a force that depends on knowledge and speed for effectiveness."[65] While time for BlueFor is an opponent—stemming from loss of shock effect, force sustainment costs, and changing public attitudes—for Black, it is an ally. Black is a force that depends on anti-knowledge and bond/relationship targeting for its effectiveness much like the Vietcong and other non- Western groups. Unlike BlueFor, it does not seek to engage in quick and decisive Clausewitzian-like battles. Black CONOPS are as follows:

Stealthing: The application of sensory defeating procedures and technologies to allow military forces to seemingly exit four-dimensional space by means of spatial warping. This is a primary form of defense for light forces which seek five-dimensional space (cyberspace) as a defensive bastion. This capability can be derived from either violating the modern rules of war or by employing advanced technologies.

Cybershielding: The capability of defeating a precision strike by means of generating an invisible shield around a force which has been stripped of its stealthing and acquired in time and space. The shield could either prematurely detonate a precision guided munition via electronic impulses, or potentially project a semi-solid "phase state" as a physical barrier. This secondary form of defense is derived from advanced non-lethal weaponry with dimensional shifting capability.

Cybermaneuver: The capability of maneuvering outside of traditional four-dimensional space (humanspace) into five-dimensional space (cyberspace). This capability is derived from the stealthing of military forces. It allows maneuver to take place outside of BlueFor's "battlespace cube" which represents the spatial killing ground of future war.

Bond/Relationship Targeting: The capability to precisely break the bonds/relationships giving form and substance to physical, and potentially five-dimensional, structures. Derived from concepts of terrorism, synergistic attack, and cross-system effects, this offensive CONOP can be applied against targets ranging from nation-states to military systems to individuals. An example of this form of targeting can be seen in Figure 7, which represents the Clausewitzian Target Set being assaulted by BlackFor beginning with its initial terrorist campaign against Blue's homeland.

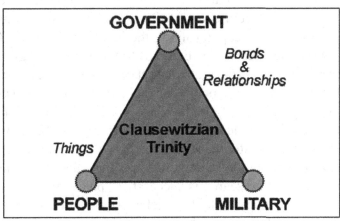

Figure 7. Clausewitzian Target Set.

What is significantly different between BlueFor and BlackFor CONOPS is their relationship to information. BlueFor CONOPS based on the Joint Vision 2010 Legacy, while said to be derived from information superiority, require information operations to take place in addition to the CONOPS themselves, much like an appliqué. BlackFor CONOPS, however, represent organic information operations applied to warfighting. Each one is seamlessly post-mechanical in orientation unlike the unwieldy "bolt-on" between BlueFor mechanical CONOPS and post-mechanical information operations.

In the ground war, BlackFor will focus on employing military forces based on advanced non-lethal weaponry, phase technology (projected), and machine systems from complex terrain.[66] Advanced non-lethal weapons will be used primarily to target the bonds/relationships of Blue materiel, personnel, and infrastructure (both informational and physical). Long-term disabling and disruption of BlueFor personnel is preferred over lethal force because of the logistical burden it will create on BlueFor support services and the further undermining of Blue's trinitarian bonds and relationships that it will create.

Counter-optical lasers, radio-frequency and microwave devices, software weapons, acoustic projectors, acetylene rocket propelled grenades (RPGs), and EMP mortars will be stressed rather than conventional armaments, which will serve in a subordinated role. Many of these advanced non- lethal weapons systems can be expected to have either smart or brilliant guidance systems like more traditionally based aircraft- and artillery-delivered munitions such as the Sensor Fuzed Weapon (SFW), the Sense and Destroy Armor (SADARM) projectile, and the Brilliant Antiarmor (BAT) glider.[67]

Anti-lethal weaponry, as a subset of non-lethal weaponry, will also be employed. Such weaponry can range from those which provide cybershielding, such as a "Faraday Cage" variant against microwave attack, to stealthing via active and metamorphic camouflage systems. [68] Direct research into phase technology will have taken place as will capitalization upon research programs that Blue starts and then drops. If this line of research is successful, "phase state" weaponry will be utilized by BlackFor for both defensive and offensive purposes.

Robotics platforms and machine soldiers, specifically small cheap systems, will be used in mass in support of Black forces. These unmanned systems can either be human or independently controlled with emphasis on the latter. Static systems, biomorphic robots, microelectro-mechanical systems (MEMS), and UAVs will make BlueFor operations in complex terrain extremely hazardous. Such machine forces will not surrender and can be used to reinfest BlueFor rear areas, and urban zones which have been cleared out and pacified, by means of artillery and air-delivery systems.

In addition, mercenaries will be employed to augment Black's non-nation state soldiers. They can offer additional capabilities not normally possessed by Black forces. Further, since they can be hired for short duration contract work, they offer potential cost savings for Black. Such mercenaries can range from terrorists to private security and intelligence firms. (See Table 3.) The precedent for the use of such forces took place back in the 1990s with Executive Outcomes' corporate contracts in failed African states and Mexican drug cartels hiring of ex-foreign and ex-U.S. special forces soldiers.[69]

Finally, Black forces will rely upon a networked form of command and control (C^2) rather than a traditional hierarchical onewhich is susceptible to leadership decapitation and easy disruption. This more robust system will capitalize on command-by-influence concepts, not only for human forces, but also for machine forces. Its exploitation of a C^2 method based upon a symbolic imagery process coupled with a nonliner defense in complex terrain makes BlackFor a very resilient, complex and adaptive opponent. In some ways, this form of defense is similar to the Swedish military's proposed defensive "cell concept."[70] However, in this instance, BlackFor's employment of advanced non-lethal weaponry and machine soldiers would be technically superior to BlueFor's legacy based armor forces.

Type	Capability
Terrorists	Bombings, RF Weaponry, WMD
Hackers	Internet Based Attacks, Misleading Intelligence Postings
Media	Real Time News Feeds, Websites, News Bias, Disinformation
Ex-Special Forces	Assassinations, Kidnappings
Drug Cartels	Drug Flow Manipulation, Dosage Tampering, Additive/Toxin Tampering
Mercenary Corporations	Ground Fighting (High Tech) & Operational Intelligence Services
Private Militias & Guerrillas	Ground Fighting (Low Tech)
Private Security & Intelligence Firms	Key Asset Protection & Strategic Intelligence/Counter-Intelligence

Table 3. Black's Employment of Mercenaries.

Can the AAN Be Defeated?

> *Our leaders called them criminals, not soldiers. How does that explain what happened to my platoon?*
> —Surviving BlueFor Soldier

The overriding question, based upon the above five-dimensional warfighting scenario, is: Could BlackFor defeat BlueFor? If we accept the June 1993 FM 100-5 *Operations* concept of decisive victory as the only way BlueFor can "win," then BlackFor will come out victorious:

> *The Army must be capable of achieving decisive victory.* The Army must maintain the capability to put overwhelming combat power on the battlefield to defeat enemies through a total force effort. It produces forces of the highest quality, able to deploy rapidly, to fight, to win quickly with minimum casualties. That is decisive victory.[71]

Based upon this scenario, BlueFor would be denied the following key components of its definition of victory:

- "the capability to put overwhelming combat power on the battlefield..."
- "..., to win quickly..."
- "... with minimum casualties..."
- "... [achieve] decisive victory."

The traditional four-dimensional battlefield, based upon open spaces and non-complex terrain, which BlueFor dominates was surrendered by BlackFor the moment hostilities began because it represents killing ground. Instead, BlueFor would be required to place its combat power directly within complex terrain containing BlackFor's stealth-masked forces, both human and machine, mixed in with innocent civilians. BlueFor's legacy mechanized forces would lose much of their qualitative superiority in such terrain and be susceptible to BlackFor's advanced technologies and CONOPS.

In heavily urbanized coastal zones containing sprawling slums such as a massive Mogadishu-like environment, BlackFor would be defending in the equivalent of a number of World War II Stalingrads. The German army fighting over that city lost tens of thousands of men prior to being cut off and decimated. If BlueFor lost a fraction of that number, the operation would be deemed a disaster. The question arises whether BlueFor would possess sufficient soldiers in its ranks to even engage in such an undertaking. Time also becomes a factor. Large scale urban operations and the ensuing terrorist/guerrilla campaign likely to follow, even if the urban centers could be occupied, far exceed any notion of a quick win on BlueFor's behalf. BlueFor would have to counter terrorists, narco-groups, and gangs in a "police" type setting for which its forces are not suited.

To further erode BlueFor's potential for victory, its ability to defeat Black decisively comes into question. Black represents a new warmaking entity based on a heavily internetted command structure—its relationships are more weblike than hierarchical. Physical terrain is meaningless to this entity, it does not field an army which can be decisively defeated in open battle, and its leadership is stealth-masked and transnational. As a result, traditional Clausewitizian centers of gravity or, for that matter, concepts of defeat do not apply.

What is most striking about these observations is that they appear to support three of the emerging impressions of the 1997 Summer AAN Wargame held in September:

- Future conflicts may have very unique characteristics.
- Conflict may be about controlling time and influence, not about seizing terrain or defeating military forces.
- Resolution of such conflicts may not imply "victory" in the conventional sense.[72]

That wargame saw Blue facing an Orange opposing force, modeled on a hybrid insurgency, conducting operations within the territory of the Green nation-state which represented a fragile, corrupt democracy. While Orange in that wargame represented an "expanding non-nation state," in this report Black represents a "post-nation state entity."[73] The difference is the political perception of the opposing force as a non-nation-state insurgency as opposed to a nation-state killer—something far more threatening to the Western nation-state form because it seeks to replace it.

Implications

We don't have to get the future right, just less wrong than our
opponents.
—A Black Military Analyst

The emergence of complex, adaptive socio-political entities as challengers to the nation-state form raises immense concerns for the Army After Next. Such a network-like entity, should its network expand to take on the form of a major military competitor, would represent a national security threat alien to the American view of war and the strategic context in which it is waged.[74] Given the historical emergence of medieval structures (as the successor to the classical city-state) and the modern nation-state (as the successor to the Church, empire, and fief) during periods of epochal change as we may now be in, such a development is not infeasible.

Conceivably in the decades to come, such a network-like entity could develop from a wide range of sources including the drug cartels of Latin and South America, the organized crime groups found in parts of the Far East, or the Russian successor state if it continues on its current path of becoming a "kleptocracy." Stemming from its unique organizational strengths, criminally derived ethics and ability to engage in five-dimensional warfighting this entity would likely defeat an Army After Next based upon current concepts of decisive victory and the traditional four-dimensional perceptions underpinning it. Derived from this perception and others raised in this report, a number of implications for 21st century land warfare exist:

Newtonian views of warfighting are rapidly becoming representative of a spatially obsolete battlefield form. Complex concepts and technologies are promoting a new form of warfighting based upon five-dimensional space. Such radically new means of waging war are at variance with the institutional Army and the society which it defends. As a result, five-dimensional warfighting will likely be proscribed by an Army leadership wedded to heavy mechanized forces, overwhelming firepower and seizing ground, until faced with catastrophic defeat on the battlefield.

The *Force XXI Operations* perception of complex, adaptive armies belonging solely to developed nations (e.g., post-industrial) appears to be in error.[75] Such "armies" may more often be initially characteristic of non-nation state entities configured around the new-warrior class and former military personnel. Many of these "armies" will form themselves into mercenary companies offering their services to the highest bidder and employ five-dimensional, rather than four- dimensional, warfighting principles. They could usher in a new global "Age of Mercenaries" and, if left unchecked, may result in U.S. firms such as MPRI competing with the U.S. Army over foreign military operations.

Achieving decisive victory, as it is currently defined, against complex and highly adaptable non-nation state entities will become untenable. As a consequence, traditional concepts of ground based military deterrence will also become insufficient. This will require the U.S. Army to reexamine both its concepts of victory and defeat and deterrence as it develops the AAN project. Such a strategic reexamination would come into conflict with deeply held American views of warfare.

Bond/relationship targeting represents a powerful new offensive CONOP. This is in direct opposition to the warfighting perceptions based on precision engagement in JV 2010. While precision engagement may serve as a means toward bond/relationship targeting, on its own it only represents an incremental increase over today's four-dimensional capabilities by making attrition warfare more precise. Bond/relationship targeting offers the conceptual means of disrupting entire systems and entities rather than gradually attriting them via precision based physical destruction as was attempted and failed in Vietnam.

The potential fusion of non-state soldiers with an advanced form of battlespace (i.e., five-dimensional) and weaponry (i.e., upper-tier non-lethals and information based) along with new CONOPS (i.e., stealthing, cybershielding, et al.) makes for an increasingly dangerous threat to American national security. To date, this synergistic threat has not been addressed in Army literature on future warfighting and as a result currently represents a "gaping hole" in Army futures threat analysis.

Failed-state environments may be conducive to the growth of successor forms of social and political organization to the nation-state. New warmaking entities which evolve in these environments and are allowed to grow and expand to create vast global "criminal" networks may represent an emergent threat to our national security.

By 2020-2025, the appearance of the 21st century equivalent of *The Prince* could be expected to take place. It would provide a more concise methodology and ideological rationale for breaking America's domination of warfare than V.K. Nair's *War in the Gulf: Lessons for the Third World*, published in 1991, ever did. Distributed by means of the internet, such a manifest could serve to fully shatter the Western nation-state's monopoly on warfare in much the same manner as Machiavelli's work broke the monopoly then held by the Medieval Church.

These implications suggest that warfighting as the Army understands it is undergoing a massive transformation. This change transcends the military arts at the RMA level and encompasses the fundamental social and political organization of human civilization based upon emergent sciences, technologies, and motive sources. [76] As a result it faces a revolution in political and military affairs

(RPMA) and not a much smaller RMA. The danger now exists that the Army After Next may be configured around an increasingly obsolescent form of warfighting, with the addition of advanced technology and concept appliqués, rather than attempting to make a break with the past and fully reconfigure itself around advanced warfighting principles as nation-state successor forms will do.

This creeping trend is evident in the Army's unwillingness, or inability, to question its basic assumptions of warfighting. Since the advent of the Force XXI program, Army modal warfare analysis—earlier Tofflerian and now Cycles of War based—has centered on the change from the industrial to the information age. This represents the time period which has defined our nation's and army's institutional existence. The current form of analysis for the AAN centers on change between the Napoleonic era, the American Civil War, the First World War, the early 1960s, and the Gulf War.[77] It represents a linear projection of a past based upon both Newtonian and Clausewitzian concepts of warfighting.

Such traditional analysis is in direct variance with the non-linear concepts and technologies discussed in this monograph. Further, it fails to recognize the greater patterns of Western modal warfare change. As a result, it must now be considered to represent a direct impediment to the AAN project. If the institutional mindset such analysis is derived from is not overcome, it will potentially set up the Army After Next and the American public for a strategic defeat many magnitudes greater than anything ever before experienced in our nation's history. Regardless of the personal and career sacrifices involved in facing this sobering reality, such a strategic defeat is something which our senior Army leadership can never allow to take place.

End Notes

[1]. Xavier Raufer, "Gray Areas; A New Security Threat," *Political Warfare*, Spring 1992, p. 1.
[2]. Robert J. Bunker, "Failed-State Operational Environment Concepts," *Military Review*, Insights, Vol. 77, No. 5, September-October 1997, pp. 90-92.

[3]. Robert J. Bunker, "Epochal Change: War Over Social and Political Organization," *Parameters*, Vol. 27, No. 2, Summer 1997, pp. 15-25.

[4]. Hendrik Spruyt, *The Sovereign State and Its Competitors*, Princeton Studies in International History and Politics, Princeton, NJ: Princeton University Press, 1994, p. 184.

[5]. For early work in this area, see J.K. Zawodny, "Infrastuctures of Terrorist Organizations," in Lawrence Z. Freedman and Yonah Alexander, eds., *Perspectives on Terrorism*, Wilmington, DE: Scholarly Resources, 1983, pp. 61-70.

[6]. United States Army, Training and Doctrine Command (TRADOC), *The Annual Report on The Army After Next (AAN) Project, July 1997*, Washington, DC: U.S. Government Printing Office, July 18, 1997, p. 9.

[7]. Steve Metz, "Which Army After Next? The Strategic Implications of Alternative Futures," *Parameters*, Vol. 27, No. 3, Autumn 1997, p. 15. Shortened version of *Strategic Horizons: The Military Implications of Alternative Futures*, Carlisle Barracks, PA: U.S. Army War College, Strategic Studies Institute, 1997.

[8]. This major military competitor represents one potential warmaking entity which could develop out of the alternative future security systems proposed by Steve Metz, pp. 15-26.

[9]. Robert J. Bunker, "Epochal Change: War Over Social and Political Organization," p. 19.

[10]. See Ralph Peters, "The New Warrior Class," *Parameters*, Vol. 24, No. 2, Summer 1994, pp. 16-26; and Charles J. Dunlap, Jr., "How We Lost the High-Tech War of 2007: A Warning for the Future," *The Weekly Standard*, January 29, 1996, pp. 22-28.

[11].11. Such perceptions began to develop immediately after the Gulf War. See Brigadier V.K. Nair, VSM (Ret.), *War in the Gulf: Lessons for the Third World*, New Delhi: Lancer International, 1991.

[12]. This box is presently 200 x 200 miles; by 2020-2025 it will conceivably be expanded based on linear projections. Derived from William Owen's "system-of-systems" concept. For the perceived advantage this concept provides, see Joseph S. Nye, Jr. and William A. Owens, "America's Information Edge," *Foreign Affairs*, Vol. 75, No. 2, March-April 1996, pp. 20-36.

[13]. TRADOC, *The Annual Report on The Army After Next (AAN) Project, July 1997*, p. 14.

[14]. *Ibid.*, p. B-2.

[15]. Robert J. Bunker, "Advanced Battlespace and Cybermaneuver Concepts: Implications for Force XXI," *Parameters*, Vol. 26, No. 3, Autumn 1996, pp. 109-110.

[16]. Alan G.R. Smith, *Science and Society in the Sixteenth and Seventeenth Centuries*, History of European Civilization Library, Geoffrey Barraclough, ed., Harcourt Brace Jovanovich, Inc., 1972., pp. 9-27.

[17]. For this process of change, see Robert J. Bunker, "Epochal Change: War Over Social and Political Organization," pp. 15-25.

[18]. This figure was originally included in a featured presentation by the author at U.S. Army Test and Evaluation Command (TECOM), Test Technology Symposium '96 "Visions of Future Conflict—Test Technology Drivers," Johns Hopkins University, Laurel, MD, June 4, 1996.

[19]. An earlier shift from one- to two-dimensional warfighting took place during the transition from the classical to the medieval world. It represents a second baseline of dimensional warfighting change not discussed in this manuscript.

[20]. For a synopsis of this view of war, see John F. Schmidt, "Command and (Out of) Control: The Military Implications of Complexity Theory," David S. Alberts and Thomas J. Czerwinski, eds., *Complexity, Global Politics and National Security*, Washington, DC: The Center for Advanced Concepts and Technology, Institute for National Strategic Studies, National Defense University, June 1997, pp. 222-224.

[21]. National Research Council, *STAR 21: Strategic Technologies for the Army of the Twenty-First Century*, Washington, DC: National Academy Press, 1992; National Research Council, *STAR 21: Technology Forecast Assessments*, Washington, DC: National Academy Press, 1993; Brian Nichiporuk and Carl H. Builder, *Information Technologies and the Future of Land Warfare*, Santa Monica, CA: The Rand Corporation, Arroyo Center, 1995; and John Arquilla and David Ronfeldt, *The Advent of Netwar*, Santa Monica, CA: The Rand Corporation, 1996.

[22]. For early thinking in the application of such emerging technologies, see Steven Metz and James Kievit, *The Revolution in Military Affairs and Conflict Short of War*, Carlisle Barracks, PA:

U.S. Army War College, Strategic Studies Institute, July 25, 1994, pp. 5-11.

[23]. Originally termed four-dimensional warfighting, with time considered a fifth dimensional attribute. In order to avoid conflict with scientific writings, time has been reordered as the fourth dimensional attribute and cyberspace as the fifth dimensional attribute of advanced battlespace. See Robert J. Bunker, "Advanced Battlespace and Cybermaneuver Concepts: Implications for Force XXI," pp. 108-120. Further concept development can be found in Robert J. Bunker, Chapter 10, "Technology in a Neo-Clausewitzian Setting," in Gert de Nooy, ed., *The Clausewitzian Dictum and the Future of Western Military Strategy*, Boston, MA: Kluwer Law International, 1997, pp. 137-165.

[24]. The possible (theoretical) folding of space leading to a space warp represents a more mature projected capability of fifth-dimensional warfighting. This insight is reminiscent of the higher dimensional spaces invoked and required for advanced physics problems such as unified field theories. For one application of these concepts, see K.C. Cole, "Scientists Report Primitive Step in Teleportation," *Los Angeles Times*, December 11, 1997, p. A30.

[25]. Spatial warping concepts partially derived from the paper, "Technology in a neo-Clausewitzian Setting," Experts-workshop for *The Clausewitzian Dictum and the Future of Western Military Strategy*, Netherlands Institute of International Relations, Clingendael, in cooperation with the Netherlands Defence Staff and The Netherlands Defence College, The Hague, Netherlands, February 13-14, 1997.

[26]. Pat Cooper and Jeff Erlich, "U.S. Troops to Field Shortstop Against Shells in Bosnia," *Defense News*, Vol. 22, February 5-11, 1996, p. 22.

[27]. One such weapon is the Chinese ZM-87 Portable Laser Disturber. A brochure exists which cites its main specifications and provides manufacturer contact information. Its major application is to injure or dazzle the eyes of an enemy combatant.

[28]. Robert J. Bunker, ed., *Nonlethal Weapons: Terms and References*, INSS Occasional Paper 15, Colorado Springs, CO: Institute for National Security Studies, U.S. Air Force Academy, July 1997.

[29]. F.M. Lorenz, "Non-Lethal Force: The Slippery Slope of War?," *Parameters*, Vol. 26, No. 3, Autumn 1996, p. 61.

[30]. Martin N. Stanton, "What Price Sticky Foam?," *Parameters*, Vol. 26, No. 3, Autumn 1996, p. 68. Reprinted from *Proceedings*.

[31]. This is far in advance of earlier projections based upon the 21st Century Politico-Military Force Spectrum which was developed prior to those regarding advanced battlespace. See Robert J. Bunker and T. Lindsay Moore, *Nonlethal Technology and Fourth Epoch War: A New Paradigm of Politico-Military Force*, LandWarfare Paper No. 23, Arlington, VA: The Institute of Land Warfare, Association United States Army, February 1996, p. 4.

[32]. Robert J. Bunker, ed., *Nonlethal Weapons: Terms and References*, pp. 2-3.

[33]. Scientific insights attributed to John Dering.

[34]. Arthur Knoth, "Disabling Technologies: A Critical Assessment," *International Defense Review*, July 1994, pp. 33-39.

[35]. Robert J. Bunker, ed., *Nonlethal Weapons: Terms and References*, p. 22. See Rolan K. Mar, "Bang-Less Tank Killer," *U.S. Naval Institute Proceedings*, Vol. 112, September 1986, pp. 112-113; and Stephen Budiansky, "All stuck up, no way to go," *U.S. News and World Report*, July 20, 1987, p. 62.

[36]. Term attributed to Lieutenant Colonel Matt Begert.

[37]. For early military applications of these concepts, see Steven Mann, "Chaos Theory and Strategic Thought," *Parameters*, Vol. 22, No. 3, Autumn 1992, pp. 54-68; and Alan Beyerchen, "Clausewitz, Nonlinearity, and the Unpredictability in War," *International Security*, Vol. 17, No. 3, Winter 1992-93, pp. 59-90.

[38]. See M. Mitchell Waldrop, *Complexity: The Emerging Science at the Edge of Order and Chaos*, New York: Touchstone, 1992, pp. 9-13.

[39]. Thomas J. Czerwinski, "Command and Control at the Crossroads," *Parameters*, Vol. 26, No. 3, Autumn 1996, p. 126.

[40]. This manual can be accessed at the Marine Corps Doctrine Division Home Page: http://138.156.107.3/../docdiv/index.html. It was approved June 20, 1997, by General Krulak, USMC, and Gen. Gray, USMC (Ret).

[41]. Steven M. Rinaldi, "Complexity Theory and Airpower: A New Paradigm for Airpower in the 21st Century," David S. Alberts and Thomas J. Czerwinski, eds., *Complexity, Global Politics and National Security*, Washington, DC: The Center for Advanced Concepts and

Technology, Institute for National Strategic Studies, National Defense University, June 1997, pp. 280-290.

[42]. See the above volume published from these proceedings.

[43]. MCDP-1, *Warfighting*, Washington, DC: U.S. Government Printing Office, 1997. Downloaded from Marine Corps Doctrine Division Home Page.

[44]. Steven M. Rinaldi, pp. 291-294.

[45]. See Robert J. Bunker, "Failed-State Operational Environment Concepts," p. 91.

[46]. Robert J. Bunker, "Technology in a Neo-Clausewitzian Setting," pp. 147-148.

[47]. Thomas J. Czerwinski, pp. 126-128.

[48]. M. Mitchell Waldrop, pp. 222-235.

[49]. Pat Cooper, "U.S. Navy Scientists Tap Sun for Radar," *Defense News*, May 13-19, 1996, pp. 1, 33.

[50]. Pat Cooper, "U.S. Mulls Lethal Robots: DoD Takes Second Look at Unmanned Weaponry," *Defense News*, July 17-23, 1995, pp. 3, 29.

[51]. Some bomb disposal robots used by law enforcement mount shotguns to blast open suspicious briefcases. At best, such robots have been used against barricaded suspects only a few times. While U.S. military forces do not currently employ what would be considered armed robots or even have such a requirement, this may change in the near future because of industry competition. The Navy and Marine Corps are now being sold UAVs with dual reconnaissance and attack mission capabilities. Still the firing of these weapons will likely be under human control. See George I. Seffers, "U.S. Industry Pushes Lethal UAVs," *Defense News*, October 27-November 2, 1997, pp. 3, 19.

[52]. National Research Council, *STAR 21: Technology Forecasts*, Washington, DC: National Academy Press, 1993, p. 113.

[53]. *Ibid.*, pp. 114-115.

[54]. Arthur Knoth, "March of the Insectoids," *International Defense Review*, November 1994, pp. 55-58.

[55]. Lisa Burgess and Neil Munro, "Tiny terrors: Microscopic weapons may reshape war," *Navy Times*, March 7, 1994, p. 34.

[56]. U.S. Army thinking concerning battlefield robots is centered around the Unmanned Terrain Domination Integrated Concept Team

at Fort Leonard Wood, MO. This team has no budget and concentrates on concept development primarily *via* email with academia and industry. See George I. Seffers, "Robots Aid Army Terrain Control," *Defense News*, March 10-16, 1997, pp. 1, 66.

[57]. See Mark Walsh, "Pilotless warplane gets a close look," *Navy Times,* Marine Corps Edition, July 14, 1997, p. 32; George I. Seffers, "U.S. Industry Pushes Lethal UAVs," *Defense News*, October 27-November 2, 1997, pp. 3, 19; and Robert H. Williams, "Unmanned Combat Aircraft Age Is Rapidly Approaching," *National Defense*, January 1998, pp. 22-23.

[58]. See Endnote 18.

[59]. Black's philosophy inspired by Maas Biolabs GmbH, "Maas. Small, fast, ruthless. All Edge." See William Gibson, *Burning Chrome*, New York: Ace Books, 1987, p. 116.

[60]. Samuel P. Huntington, "The Clash of Civilizations," *Foreign Affairs*, Vol. 72, No. 3, Summer 1993, pp. 22-49; and "If Not Civilizations, What?," *Foreign Affairs*, Vol. 72, No. 5, November/ December 1993, pp. 186-194.

[61]. TRADOC, *The Annual Report on The Army After Next (AAN) Project*, July 1997, pp. C-19 to C-22.

[62]. *Ibid.*, p. 14.

[63]. See Joint Chiefs of Staff, *Concept for Future Joint Operations: Expanding Vision 2010*, Fort Monroe, VA: Joint Warfighting Center, May 1997.

[64]. TRADOC, *The Annual Report on The Army After Next (AAN) Project*, July 1997, pp. 17-20.

[65]. *Ibid.*, p. 19.

[66]. While weapons of mass destruction (WMD) exist in the Black arsenal, their direct contribution to BlackFor warfighting capabilities will not be considered because of the immense damage they would cause to Black territories. They may, however, be utilized by terrorists employed by Black against Blue's homeland so that Black is not left holding a "smoking gun."

[67]. Glenn W. Goodman, Jr., "Nowhere to Hide: New Smart Munitions Rain Certain Destruction from the Sky," *Armed Forces Journal International*, Vol. 135, Vol. 3, October 1997, pp. 58-64.

[68]. Robert J. Bunker, ed., *Nonlethal Weapons: Terms and References*, pp. 4-6.

[69]. For the rise of such groups, see David Isenberg, *Soldiers of Fortune Ltd.: A Profile of Today's Private Sector Corporate Mercenary Firms*, Washington, DC: Center for Defense Information, November 1997. For Mexican cartel employment of former U.S. soldiers, see "Around the Nation: Texas," *Law Enforcement News*, October 31, 1997, p. 3.

[70]. Brian Nichiporuk and Carl H. Builder, pp. 52-54.

[71]. United States Army, FM 100-5, *Operations*, Washington, DC: U.S. Government Printing Office, June 1993, p. 1-5.

[72]. TRADOC Analysis Center, *Emerging Impressions Report: Army After Next Summer Wargame 1997*, Briefing Slides, September 24, 1997.

[73]. *Ibid.*

[74]. United States Army, FM 100-5, *Operations*, pp. 1-2 to 1-5.

[75]. United States Army, TRADOC Pamphlet 525-5, *Force XXI Operations*, Fort Monroe, VA: Training and Doctrine Command, August 1, 1994, p. 2-5.

[76]. For an overview of the traditionalist view of the RMA and what a strategic revolution would entail, see Steven Metz, "The Revolution in Military Affairs: Orthodoxy and Beyond," in Earl H. Tilford, ed., *World View: The 1997 Strategic Assessment from the Strategic Studies Institute*, Carlisle Barracks, PA: U.S. Army War College, Strategic Studies Institute, February 3, 1997, pp. 23-27.

[77]. TRADOC, *The Annual Report on The Army After Next (AAN) Project*, July 1997, pp. A-1 to A-7. See also Major General Robert H. Scales, Jr., USA, "Cycles of War: Speed of Maneuver Will Be The Essential Ingredient Of An Information-Age Army," *Armed Forces Journal International*, Vol. 134, July 1997, pp. 38-42; and Dr. Robert J. Bunker, "Cycles of War?" *Armed Forces Journal.*

Section 3:
Higher Dimensional Warfighting

Robert J. Bunker

Originally published in
Military Review, September-October 1999: 53-62.

Modern American military perceptions articulated in *Joint Vision 2010* and *Concept for Future Joint Operations: Expanding Joint Vision 2010* are designed to achieve the required capabilities for the challenges that our nation faces in the 21st century.[1] These visions increasingly speak more to the present era than to the emerging one. Qualitative advances in human civilization periodically redefine the military arts and sciences. The introduction of the stirrup and gunpowder into the European system represents two such seminal events. They helped define land warfare in terms of animal energy in the three-dimensional medieval era and mechanical energy in a four-dimensional modem world.[2]

The military arts and sciences are again being redefined— this time without supporting bureaucracies. The sheer magnitude of the change is beyond our national experience. Instead of looking to the 1920s and 1930s for indicators of coming change, our leaders should look to the Dark Ages and the European Renaissance. That notion, however, seems a bit too farfetched for today's global vision. Scientific sectors of society are well aware of the current changes. Research increasingly focuses on emerging sciences— bioengineering, advanced biometrics, cloning, chaos and complexity theory, non-linearity, post-mechanical energy and even psi-based research. In theoretical physics:

> Many of the world's leading physicists now believe that dimensions beyond the usual four of space and time might exist. This idea, in fact, has become the focal point of intense scientific investigation. Indeed, many theoretical physicists now believe that higher dimensions may be the decisive step in creating a

comprehensive theory that unites the laws of nature—a theory of hyperspace... This seminal concept has sparked an avalanche of scientific research: several thousand papers written by theoretical physicists in the major research laboratories around the world have been devoted to exploring the properties of hyperspace. The pages of *Nuclear Physics* and *Physics*, two leading scientific journals, have been flooded with articles analyzing the theory. More than 200 international physics conferences have been sponsored to explore the consequences of higher dimensions.[3]

Fifth-dimension research, referred to as "hyper" when describing higher-dimensional geometric objects and "cyber" when referring to the higher—dimensional qualities of information, does not influence the majority of our military scholars. US military journals and publications almost completely omit research, speculation or even debate concerning higher-dimensional space and its potential impact upon future warfighting. Military logic remains literally within the "box" of the three dimensions of space {x,y,z} and the fourth dimension of time {t}. Information operations and warfare, while increasingly discussed and recognized for their importance, lack any real form of dimensional residence. They are relegated to the electromagnetic spectrum, an uneasy addition to modern battlespace perceptions.

This article will build upon earlier battlespace research by discussing higher dimensional warfighting and its potential impact upon future operations.[4] Further, it will cover linear and nonlinear projections of the future battlefield, highlight recent research concerning five-dimensional {cyber} battlespace, analyze concepts and technologies underlying bond-relationship targeting and cybershielding and explore warfighting implications of redefined battlespace.[5]

A Linear or Nonlinear Dimensional Future?

Future warfare projections have crystallized in DOD initiatives based upon the revolution in military affairs.[6] This traditionalist school of thought predicts rapid advances in the information sciences will revolutionize modern warfare. This logic principally derives from early military technical revolution writings of Soviet authors [7]; studies and research promoted by the Pentagon-based Office of Net Assessment; and Alvin and Heidi Tofflers' popularized view of an emergent Information Age, "The Third Wave."[8] Joseph Nye and William Owens envision the United States with a qualitative change in its "system-of-systems" permitting "dominant battlespace knowledge."[9] George and Meredith Friedman repeat the siren's call in their writing on future war—a future based on precision guided munitions and America's undisputed military domination of war.[10]

The traditionalist school of thought has gone on to dominate future US joint force perceptions of war. In *Concept for Future Joint Operations*, new warfighting techniques derive from US information superiority and technological innovation. These operational concepts—dominant maneuver, precision engagement, fall-dimensional protection and focused logistics—are considered the epitome of modem US military thinking that is greatly influenced by its stunning coalition battlefield successes in the 1991 Gulf War. Embedded in these operational concepts are precision targeting, informational superiority, a systems-of-systems approach to warfighting and, most significant, a linear spatial projection of the future battlefield.

This linear spatial projection, however, is never mentioned. It is implicitly assumed by traditionalist thinkers that battlespace is historically defined by three spatial dimensions {x,y,z} and one temporal dimension {t} just as it is implicitly assumed by the thinkers that our most dangerous future opponents will be peer-competitor nation-states rather than emergent warmaking entities which defy our perceptions of crime and war. Such global visions and images of reality portray a modem hubris that expects other peoples and cultures to blindly follow Western military and ethical norms derived from the Treaty of Westphalia in 1648. However, Nye and Owens argue that "because the United States will be able to dominate in battle, it has to be prepared for efforts to test or undermine its resolve off the battlefield with terror and propaganda."[11]

Reformists argue that what traditionalist thinkers consider "off the battlefield," *is* the future battlefield. Reformist thinkers increasingly recognize a fifth-dimensional battlespace attribute. In addition to space and time, they include another characteristic, commonly referred to as cyberspace {c}. This attribute is required to account for both the impact of the Internet and a stealth-masked terrorist on the advanced battlefield. The National Defense Panel's report *Transforming Defense* defines cyberspace as both benign and potentially dangerous: "The Global Information Infrastructure; That aspect of the area of conflict composed of the electromagnetic spectrum and nonhuman sensing dimension in which stealth-masked forces either stage attacks or seek refuge from them."[12]

Such a nonlinear projection of the future battlefield is at odds with *Joint Vision 2010* perceptions. It incorporates both the traditional humanspace found in modem definitions {x,y,z} + {t} along with the higher dimension of cyberspace {c} derived from post-mechanical energy sources. On this future battlefield, the United States will be unable to achieve anything even remotely near "dominant battlespace knowledge" because stealth-masked forces are able to seek higher-dimensional battlespace for defensive purposes. Reformist thinkers hold that the future principal threat to Western nation states will be non-state (criminal) forces who exploit advanced battlespace— both upper-tier cyberspace (such as the Internet and electromagnetic spectrum) and lower-tier cyberspace (such as the stealth-masking of physical forces). Rather than envisioning revolution in only military affairs, reformist scholars argue that fundamental social and political changes are also taking place; together these shifts are transforming the very nature of war.

Five-Dimensional (Cyber) Battlespace

As noted earlier, to recognize that we have entered the information age is now cliché in most US military circles. The perceived primacy of information is an illusion, however, analogous to the peak of an iceberg visible above the waterline.

Inherently linked to it, yet unseen, is a foundation derived from nonlinear, post-mechanical, chaotic and complex technologies and sciences. Hence, information does not independently drive change as proponents of the revolution in military affairs suggest, any more than industrialization before it. Instead, information is an outcome of underlying strata. This being the case, five-dimensional battlespace will allow us to overcome the limitations inherent in four-dimensional, or modern, battlespace for advanced warfighting purposes.

To better understand the new potentials that cyberspace offers, three limitations of modern battlespace must be addressed. The first limitation is that of physical distance and orientation. In modern warfighting an object at $\{x,y,z\}_1$ resides at a measurable distance from another object at $\{x,y,z\}_2$. The distance between the objects and their orientation to each other is fundamentally important. Terms such as *frontal*, *flank*, *rear*, *stand-off* and *close-in* describe this mutual relationship. Cyberspace warps that mutual relationship through spatial expansion and contraction as demonstrated in Figure 1. Spatial expansion takes two military objects that are close to each other and makes them far away from each other. Stealth fighters were able to fly over Baghdad at night because, to the unaware, they did not exist. If they had, they would have been targeted by severe air defense fires. The same process works for terrorists. A terrorist standing five meters from a US soldier may as well be thousands of kilometers away because stealth-masking protects him.[13] Spatial contraction takes two military objects that are far away from one another and brings them close together. The use of the Internet, telemedicine and even real-time media broadcasts for military purposes are all examples of spatial contraction. Individuals thousands of kilometers away can be brought right to the battlefield for either virtual support or psychological warfare purposes as in the case of American citizens sitting in their living rooms watching world events unfold on CNN.

The second limitation is that of the time $\{t\}$ it takes to travel between two military objects. If one object is at $\{x,y,z\}_1$ and the other at $\{x,y,z\}_2$, a time window exists between them. In the case of a fired projectile, this would be its time of flight from shooter to target. Cyberspace can either compress this window or make it totally nonexistent. A directed-energy weapon, such as a laser, for all practical purposes has no time of flight; firing the weapon and impact are virtually simultaneous. No warning of attack will exist because no defensive mechanism can approach the absolute speed of light. As a result, based upon any warning, four-dimensional limitations have been overcome.

The last limitation of modern battlespace is dimensionality, the physical structure of an object {x,y,z}. Historically, defensive matter has been an impediment to military forces—it must be defeated in some manner. For example, the armor protecting a tank is designed to withstand an antitank projectile. The post-mechanical nature of fifth dimensional battlespace overcomes this offensive limitation. Rather than matter, electromagnetic energy is employed as a weapon. Such weaponry, be it infrasound or high-power millimeter waves (HPMMW), bypasses such physical armor and defenses by being out of phase with them. In a worst case scenario, criminal forces using such weaponry in a failed state's sprawling slum would be able to overcome US armored vehicles and incapacitate or injure their crews with little effort.

All of these examples suggest that cyberspace will offer new warfighting capabilities that are currently little understood or even discussed. We do know that the battlefield advantages of higher-dimensional space must be fully exploited by US forces and denied to their opponents. Earlier research on this new form of battlespace has focused on its basic spatial constructs: humanspace and cyberspace, which define its parameters, and data fusion and stealth that allow for dimensional transcendence.

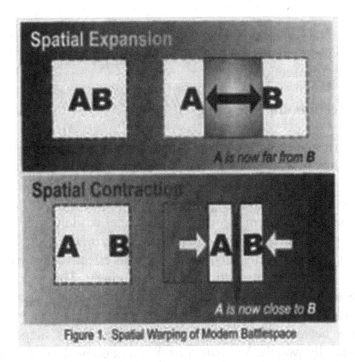

Figure 1. Spatial Warping of Modern Battlespace

Research also developed basic defensive concepts of stealth—"The application of sensory defeating procedures and technologies which allow military forces to enter cyberspace"— and cybermaneuver—safely moving military forces outside four-dimensional humanspace.[14] Notably, this cybermaneuver concept conflicts with the *Joint Vision 2010* concept of full-dimensional protection. While full-dimensional protection concerns itself with protecting US forces that reside in the kill zones of modern battlespace, cybermaneuver is meant to protect them from danger in the first place.

To these advanced operational concepts can now be added bond-relationship targeting and cybershielding.[15] While historical precedents exist, their potential can only now be fully recognized because of technological advances. Bond-relationship targeting represents the principal offensive component of cyberwarfighting, while cybershielding offers a secondary form of defense for military forces who have had their stealth-masking compromised. Bond-relationship targeting is at odds with the *Joint Vision 2010* concept of precision engagement, which is viewed as simply a precise form of attrition warfare; cyber-shielding appears to have no *Joint Vision*

2010 corollary operational concept. These concepts and the various technologies that support their emergence will be discussed in the following two sections.

Bond-Relationship Targeting

In modern four-dimensional warfighting, the US Army is renowned for its ability to seize ground, destroy enemy armored fighting vehicles and aircraft and kill opposing forces. This type of warfare focuses on personnel, material and terrain using operational styles of attrition, precision strikes and maneuver. Conventional wisdom suggests that as an opposing force is worn down by a meat grinder effect, surgical-like strikes or physically cut off, it will lose its effectiveness in combat and at some point cease to be militarily viable. This logic works well when facing opposing armies fielded by other nation-states but breaks down when applied to non-state opponents. An immense disparity between US and Vietcong casualty figures suggests that we physically won the Vietnam War. We cannot overlook that the Tet Offensive physically broke the back of the communist insurgency. Using this logic, the rescue attempt in Somalia also indicates we were physical victors with 18 Rangers killed versus perhaps up to 6,000 to 10,000 Somali casualties.[16] However, both the conflicts in Vietnam and Somalia are considered failures because they did not achieve our political goals and eventually resulted in US military withdrawal.

The two previous examples imply that crude "body counts" short of genocide poorly measure future operational success against the non-state (criminal) soldier and the new warmaking entities within which he or she will be organized.[17] Bond-relationship targeting overcomes these limitations by attacking the linkages between things rather than things themselves. This targeting capability would extend to the concept of embedded information proposed by John Arquilla and David Ronfeldt's *In Athena's Camp*.[18] This form of targeting functions along a continuum from the micro to macro level from subatomic particles to states and their coalitions to the environments in which they exist. Rather than gross physical destruction or injury, the desired end state is a tailored disruption within a thing, between it and other things or between it and its environment by degrading, severing or altering the bonds and relationships which define its existence.[19]

This operationalized end state greatly broadens Richard Harknett's *cyberwar*, which he refers to as "conducting and preparing to conduct military operations against or in defense of military connectivity." [20] The operationalization also highlights those unique properties of nonlethal weapons, means other than gross physical destruction that prevent a target from functioning.[21]

Bond-relationship targeting at a micro level can affect inorganic materials like metal and ceramic tank armor and the rubber tires of jet aircraft or ground vehicles. Liquid metal embrittlement (LME) agents alter the molecular structure of base metals or alloys and biodegrading microbes and can produce enzymes that break down rubber products.[22] Timothy Thomas has discussed the disruptive effects using strobe lights, VHF generators, noiseless cassettes and other forms of psychotronic weapons against organic forms such as human beings.[23] Such weapons, according to a Russian source, are "used against the human mind to induce hallucinations, sickness, mutations in human cells, 'zombification' or even death."[24] Many such effects may violate current arms control treaties and international norms, but as components of bond-relationship targeting, they must be openly recognized and debated for ethical and operational implications.

Against military systems such as tanks, this form of targeting can not only degrade tank armor but also cause engines to fail by means altering combustion via vapor ingested through air intakes, disrupt crew vision with rapid-hardening agents applied against vision ports and optics and disable onboard fire control computers using an energized pulse.[25] Other target sets, such as aircraft and naval vessels, can also have their functioning disrupted and degraded in a similar manner. When applied against armies and criminal-military fighting structures, bond-relationship targeting will focus on their military connectivity as currently proposed by cyberwar theorists. This disruption will require manipulating the electromagnetic spectrum that channels waves and Internet messages, isolating and overwhelming key nodes in these networks, thus creating cascading failures.[26]

Societal and political groups such as traditional and emergent state forms are vulnerable at the bonds which hold them together. Among Westphalian nation-states, the linkages within the Clausewitzian trinity represented by the government, the people and the military can be targeted as illustrated in Figure 2.[27] Rather than seeking victory on the traditional battlefield, the Vietcong engaged us on a higher dimension, eroding the bonds between our people and the government and military that served them. Terrorism also operates at this level, undermining societal security. A government that fails to stop terrorist attacks or overly infringes upon personal liberties while doing so alienates its people. We currently know very little about the bonds and relationships which hold warmaking entities, such as drug cartels, together, but this target set scheme appears to offer great possibilities over current methodologies such as "bale count" and "bag count."

Whether its structure looks like the Clausewitzian trinity conception or something else is unknown.[28] Using bond-relationship targeting and environmental warfare appears to be effective against state forms and their physical surroundings. Iraqi forces employed a crude form of this concept, setting countless oil well fires, causing environmental damage to Kuwait. Weather modification and the use of biological agents to disrupt crop yields or dairy milk production represent more sophisticated attacks, as does the detonation of radio frequency weapons that can "pollute" a nation's electromagnetic spectrum.[29] An assault upon the Internet-based communication infrastructure of a country would also be considered a bond-relationship attack. While clearly violating our modern rules of warfare, these methods point ominously toward some non-state groups posing a threat in the future.

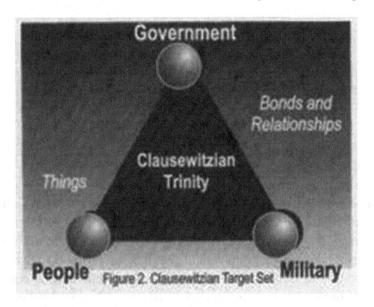

Figure 2. Clausewitzian Target Set

Both intrastate and interstate bond-relationship targeting raise important concerns. Perhaps future strategic-level warfare will evolve from weapons of mass destruction that target things to weapons of mass disruption which target linkages between those things. Recent demographic trends and Army war games suggest that opponents of the United States will defend in complex terrain such as massive urban zones. Instead of solely developing a capability to fight in such "urban death traps," our forces should be able to send a city into chaos instead of physically invading it at all. Abstracting this possibility to a higher level suggests future US defense policy option—sending a belligerent state, society or city into chaos, rather than physically invading or destroying it, by using a fifth-dimensional attack.

Cybershielding

The initial operationalization of the term *cybershielding* was as a defensive contingency operation (CONOP) against a BlueFor *Joint Vision 2010* legacy force:

> "The capability of defeating a precision strike by means of generating an invisible shield around a force which has been stripped of its stealthing and acquired

in time and space. The shield could either prematurely detonate a precision-guided munition via electronic impulses, or potentially project a semisolid 'phase state' as a physical barrier. This secondary form of defense is derived from advanced nonlethal weaponry with dimensional-shifting capability."[30]

However, against a more advanced opposing force with bond-relationship targeting capabilities, this operationalization proves insufficient. While the capability of disrupting or neutralizing a physically based precision strike is critical and should be retained, a defense against bond-relationship targeting is also required. Further, generating defensive nonphysical barriers to protect our soldiers also appears to fall within the purview of this operational concept. None of these capabilities appears in the *Joint Vision 2010* concept of full-dimensional protection.[31] Cybershielding has more in common with the concepts of antilethal weapons and weapons of mass protection suggested by Chris and Janet Morris and Thomas Baines.[32] Primarily, cybershielding protects bonds-relationships within thing, between it and other things or between it and the environment. Secondarily, it defends against a precision strike from a less technologically advanced opponent.

The desired primary end state concerns shielding against bond-relationship targeting.[33] At the lowest level of shielding, some sort of cyberbarrier could be developed for the individual solider. Such a barrier would complement the personal battle armor of the Land Warrior modular fighting systems. These systems' "basic components are a helmet-mounted display, an improved image intensification (I^2) modular weapon, improved protective clothing to include improved modular body armor, a computer and radio setup and special software for battlefield communications."[34] Additional shielding would offer protection against advanced nonlethal weaponry. The power source to generate this shield, which would be projected immediately over the battle armor and visor, would already be organic to the soldier system for other component power needs.[35] Aircraft and ground vehicles could also be considered for cybershielding, protecting systems, crews and passengers from radio frequency (RF) and high-powered microwave (HPM) weaponry or barriers.

With regard to military connectivity, Martin Libicki of the National Defense University suggests that the true dangers from hacker attacks are corrupt information and the decisions that depend on it.[36] To counter this warping of data, he suggests a number of defensive measures:

> "cryptographic methods to hide information, regulate external access to a system or tag internal changes to its data; filters that permit only a limited number of set messages to be transferred among machines; unerasable media to archive information and protect against viruses; air-gapping for a few systems [removing outside access to a nuclear power plant] as well as more quotidian defenses [such as firewalls, anomaly detection, heightened awareness]."[37]

Once a network has been penetrated, antiviral programs represent another form of cybershield. This digital struggle pits virus and antivirus software programs against one another. Possibly the immune system metaphor is useful when discussing defensive measures against bond-relationship attacks targeting out information systems.[38]

The shielding of social and political groups also potentially benefits from fifth-dimensional thinking. This approach would likely center on how the psychic effects of a terrorist incident, such as the bombing of American servicemen in Lebanon and Saudi Arabia, could be degraded or mitigated. It would require a better understanding of the Clausewitzian trinity and the bonds-relationships among the government, military and people. Currently, our knowledge is very limited in this regard. Additionally, regardless of whether the United States seeks the capability to send a belligerent state or entity into chaos by using weapons of mass disruption, it would be prudent to develop shielding countermeasures against such attacks. Preventing a "digital or radio frequency Pearl Harbor" is common sense.

With regard to its secondary end state, a cybershield would represent a nonphysical or semisolid barrier which against a precision strike. Unlike three-dimensional based armor for individual vehicles and soldiers, this protective barrier would be projected out around a defending force. The best known example of this principle is the *Shortstop* system deployed in Bosnia. It generates an electronic barrier, prematurely detonating mortar rounds by sending false messages to their fuzing.[39] Radio frequency (RF) and high-powered microwave (HPM) devices are be able to generate similar defensive barriers. Unshielded precision missiles and munitions entering their electromagnetic fields would have their circuitry burned out or fused, rendering them inoperable. Such barriers could also be used against attacking aircraft. Several early crashes of Army UH-60 Black Hawk helicopters have been attributed to their flying too close to large microwave transmitters.[40]

Cybershielding used to generate nonphysical defense falls within the parameters of the secondary end state. Likewise, this specific capability is conceptually problematic and might also be considered offensive. It does have immediate applicability in domestic not control and foreign failed-stated environments. One form of this shielding would be an "acoustic curtain" projected in front of soldiers protecting a contested facility, such as a radio station in Bosnia. Such curtains could also be generated across a bridge, at a road block or even at a choke point in a sewer system. The biophysical effects generated by these curtains could range from nausea and loss of bowel control at their edges to more severe effects closer to their centers.[41] To mark these barriers, specially designed holograms could be projected within their confines with either wording or symbols to designate their danger levels.[42]

Holograms, remarkably, make for another form of defensive shielding. They can create the illusion of solid walls, roadblock barriers and other terrain obstacles such as fences, and as a means to hide spike strips and caltrops. While the two above technologies with barrier capability are projected, a new state-of-the-art laser technology is currently being field tested. The *Laser Dazzler* is a handheld 532nm diode-pumped laser that resembles an oversized flashlight, This *eye-safe* laser-baton generates an "optical wall" out to over 500 meters that causes most individuals to turn away from the light source. In addition, a "strobe" effect is built into the laser's programmable power supply, increasing disorientation effects. Such an optical wall not only provides a time cushion to US soldiers but could potentially distract, disorient and temporarily immobilize an approaching group of rioters. Such a group would be unlikely to continue its advance or aggressive activities.[43] As a modification on this theme, variants of the *Laser Dazzler* placed on 360-degree mounts on a high mobility multipurpose wheeled vehicle (HMMWV) could provide a close-in-defense system to protect troop convoys against urban mobs.

Warfighting Implications

Many ideas in this article concerning the influence of five-dimensional (cyber) battlespace, bond-relationship targeting and cybershielding in future land warfare may range from mild inaccuracy to something much further off the mark. Such an attempt is in some ways analogous to the effort made by Mr. Square who lives in flatland {x,y} to visualize the higher third dimension {x,y,z} after an encounter with Lord Sphere in Edwin Abbott's celebrated 1884 work *Flatland*.[44] Such attempts to understand the implications of higher-dimensional space, even if they partially fail, go beyond thinking that overlooks cyberspace's impact on future warfare.

    Joint Vision 2010 is probably the most advanced document ever written concerning four-dimensional {x,y,z}+{t} warfighting, but the form of warfighting based on mechanical, linear, reductionist, synchronized and proportional concepts and technologies is becoming increasingly obsolete. Human civilization is qualitatively changing based on post-mechanical and nonlinear sciences that generate cyberspace {c}. With this change comes the expectation that the military arts and sciences will be redefined. It is only a matter of time before seminal technology on the scale of the stirrup or gunpowder will emerge or become fully recognized after its successful demonstration on the battlefield—possibly some sort of electromagnetic energy-generating device of the Internet itself. Unfortunately, such a demonstration may be conducted by a hostile warmaking entity.

    The warfighting challenge we now face is maintaining the ability to fight and win the four-dimensional conflicts of the past, which take center stage in *Joint Vision 2010*, while simultaneously obtaining a growing capacity to fight the five-dimensional wars of the future. Victory in those new types of wars will likely not be obtainable quickly.[45] To face this challenge, military scholars and officers must ask difficult questions concerning the dimensional parameters of the battlefield, its influence on future land warfare and how matter-energy and space-time analysis can develop future operational concepts suited to higher-dimensional warfighting. Military thinkers have no choice—one of the greatest sins a professional force can commit is not understanding the parameters of its next battlefield.

End Notes

[1]. *Joint Vision 2010*, Chairman Joint Chiefs of Staff (Fort Monroe, VA: Joint Warfighting Center, July 1996); and *Concept for Future Joint Operations: Expanding Joint Vision 2010*, Chairman Joint Chiefs of Staff (Fort Monroe, VA. Joint Warfighting Center, May 1997).

[2]. Medieval battlespace is three-dimensional in nature. It is based upon {x,y} + {t}. {x,y} =the two physical dimensions of depth and width and {t} = time. The knight and the castle represent the dominant weapon system and fortification type of this epoch based upon an animal motive source. Modern battlespace is four-dimensional in nature based upon the incorporation of the physical dimension of height {z}. This was only made possible by the harnessing of mechanical motive sources that allowed for the development of the firearm, cannon and later aircraft and missile weaponry.

[3]. Michio Kaku, Hyperspace. *A Scientific Odyssey Through Parallel Universes, Time Warps, and the 10th Dimension* (New York: Anchor Books. 1994), 9.

[4]. Robert J. Bunker, "Advanced Baftlespace and Cybermaneuver Concepts: Implications for Force XXI," *Parameters* (Autumn 1996), 108-120; and *Five-Dimensional (Cyber) Warfighting Can the Army After Next be Defeated Through Complex Concepts and Technologies?* (Strategic Studies Institute [SSI], US Army War College [USAWC]: Carlisle, PA., March 10, 1998), 142.

[5]. For background information see Jeffery R. Cooper, *Another View of the Revolution in Military Affairs* (Carlisle, PA: SSI, USAWC, 15 July 1994), 1-46.

[6]. Mary C. FitzGerald, "The Soviet Image of Future War: Through the Prism of the Persian Gulf," *Comparative Strategy* (October-December 1991), 393-435 and "The Russian Image of Future War" *Comparative Strategy* (April-June 1994), 167-180. See MG Vladimir I. Slipchenko (Ret). "A Russian Analysis of Warfare Leading to the Sixth Generation," *Field Artillery* (October 1993), 38-41.

[7]. A.W. Marshall, "Some Thoughts on Military Revolutions" (Office of Net Assessment Memorandum, 27 July 1993); and Andrew Krepinevich, "Cavalry to Computer: The Pattern of Military Revolutions." *The National Interest* (Fall 1994), 30-42.

[8]. Alvin and Heidi Toffler, *War and Anti-War Survival at the Dawn of the 21st Century* (Boston: Little, Brown and Company, 1993).

[9]. Joseph Nye and Williams Owens, "America's Information Edge," *Foreign Affairs* (March-April 1996), 20-36.

[10]. George and Meredith Friedman, *The Future of War: Power, Technology & American World Dominance in the 21st Century* (New York: Crown Publishers, 1996).

[11]. Nye and Owens, "Americas Information Edge," 25.

[12]. Report of the National Defense Panel, Transforming Defense: National Security in the 21st Century (Arlington, VA, December 1997), 90.

[13]. Bunker, "Advanced Battlespace and Cybermaneuver Concepts: Implications for Force XXI," 116-117.

[14]. Ibid., 111.

[15]. Bond-relationship targeting and cybershielding as operational concepts were first discussed in Robert J. Bunker, Five-Dimensional (Cyber) Warfighting. Prior to that paper, the concept of bond-relationship targeting being used by non-state forces was proposed in my article "Failed-State Operational Environment Concepts," *Military Review Insights* (September-October 1997), 91.

[16]. Malcolm H. Wiener, Chairman, Non-Lethal Technologies: Military Options and Implications. *Report of an Independent Task Force* (New York: Council on Foreign Relations, 1995), 4.

[17].-This form of warfighting also offers great potential against rogue nation-states willing to suffer massive human causalities to further their causes. Of concern is the great likelihood that the development of five-dimensional offensive operational concepts such as bond-relationship targeting has already been realized by nonstate

entities against the Western nation-state form. Such concepts would likely develop from a trial-and-error process rather than a focused research effort.

[18]. John Arquilla and David Ronfeldt, ad., *In Athena's Camp: Preparing for Conflict in the Information Age*, Chapter Six, "Information, Power, and Grand Strategy. In Athena's Camp-Section 1" (Santa Monica, CA National Defense Research Institute, RAND, 1997), 148-149. Such targeting could be considered "hyper" rather than "cyber" based. Hyper targeting corresponds to novel technologies that attack, alter or influence embedded information as in the case of a genetic or chemical code. Cyber targeting attacks, alters or influences the higher-dimensional qualities of processing information within or outside the electromagnetic spectrum. I am indebted to Deputy John Sullivan for this observation.

[19]. Concepts of weapons of disruption and the employment of mass disruption as an operational concept first originated in discussions held by members of the Los Angeles County Terrorism Early Warning Group (TEW) in 1996.

[20]. Richard J. Harknett, "Information Warfare and Deterrence," *Parameters* (Autumn 1996), 97. This term first developed by John Arquilla and David Ronfeldt when used by Harknett focused upon command and control warfare. See John Arquilla and David Ronfeldt, *Cyberwar is Coming!* (Santa Monica, CA: RAND, P-7791. 1992).

[21]. Department of Defense, Policy for Non-Lethal Weapons, No. 3000.3, 9 July 1996.

[22]. Arthur Knoth, "Disabling Technologies: A Critical Assessment," *International Defense Review* (July 1994), 33-39.

[23]. Timothy L. Thomas, "The Mind Has No Firewall," *Parameters* (Spring 1998), 84-92. For other publications by this author on this theme go to the Foreign Military Studies Office website located at http://leav-www.army.mil/fmso/ fmsopubs/ fmsopubs.html.

[24]. Ibid., 89.

[25]. Roland K. Mar, "Bang-Less Tank Killer," *U.S. Naval Institute Proceedings* (September 1986), 112-113, Stephen Budiansky, "All stuck up, no way to go," *U.S. News & World Report* (20 July 1987). 62; and Knoth, "Disabling Technologies: A Critical Assessment," 33-39.

[26]. Steven M. Rinaldi, "Chapter 10: Complexity Theory and Airpower: A New Paradigm for Airpower in the 21st Century," in David S. Alberts and Thomas J. Czerwinski, ed., *Complexity, Global Politics and National Security* (Washington. DC: The Center for Advanced Concepts and Technology, Institute for National Strategic Studies, National Defense University, June 1997), 247-302.

[27]. The actual Clausewitzian trinity is chance, rationality and passion This trinity is loosely associated and has been promoted by modern military scholars such as Harry Summers, Jr., Martin van Creveld and David Jablonsky. For more on this controversy see Edward J. Villacres and Christopher Bassford, "Reclaiming the Clausewitzian Trinity." *Parameters* (Autumn 1995). To access this article within the Clausewitz homepage go to [http.//www.mnsinc. com/cbassfrd/CWZHOME/ Trinity/TRININTR.htm]. I am indebted to Dr. Steven Metz for this observation.

[28]. Mark T. Clark, "The Continuing Relevance of Clausewitz," *Strategic Review* (Winter 1998). 60.

[29]. Numerous documents and articles address the dangers that RF weapons pose to modern infrastructure. A number of these can be accessed at infowar.com. This threat is increasingly coming to the attention of the US government. See "GAO Launches Review of How DoD Handles the Radio Frequency Threat," *Inside the Pentagon*, 30 April 1998, 12.

[30]. Bunker, *Five-Dimensional (Cyber) Warfighting*, 24.

[31]. Joint Chiefs of Staff, *Concept for Future Joint Operations: Expanding Joint Vision 2010*, 52-54.

[32]. Chris and Janet Morris and Thomas Baines, "Weapons of Mass Protection: Nonlethality, Information Warfare, and Airpower in the Age of Chaos." *Airpower Journal* (Spring 1995), 15-29.

[33]. This proposed capability has not been discussed within the Department of Defense nonlethal weapons program. Instead, that program supports the Joint Vision 2010 operational concept of full-dimensional protection. See Department of Defense Non-Lethal Weapons Programs, "A Joint Concept for Non-Lethal Weapons," *Marine Corps Gazette* (March 1998), A-1 to A-13.

[34]. Barbara A Jezior, "Chapter 2: The Revolutionized Warfighter Circa 2025," in Douglas V. Johnson 11, ed., *AY 97 Compendium Army*

After Next Project (Carlisle, PA: Strategic SSI, USAWC, 6 April 998), 41.

[35]. The battery issue is one of the major hurdles facing the Land Warner system. See John G. Roos, "Power to Spare: Revolutionary Fuel Cell Could Be The Cure For the Army's 'Battery Blues,'" *Armed Forces Journal International* (May 1998), 17.

[36]. Martin C. Libicki, "Information War, Information Peace," *Journal of International* Affairs (Spring 1998), 419.

[37]. Ibid.

[38]. See Martin C. Libicki, *Defending Cyberspace and Other Metaphors* (Washington, DC: The Center for Advanced Concepts and Technology, Institute for National Strategic Studies, National Defense University. February 1997).

[39]. Pat Cooper and Jeff Erlich. "U.S. Troops to Field Shortstop Against Shells in Bosnia," *Defense News* (February 1996), 22.

[40]. Glenn W. Goodman Jr., "US Electronic Systems Highly Vulnerable to Radio-Frequency Beam Weapons," *Armed Forces Journal International* (May 1988), 20.

[41]. See Barbara Starr, "Non-lethal weapon puzzle for US Army" *International Defense Review* (April 1993), 319-320; and Sid Heal and Paul Evancoe, "Nonlethal Disabling Technoogy: A Future Reality," *Police and Security News* (September-October 1996), 3-16.

[42]. For recent Army work, see "Army Researchers Work on Realistic Holograms," News Briefs. *Army RD&A* (March-April 1998).

[43]. Jack Kehoe, "Laser Dazzler for Non-Lethal Force Applications," LE Systems Inc., Glatstonbury, CT, Presented at Non-Lethal Defense II, National Defense Industrial Association, Johns Hopkins University, Laurel, MD, 25-26 February 1998.

[44]. Michio Kaku and Jennifer Thompson, *Beyond Einstein: The Cosmic Quest for the Theory of the Universe*, revised and updated (New York Anchor Books, 1995), 165-167.

[45]. Earlier recognized by Ralph Peters. See his "The Culture of Future Conflict," *Parameters* (Winter 1995-96), 25.

Section 4:
The Fifth Element:
High-tech information-gathering tools are becoming a critical weapon in the tactical officer's arsenal

Lois (Pilant) Grossman

Originally published in
Police Magazine, Vol. 26. Iss. 8., 1 August 2002: 24-26, 28.
Copyright Police Magazine/PoliceMag.com. Used with permission.

When the United States was attacked by terrorists on 9-11, it was a blow beyond our wildest imagining, devastating beyond belief. Thousands died at the hands of enemies most of us never even knew we had. The ripple effect damaged everything from the economy to our relationships with our government and with one another. Which was exactly the point.

Welcome to the new battleground. Called "fifth-dimensional battlespace," it takes the old three-dimensional battlefield (the spatial dimensions of length, width, height or depth of an area), and the temporal dimension of time, and adds the fifth dimension of cyberspace. It is a place where none of the old rules apply, where attacks can come out of nowhere, and your sworn enemy might be your next-door neighbor.

Fifth-dimensional battlespace is the perfect playground for terrorists, who require anonymity to operate. Yet it also is the very thing that, when used appropriately, can keep the good guys safe.

The concept of fifth-dimensional battlespace, while typically applied to military operations, is beginning to affect law enforcement, especially in the area of SWAT tactics. It moves SWAT officers out of the predictable dance of symmetrical response, where officers respond to a show of force with an equal or greater force, and into an asymmetrical response, where they too can operate with anonymity and exploit their adversary's weaknesses.

Sensory Perceptions

"The old idea was to rush in and dominate the geography as fast as possible," says Sgt. Don Kester, SWAT Supervisor for the Pima County (Ariz.) Sheriff's Department. "Now the emphasis is on officer safety, slowing down, and the ability to switch tactics in the middle of an operation if the circumstances call for it. The way to manage that is through information, and the way to get that is to use different technologies."

Information is the new tool, the fifth element, that lets SWAT officers overcome the physical limitations of the three-dimensional crime scene, where the biggest, the baddest, or the best armed win. It also overcomes the fourth dimension of time, where tactics be damned if the timing is wrong.

Maneuvering in cyberspace means using GPS to locate a suspect or do surveillance from space. It is the ability to intercept cell phone calls or use radar to monitor a suspect's movements inside a building. It is what will allow law enforcement to remotely shut down vehicles, lock and unlock cars, or open and close garage doors.

Dep. Brice Stella of the Los Angeles County Sheriff's Department demonstrates some of the more high-tech devices available to SWAT teams, including Remotec's Mini-Andros robots and portable video systems and monitors from Chang Industries.

"The new weapons will be sensing technologies," says Capt. Sid Heal, who heads the Los Angeles Sheriff's Department's Special Enforcement Bureau. "[The bad guys] send a message from one point to another. If we can acquire, manipulate, or deprive them of information of all types, including the message, and if we can do it while it's in transit, then we have the advantage."

"It's not technically difficult to kill people. What is really hard is trying not to kill them. What is really difficult is dealing with the ambiguity of making the right decision. Our intent is to make better decisions, not develop better weapons."

Improving Intel

Better decision making requires the ability to gather information. New technologies are being employed by SWAT departments for just this purpose. Some have been developed by SWAT officers, while others come from research facilities, government labs, or private industry. Some are nothing more than a developer looking for the problem that fits his solution, but others are appropriate, workable tools that can have a dramatic effect on officer safety.

"Our goal is to not be shot at. Period," says Kester. "We use cameras, under-the-door scopes that we can slide in and look around an entire room. We put them in vents or through holes drilled in walls. They can work on radio frequency or a hard line, and transmit a picture back to the team leader at the scene or to the command post. We use microphones that we can slip under doors or attach to windows. Using these things means we don't have to engage people in the same way we used to. If we know what room they're in, we can have the team do a stealth entry. The microphones let us listen to the hostage taker and get an idea of his mental state and his intentions. All of these things help us decide what tactics to use."

Optical Awareness

Night vision and thermal imagers, once the expensive province of the military, are becoming the norm in SWAT operations. Not only has the price dropped considerably since these technologies were first introduced, there are grant programs, most notably from ITT Night Vision, that help underfunded agencies afford them. State-of-the-art night vision devices, dubbed GenIII, are small, light, and provide clearer images than previous generations. They can be handheld or take the form of a monocular that attaches to a helmet.

Pole cameras also are becoming more popular, allowing officers to safely peer around corners, over walls, or into areas outside their field of vision. The Royal Canadian Mounted Police (RCMP) equips its officers with pole cameras, a vest-mounted flat-screen monitor, and a battery pack that operates both units.

An emerging technology that holds some promise is radar that can "see" through walls. One device is being developed by Time Domain Corp. in Huntsville, Ala. Called RadarVision 2000, it broadcasts short, low-powered pulses over wide-band frequencies to show the location of a person and the direction of movement. RadarVision 2000 can detect gross motions, such as walking, running, bending, or turning, through almost everything but solid metallic surfaces. It could be used outside of a house, from the roof of an apartment building, or inside a building to scan the attic, basement, crawlspace, or individual rooms or offices.

The National Institute of Justice has funded the venerable Georgia Tech Research Institute in Atlanta to create a Radar Flashlight. This device transmits a beam and detects anomalies in the frequency of the returning beam. The results are plotted on a bar graph. Although the Radar Flashlight is in the prototype stage, the NIJ offered it to rescue workers at the World Trade Center site. The hope was that it would detect the movement of survivors, but the device was never used.

One of the most popular technologies is the robot. It has been used to batter down doors, clear rooms, or make contact with a suspect. In many instances, robots have saved lives.

A case in Pima County, Ariz., had three suspects wanted for aggravated assault hiding in a house. An explosive entry in the rear door got no response, so the team sent in its robot. Two of the suspects were contained, but the third proved elusive until the robot pushed open the door to a darkened laundry room. There stood the drug-addled suspect swinging a samurai sword high over his head. By communicating through the robot, officers convinced the man to surrender. "If we'd have gone in, we'd have been forced to kill him," Kester said.

Robots also have been used to toss "throw" phones, lob tear gas into buildings, or plant cameras or microphones to gather information for SWAT commanders. The disadvantage to deploying robots is that the technology typically has been adapted from bomb disposal teams, which means robots also have limited capabilities. Some cannot climb stairs, for example, or record conversations. Robots engineered specifically for SWAT purposes are a somewhat new device and are still relatively expensive.

Information Sharing

All of these devices and technologies can increase officer awareness at the scene, but may not be of much help if the information cannot be transmitted to a command post or shared with other officers. Thus far, bringing everybody involved into the information loop has been almost impossible. There are two systems, however, that are in the development and prototype stages that may alleviate the problem.

Gord Scott, a 31-year RCMP veteran who now works in the agency's Bomb Data Center, recently rolled out the prototype of a tactical video system that takes the images of up to 12 cameras and displays them on a 13-inch flat screen that is housed in a small suitcase. Although the system can transmit via radio frequency, Scott prefers using cables "because RF only works about 5 percent of the time."

Video cameras on extensible poles, like this Chang Industries model with an infrared attachment, help SWAT officers achieve their primary tactical goal: to avoid taking fire.

Such a system would supersede the use of robots, which are restricted to a forward view and to a monitor held by the operator. Scott's battery-operated system sends pictures from anywhere a camera is placed, transmitting it to the vest-mounted monitors of field officers and to a command post up to 2,000 feet away. It can use thermal imagers or night vision, with views appearing individually or multiplexed on the commander's screen. The system has a VCR input to play reconnaissance video, and will send scanned photos of suspects or floor plans from the command post to team members.

The LASD is working with private industry to create a similar system, only one that is wireless and can transmit to officers' PDAs, a nearby command post, an operations center, and finally, that is accessible via the Internet to experts at national labs, university research centers, or other government agencies.

This "ground-link video system" is part of the LASD's Technology Exploration Program, which has officers working with developers to make sure new gadgets meet operational needs. The system's most recent incarnation combined wireless handheld technology with encrypted digital video surveillance and a secure mobile intranet. It would receive images and audio from the field and make them available to command and field personnel, and to a remote emergency operations center. The goal was to create a cyber command post where the limitations of geography and time were irrelevant. The only problem was, it didn't work.

The department stopped working with the developer and has forged relationships with other companies in search of one that can build such a system. Heal envisions using it in any number of situations, whether a chem/bio incident that requires the expertise of scientists from Utah's Dugway Proving Grounds, or a hostage situation where profilers from other agencies or university behavioral scientists lend their expertise while remotely viewing the negotiations. It also could link to any number of local, statewide, or national databases. Such a system forms the basis of what Heal foresees as the LASD's ability to operate in fifth-dimensional battlespace.

"We want our deputies to see through a window or under a door and determine what type of weapon a suspect has so they'll know what level of force they need to respond. We want them to determine whether a less-lethal option is appropriate without making a risky entry into the building. We want them to view the scene without sticking their heads in a window or above a fence. Therefore, we'll continue to use thermal imagers, night vision, infrared, and anything else that works, and we'll continue to find ways to maneuver in cyberspace. Our goal is reliable, accurate, and timely information, which defines every tactical operation. It is the bedrock for dependable intelligence, effective decisions, and efficient operations."

High-Tech is Nice, But...

High-tech gizmos may be the thing of the future, but field officers are interested in only one thing: Does it work?

Such is the disconnect between the front lines and command staff, between the users and the inventors. In an interview with officers of the Los Angeles County Sheriff's Department's specialized SWAT teams, the message was clear. They rely on training and those things that have been proved effective.

Technology is nice, they say, but it is often only applicable in special circumstances. "Take our robot," says Dep. Jim Corrigan. "In the four years we've had it, we've only used it nine or 10 times."

Necessity, coupled with the lack of technology, has forced enterprising officers to come up with a few inventions of their own. Although they are unabashedly low tech, they work like a charm.

Giant Fish Hooks-These enormous iron hooks can rip the door off just about any building. In one instance, officers planned to serve a warrant on an armed robbery and kidnap suspect, who was holed up inside a home barricaded with bars and a steel door. No amount of ramming would break down the door, so in the wee hours of the morning, they quietly attached the hooks to the door and the other end to the hitch on their truck. When the time was right, they drove off, taking the door of the house with them, and allowing other officers to enter and arrest the suspect.

Giant Fish Hooks

The Burn Safe—This crude metal container is used as a carrier for tear gas canisters when the goal is to arrest a suspect without burning down the house. Created by an officer in the San Diego area, the container is large, heavy, and cumbersome, yet when lobbed into a home, it allows for the dispersal of hot gas without allowing the resultant heat and flame to ignite the area.

The Burn Safe

The Gas Ax—Developed by the same San Diego officer, the gas ax is yet another inventive way to disperse gas. It looks remarkably like an ax, but with a handle attached to a gas canister that feeds into a hollow, metal pole with holes drilled in the end. It has been used in apartment entries, where the only way to inject gas was to get into the apartment next door to the suspect's, and ram the pole end of the ax through the wall between the two apartments.

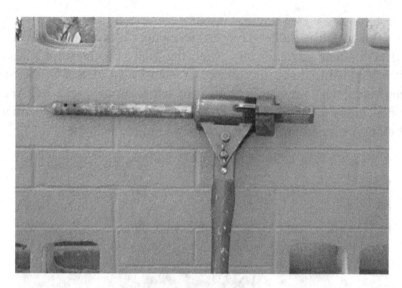

The Gas Ax

"This stuff is high-tech when you think about some of the other things we do," says Dep. Rick Rector. "We've drilled holes in old military ammo cans, put the gas in there and thrown them into the house. Or if we need to put gas in an attic and we're in the house, we'll put the canister in a big spaghetti pot and slide it into the attic."

Clearly, SWAT officers are not picky about their equipment; they'll use just about anything. They have only one single, non-negotiable demand: It has to work. This is not to say they are averse to working with technology developers or trying out new equipment and offering feedback on its performance. "What we want them to understand," says Sgt. Scott Walker, LASD's Blue Team Leader, "is that while we are happy to help and we certainly benefit, nothing is ever going to take the place of a person. Technology can increase our awareness prior to entry, but there is no technology they can come up with that will replace a trained officer and proven SWAT tactics."

Section 5:
Information Warfare and Mimicking Operations

Christopher Flaherty

Originally published in
Australian Army Journal, Vol. 1. No. 2. Summer 2003: 11-14.

In the 21st century, the Australian Defence Force (ADF) cannot afford to ignore the role that mimicry will play in contemporary conflict, particularly in unconventional or asymmetric warfare. This article argues that the Australian Army needs to develop an information warfare concept based on mimicking operations— that is, the imitation of an adversary's methods in order to facilitate deception. The development of a concept of mimicking operations by the ADF has the potential to elevate the more generic notion of deception into the realm of a precise operational concept for use in a networked force structure.

Mimicking in Information Operations

The phrase 'mimicking operations' is commonly used in modelling and scientific simulation and is connected to the idea of shielding friendly forces from detection and deception. For example, the Australian Army's keystone doctrine, *The Fundamentals of Land Warfare*, identifies the concept of 'shielding' as a combat function in the application of land power.[1] Shielding, the manual points out, 'is achieved by measures that include avoiding detection, and [ensuring] protection against physical or electronic attack'.[2] In short, shielding is viewed as an action that contributes to combat effectiveness. The connection between mimicking in scientific research and the use of deception in the military application of information operations has been described in a paper delivered by two researchers, Carlo Kopp and Bruce Mills, at the 2002 Australian Information Warfare and Security Conference. Kopp and Mills pointed out:

> Deception and Mimicry/Corruption is the insertion
> of intentionally misleading information ... [deception
> and mimicry] amounts to mimicking a known signal
> so well, that a receiver cannot distinguish the phony
> signal from the real signal.[3]

Kopp and Mills define mimicry as one of 'four canonical offensive information warfare strategies'.[4] The authors go on to develop a methodology that is influenced by biology, ecology and the workings of the natural world. The authors point out that 'a species evolves the appearance of another to aid its survival'.[5] For example, animals or insects that develop a physical similarity to predators are engaged in avoiding danger. Mimicry is also found in the behaviour of more aggressive species. For instance, 'Portia spiders strum the webs of other spiders to imitate mating behaviours or the actions of distressed prey'.[6] In this case, the target is given confusing information and is encouraged to walk into what appears to be a safe situation.

In essence, then, mimicry manipulates information through the simulation of behaviour or of physical appearance. In military terms, the employment of mimicking operational strategies has the potential to create a more sophisticated understanding of the way in which information operations might be applied in combat. In addition, mimicking operations may represent an increasingly cost-effective way of achieving a desired operational effect using superior information to exploit concealment, deception and imitation techniques.

Information-based mimicking operations using principles of non-linearity have the potential to extend military action beyond traditional tactical approaches. For instance, most conventional 20th-century operations have been traditionally planned and executed by commanders using sequential methods of decision making, often in traditional headquarters. In sequential decision-making, staff organisations are hierarchically organised and employ linear models of command and control. Conventional military doctrine tends to neglect intuitive and non-linear thinking because the command-and-control implications of such an approach require decentralisation. Effective mimicking operations demand a networked structure in which component groups are either loosely connected or are almost autonomous, but where all concerned have access to common information.

The American researchers, John Arquilla and David Ronfeldt, have developed a netwar model for 'swarming' attacks in warfare whose features are similar to nonlinear organisations. They note that 'network formations can reinforce the original assault, swelling it; or they can launch swarm attacks upon other targets, presenting the defence with dilemmas about how best to deploy their own available forces'.[7] The 'Netwar' concept developed by Arquilla and Ronfeldt is concerned with how widely distributed forces may operate collaboratively. A netwar approach requires an ability to work in a relationally based mode and to retain the ability for coordination, without the need for hierarchically based command and control.

For a non-linear network model to succeed, networked groups and individuals must be capable of pooling information and knowledge, and of undertaking swift decision-making. To date, it is those that practice unconventional, rather than conventional, warfare who have been most successful in mimicking an adversary. For instance, the al-Qa'ida movement appears to be a prime example of a non-state group that possesses a networked character based on autonomous cells that infiltrate and mimic their enemy. These cells are distributed globally, but remain connected by information systems that are common to those used by the societies that the movement aims to attack. Islamic religious schools or *madrassas* and assorted training camps in the Middle East represent the key ideological–military institutions for preparing cadres for decentralised *jihad* operations in infiltrated societies. In this sense, these schools and camps seem to operate as 'network hubs' on which a cellular structure of cadres can operate globally as a virtual army.

Networks of the type envisaged in the RAND netwar concept are predicated on a belief that, ideally, human relations are fluid and non-linear in character. Participants in a network system perform any collaborative function necessary for success and treat each other as peers rather than as superiors or subordinates. The networked, cellular structure of an organisation such as al-Qa'ida confers tactical advantages since there is a reduced need for communication, control or command coordination. Such a decentralised yet connected structure aids in the launch of mimicking operations against target societies.

For instance, the al-Qa'ida cells that launched the 11 September 2001 attacks on the United States mimicked normal flight passengers. During the operation, the attackers were indistinguishable from their victims and the surprise they achieved was total. Dispersed tactical measures in a decentralised operational plan were coordinated to achieve strategic effect through the power of information networking.

Conclusion

The concept of mimicking operations simulates activity that resembles a bacterial attack on a large and complex organism. Attacking cells mimic the behaviour of their victims, but remain dormant while awaiting an opportunity to launch an attack. In order to counter a connected, non-linear enemy, the ADF needs to investigate the use of the concept of mimicking operations as a counterstrategy in its evolving network-centric warfare doctrine. Such an approach may require a radical new direction in operational art, one that empowers a dynamic networked military organisation based on non-linear units and decentralised military activity. The challenge for the 21st-century ADF will be to reform its organisation and command-and-control methods in order to make such a military approach a reality.

End Notes

[1]. Australian Army, *Land Warfare Doctrine 1: The Fundamentals of Land Warfare*, Land Warfare Development Centre, Puckapunyal, Vic., pp. 70–2.
[2]. Ibid., p. 72.
[3]. Carlo Kopp and Bruce Mills, 'Information Warfare And Evolution', paper delivered at the 3rd Australian Information Warfare and Security Conference, 2002, p. 3.
[4]. Ibid., p. 3.
[5]. Ibid., p. 6.
[6]. Ibid., p. 4.
[7]. John Arquilla and David Ronfeldt, *The Advent of Netwar*, RAND, Santa Monica, CA, 1996, p. 11.

Section 6:
21st Century Tactics: Fighting in the Fifth Dimension

Charles "Sid" Heal

Originally published in
The Tactical Edge, Winter 2003: 21-25.

When Luke Helder was arrested in Colorado, he had already planted 18 pipe bombs in mailboxes throughout the Midwest and was on his way to California with six more. He was caught after a 40-mile chase at speeds of over 100 miles per hour. Particularly interesting is that he was stopped and released by police no less than three times in the days immediately preceding his arrest. What is even more noteworthy, however, is that his eventual arrest resulted because he was targeted and attacked from the "fifth dimension."

Tactical operations always unfold in at least four dimensions. The first three, length, width and height (and/or depth), make up the realm of space.[1] In fact, the older term "battlefield" has long been replaced in modern military discourse by the more accurate term "battlespace." Loosely defined, battlespace is that domain or realm where an adversary can be acquired and engaged.

In the law enforcement community, battlespace can be readily understood in the stark reality of everyday examples. For instance, a criminal evading a tactical team by hiding in an attic has removed himself from being acquired and engaged by maneuvering behind the barrier of the ceiling and roof of a structure. He has removed himself from the team's battlespace. In order to acquire and engage this criminal, tactical personnel must choose between entering the criminal's battlespace (the attic) or forcing him into their own. Since entries into attics are particularly dangerous, tear gas is usually the preferred method to force the criminal into an area where he can be acquired and engaged. This concept plays out in innumerable ways depending upon the various circumstances making up each tactical situation.

The fourth dimension is time. Time is a "nonspace continuum" where events occur in an irreversible succession from the past through the present to the future. Time is a separate and distinct dimension but a critical component of battlespace nonetheless. Knowing where a criminal is going to be, for instance, is only half of the equation. In order to engage a criminal, a tactical commander needs to know when the criminal will be there. Indisputably, there is no member of law enforcement who can't recall an instance where the most diligent searches revealed that the location was correct, but the criminal had already left.

Until recent times, these four dimensions satisfactorily described battlespace sufficiently enough to provide a basis for planning, acquiring and engaging adversaries in support of military and law enforcement applications, whether the adversaries were criminals, terrorists or enemy soldiers. As time has passed, however, this understanding of battlespace is proving increasingly inadequate. Battlespace has acquired a new dimension.

The Fifth Dimension

The fifth dimension is cyberspace. While most people think of cyberspace[2] as the online world of computer networks, it is actually a much richer and deeper environment. It is better understood as a notional "information space." In this realm, people interact with "humanspace"[3] through the use of a myriad of devices besides computers, such as cell phones, two-way pagers, global positioning systems, personal digital assistants, and the like. Every time a person interacts with another person or machine through one of these devices, they are, in effect, moving through cyberspace.

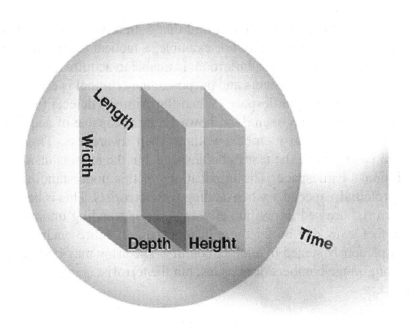

If it were possible to see battlespace, it might look something like this. Length, width and depth/height comprise the dimension of space. The fourth dimension is time. Together, space and time comprise humanspace. The fifth dimension is cyberspace.

All five dimensions interact with one another, with humans being the common "go between" or element. A business meeting, for example, involves both a place and a time. When cyberspace is added, conventional limitations are tremendously reduced or eliminated altogether because a physical location is no longer required and the limitations of time are greatly diminished. This can be readily conceptualized in a teleconference where members of a meeting at remote geographic locations participate via a closed-circuit television system. The physical location of the members is practically irrelevant, while the time to travel to a distant common locality is likewise minimized. They are operating and interacting in cyberspace.

The same concept applies in tactical operations and the arrest of Luke Helder is just one recent example. Helder had successfully been evading an intensive nation-wide manhunt for days, but once he turned on his cell phone he was quickly located and arrested. Thus, although he was moving through humanspace, he was targeted from cyberspace.

It should also be understood that both adversaries need not be in the same battlespace. For example, a tactical team searching for a criminal hiding in a dark room is unable to acquire and engage the criminal. For all intents and purposes, the criminal is effectively outside the team's battlespace. When the criminal detects the team entering through an open door, however, he is capable of acquiring and engaging team members without their awareness. Thus, the criminal is outside the team's battlespace, but the team is inside the criminal's battlespace. The implications of this understanding can be profound, especially when dealing with terrorists. This is because a terrorist dressed in civilian clothing who is standing unnoticed a few feet away can be far more deadly than an entire enemy army conspicuously staged in another country. The army may be engaged by long-range bombers or missiles, but the terrorist is impervious to attack.

Maneuvering in Five Dimensional Battlespace

Once we recognize that battlespace is five-dimensional, it raises all kinds of interesting questions, not the least of which is how to maneuver through it. Maneuver is one of the "nine principles of war"[4] and can be defined as the movement of troops and equipment to gain an advantage. Although maneuver takes on different forms in different dimensions, it transcends all five dimensions and encompasses the entire spectrum of battlespace.

Maneuver in space is so well known that little is to be gained by expounding on it. Suffice it to say that when in space, the maneuver elements are physical. They can be seen and felt. Examples include personnel, vehicles, supplies, and so forth. Moreover, maneuver in space is measured in distance and the early identification and control of key terrain takes on critical importance. Likewise, the arms used in space will also be physical, since it is superior firepower that will be required to achieve victory once the adversary can be acquired and engaged.[5]

While nearly everyone recognizes how maneuver applies in space, the more astute will also recognize the critical aspect of time. Every tactical operation is the result of a unique and temporary set of circumstances. Unique, because each circumstance is dependent only upon those factors that are present at a particular time and place. Temporary, because an outcome of any kind affects the next set of circumstances in an irreversible succession.

Because tactical operations unfold in time as well as space, it becomes clear that they are in a constant and never-ending state of change. This dynamic nature makes them inherently time sensitive since they are easily altered by actions. While all tactical operations are dynamic, the problem is especially acute when criminals are involved because they include a competing interest that is actively attempting to exploit the circumstances for their own benefit. Consequently, when tactical operations involve criminals, they are not only time sensitive, they are also time competitive. The opponent who can most quickly exploit the circumstances to his own benefit gains an advantage. Conversely, time or opportunity neglected by one adversary can be exploited by the other. While the maneuver elements involving time are just as intrinsic as those in space, they are intangible. They exist only as a mental image. Examples include actions, events and circumstances. Accordingly, when maneuvering in time, the identification and exploitation of opportunity is the compelling objective.

Impact of Tempo

Maneuver in time is measured in speed. In tactical operations and competitive games, this is most often referred to as "tempo." Tempo refers to the speed, rhythm or rate of movement of something. In a tactical operation it describes the speed at which events are unfolding. The impact that tempo has on tactical operations can be easily illustrated by recalling the advantage of the "fast break" in basketball or the "breakaway" in hockey. The team which moves the fastest gains a considerable advantage. However, tempo is relative. A rapid tempo is only useful when compared with how fast an opponent can react because sheer speed is not the critical factor. It is only relevant in that what ever you do, you are doing it faster than your adversary.

Another important maneuver factor in time is density. [6] When maneuvering in space, density refers to the number of personnel, citizens, vehicles and the like, per unit of space. When maneuvering in time, density refers to the quantity of activities per unit of time. Like space, time can be congested and cumbersome in which to operate. This results in a condition called "overwhelmed by events," often identified by the abbreviation "OBE." Like traffic congestion in space, the OBE condition ensues because the human mind is incapable of endlessly processing an infinite amount of information. A large number of events requiring decisions occurring in close succession means there is less time to analyze the situations and alternatives and more anxiety over the most appropriate course of action. When maneuvering through a congested time period, it may be necessary to "clear the landscape" by removing distractions, demanding standard formats, insisting on recommendations by trusted subordinates or delaying nonessential decisions.

The arms necessary to gain and maintain the initiative in time are those that increase the speed and effectiveness of decisions and actions. These include such things as standard formats for plans, reports and briefings to increase comprehension, vehicles and aircraft to expedite movement, and personal insight to be able to quickly recognize and exploit opportunities.

Maneuver in cyberspace requires a new paradigm, because the defining characteristic is information. Whether it is needed to locate a criminal hiding in a building or identify a terrorist concealed by anonymity, it is information that is necessary to acquire and effectively engage him. Consequently, the maneuver elements in cyberspace are data, often the "fruits" of devices designed to allow humans to interact in this dimension. Examples include the information obtained from cell phone conversations, pager messages, location reports from global positioning systems, or information gleaned from e-mail, Web sites and other on-line transactions. It also includes the information gleaned from sensors, such as thermal imaging devices and night vision goggles.

This interaction not only includes humans interacting with each other, but with machines. Examples include television tuners, garage door openers and remotely operated automobile alarms and locks. No law enforcement officer is likely to miss the tactical significance of being able to remotely open a garage door, lock a criminal out of his car or prevent him from watching a live TV broadcast. Understandably, maneuver in cyberspace is measured in knowledge, and the ability to acquire, deprive and manipulate information is critical; gaining understanding is the compelling objective.

Battlespace = Humanspace + Cyberspace

Together, the dimensions of space and time make up that portion of battlespace occupied by humans, and as such, is called "humanspace." Until recently, humanspace was the exclusive domain where combatants met and fought. When the dimension of cyberspace is added, however, combatants who remain in humanspace can be attacked with impunity from cyberspace. Luke Helder is only one of those who missed the lesson.

What separates humanspace from cyberspace is a "human sensing dimensional barrier."[7] Depending upon the circumstances, this barrier will take on different forms. When an adversary is barricaded inside a structure, for example, the barrier will be physical, but when concealed by darkness, fog or smoke, the barrier can be intangible. The barrier can also be notional, such as when an adversary is protected by anonymity. All that is necessary is that an adversary is unable to be acquired or engaged because he is outside human sensing capabilities. Understandably, cyberspace provides a refuge where weaker opponents can escape by hiding, becoming indistinguishable, or even just obscured so that the effort to identify and acquire them exceeds the value of the search. Certainly this last aspect is appealing to many crooks who understand that they need not hide indefinitely, only long enough for the tactical operation to end.

This barrier is a dynamic and contested frontier between opposing forces because terrorists and criminals will, quite understandably, take steps to avoid detection and thus remain in the safety of cyberspace, while authorities will attempt to identify and locate them to make them vulnerable to attack. Regardless of whether they are temporarily concealed by darkness or more securely protected by anonymity, they are immune from attack as long as they remain undiscovered.

Once an adversary is detected, however, he can be acquired and engaged. Thus, they are drawn into humanspace. While the essential component necessary to achieve victory in humanspace is superior firepower, firearms and other similar weapons are completely useless in cyberspace. What is necessary to succeed in cyberspace are tools to gather, deprive or manipulate information. While computers most often are the first to come to mind, they are only one of a broad range of such devices that include night vision goggles, thermal imaging devices, see-through-the-wall radar, acoustic sensing devices, remote video cameras, biometric technologies,[8] and so forth.

Dominating Cyberspace

Understanding that battlespace is five-dimensional fundamentally alters thinking and planning for tactical operations. First, recognizing that cyberspace is an inherent component of battlespace becomes a tactical imperative. Any commander who chooses to fight only in humanspace can expect to be flanked and attacked from cyberspace. This is particularly the case with terrorists who cannot win a stand up fight and must attack and return to the safety of cyberspace in order to survive, much less succeed.

Second, retooling and not rearming will be necessary. Sensors, not firearms, will be required to identify and locate criminals and terrorists hiding outside human sensing capabilities. These will take on countless forms and provide any number of advantages. On the tactical level, devices that detect explosives and weapons will tremendously diminish a criminal's ability to commit robberies or a terrorist's ability to emplace and secrete bombs. On the strategic level, biometric devices will identify terrorists and criminals and remove them from the "sanctuary of anonymity."

Third, the rules of engagement in cyberspace are not based on the appropriateness of force but the invasion of privacy. Technology already provides an ability to search electronically for contraband and weapons without the knowledge of the person being searched. So, while a "see-through-the-wall" radar or audio interception device may be easy to justify during a hostage recovery operation, screams of protest erupt when biometric devices are suggested to scan and identify terrorists among passengers arriving from another country.

Fourth, the realm of cyberspace is far more expansive than the finite limitations of space and time in humanspace. The volume of information is seemingly unfathomable. Consequently, tactics in cyberspace will not focus on the movement of personnel or equipment, but the ability to gain understanding and knowledge from a myriad of data. Information will need to be analyzed and appraised to determine meaning, relevance and significance before being incorporated into the decision-making process. Accordingly, the most effective strategies will provide an ability to quickly sort the relevant from the volume.

Fifth, cherished methods and practices will be challenged. Nowhere will this be more prominent than in the command and control function. Currently, tactical decision-making is accomplished by placing people with expertise and authority in a central location, generically referred to as a "command post," and then providing them information to make decisions. The major problem with this method is that the authority and expertise to make effective decisions lies at the command post, while the greater situational awareness [9] remains at the crime scene. Additionally, complex tactical situations, such as those involving chemical, biological or radiological threats, will require the advice of experts seldom affiliated with tactical organizations. Instead, college professors, scientists and engineers located at distant universities and research facilities will possess the essential information. Incorporating their expertise into the decision-making process becomes a compelling need for a satisfactory resolution.

These problems are greatly attenuated when a "cyber-command post" is created. Much like a teleconference, a cyber-command post does not rely on a physical location, but incorporates technology to provide the insight of subject matter experts wherever they are through the use of remote video viewing, the World Wide Web, e-mail, cell phones, and the like. Thus, the tactical decision-making process is immensely enriched with knowledge that far exceeds the capabilities of any tactical organization alone.

Well over a century ago, American Civil War Gen. Ulysses S. Grant said, "The laws of successful war in one generation would ensure defeat in another." Whether it is the war on crime or the war on terrorism, the surest way to lose a war is to use the last one as the model for the next one. While the scope of the implications of five-dimensional battlespace are staggering, there is really only one underlying requirement for success. That is to identify and locate criminals and terrorists operating in cyberspace to enable them to be attacked in humanspace. No amount of additional firepower will even the odds, because in cyberspace firepower is measured in megabytes.

End Notes

[1]. Space may be simply defined as a three-dimensional field in which matter exists.

[2]. "Cyberspace" was coined by science fiction author William Gibson, in his book *Neuromancer,* published in 1984.

[3]. "Humanspace" is used by Dr. Robert Bunker, a counter-terrorism and nonlethal weapons consultant, to describe all dimensions where humans live and interact. He defines it as "That aspect of battlespace composed of the traditional physical dimension in which humans and their machines move and fight." Consequently, humanspace will encompass both space and time.

[4]. The United States Army first published its discussion of these principles in 1921, but they were taken from the works of British Major General J.F.C. Fuller, who originally published them in 1912. Fuller's work sets forth in concise terms, nine interacting and related factors that have stood the test of analysis, experimentation and practice and are now part of nearly every Western military course of study as the "Nine Principles of War."

[5]. It should be understood that "superior fire-power" will include nonlethal options, since killing the adversary may not be necessary to defeat him. This is especially the case in law enforcement operations.

[6]. For more information on density in time, the author highly recommends the book, "Heavy Matter, Urban Operations' Density of Challenges," by Russell W. Glenn, RAND Corporation, Santa Monica, CA, 2000 (310-451-6915 or order@rand.org).

[7]. Concept and definition taken from "Advanced Battlespace and Cybermaneuver Concepts: Implications for Force XXI," by Dr. Robert J. Bunker, published in *Parameters,* Autumn 1996, pp. 108-120.

[8]. Biometric technologies are those that identify and compare the physical characteristics and personal traits of people to distinguish them from others. Examples include facial recognition, retinal scans, fingerprints, voiceprints, DNA, and many others.

[9]. Situational awareness is a concept that describes a person's knowledge and under- standing of the circumstances, surroundings, and influences with regard to an unfolding situation.

Section 7:
5th Dimension

Lois Clark McCoy

Originally published as a
White Paper. National Institute for Search and Rescue (NISUR):
Santa Barbara, CA: 2009.

The Topic "The Fifth Dimension" seems to be generating more heat than usual in these days of Rapid Change. As individuals, as organizations and as nations, it changes all the rules of social intercourse, as well as governing bodies. To make that jump into instant speed; to not be left behind as a Luddite, we need to dive into the water and learn how to swim in what is now the Main Stream. We are heading for the new "Normal" which will become our everyday world as we proceed into the 21st Century.

We in NIUSR are wrestling with this 5th Dimension. Its exponential speed has succeeded in changing our perception of our world and our new Century. In comparison to the speed of change experienced in the World after the introduction of Henry Ford's Tin Lizzie, that previous change will seem to have been a mere blip in the road. There is no comparison to the exponential increase in rates at the Speed of Light.

Carry that increase in speed from the space shuttle's travel to people. Today, each time a person uses a cell phone or such device, **they** travel with the aid of television and voice anywhere in the world instantaneously. They arrive at your door or meeting room in seconds. They are presenting as a pictograph but with all the characteristics of that particular moving, talking "live" creature.

Folks seem to be quite firey about pros and cons and once again we find ourselves lacking the "right words" to explain the intricacies of the concept. Or, even with the "right words", having differing interpretations of those words. At this transaction speeds, business decisions must be made click, click, click. There is no time for discussion or contemplation.

For me, the definitive discussion is an article by Dr. Robert Bunker. I recommend it to you. It is testimony before The U.S–China Economic and Security Review Committee, 2007.[1]

What then are my credentials to undertake a discussion on such a controversial and volatile subject? I've been reading and studying up on all I can find on the 5th dimension, cyberspace and related topics. Let me set the stage with a quick re-cap of some of my background so you can evaluate the worth of my words. I have been (among other things) a cook at Camp Pendleton for the Marines during the opening days of the Viet Nam war. I hold a Bachelor Degree in Science from Skidmore College in upstate New York.

Are you impressed with my credentials yet? Don't be. My degree in Science was awarded in Home Economics, i.e. Cooking and Sewing. Those were real "majors" for women in College in 1938 but I did graduate "cum laude".

Will a credential earned long after college add to my luster and your reassurance? I hold a NASA license for a satellite experimental ground station at L-band.

I have been studying up on Cyberspace and the 5th Dimension. So how do I presume to write my views on such an essential concept for life in this Century? Because, in my attempts to get my arms around this newly emphasized topic, I couldn't find the one book I needed. An understandable explanation in everyday language to learn all I should know about the 5th dimension

I could not find any book entitled "The 5th Dimension for Dummies." Aha. Here was my chance to write one!!! Since this knowledge is so important to our successful journey into the 21st century, permit me and my smarter friends to take a stab at explaining our versions of the 5th dimension.

"The 5th Dimension for Dummies".

Author; Lois Clark McCoy, President and CEO,
NIUSR Editors:
John Clay, SRA International, First V.P. NIUSR
Dan Lemon, Chief of Staff, NIUSR
Charles "Sid" Heal, Commander, (Ret), L.A. Sheriff's Dept.

Point One. The 5th Dimension is not a "Thing". It is a "Concept". You cannot see it under a microscope or in a telescope and there are two schools of thought on whether or not you can diagram it. It is not a version of an Internet Network Cloud. That can be diagramed if you want to spend the time. However the 5th dimension exists and is "real" in the sense of the word "concept."

To get down to basics, may I say it is as "real" as the concept of Love? Both Love and the lack of Love are real, although with wide individual interpretations. You cannot see Love under a microscope or with a telescope.

But let us leave the concept of Love to greater minds such as Shakespeare and press on to a concept where you may find yourself more comfortable: Physics 101 in High School.

High School Physics was our original testing ground for understanding the concept of three dimensions and the x, y, and z axes. In high school we struggled with equations which delineated relationships of length, width and the vertical scale of height (which included depth on the "z" axis.)

We added "Time" as the 4th dimension, at least in my Physics 101 class.

This is where it became complicated. Time is a "nonspace continuum" where events occur in an irreversible succession from the past through the present into the future. Time is a separate and distinct dimension but is a critical component of events.[2]

All would have been well if we had stuck to hours and minutes on the 24 hour clock. However when the measurement of Time was linked to Distance things became more complex. We again measured Distance in the dimension of "elapsed time of travel and speed." Although we no longer tell time and distance in the Native American fashion of "Sleeps" and "Nights", we do think of time and distance together, e.g., as days, weeks, months or years of travel, dependent upon our chosen method of transportation.

Time passes. Rules of measurement change. Let's talk about a tape; a yardstick and the Slide Rule. Dressmakers measured ladies with a tape. Every house had a yardstick. Engineers had a Slide Rule. The yardstick worked pretty conveniently during the past century but it is about to go the way of the Slide Rule which was a handy little gadget that every engineer carried in his vest pocket 40 years ago. Now computers do those equations for us. But don't overlook countries that use the metric system of meters and kilometers. I'm sure they don't call it a "yardstick"?

For a moment let's revisit our three dimensions, x. y and z. With these equations we could understand the relationships of a rudimentary shelter: a floor, a roof, and four sides- length, width and height. The original shelter grew to be a three dimensional shack. Good. Got it. **It's a BOX**.

But people weren't satisfied with living in a box, so we are, we punch holes in it for windows and doors and over the ages we wind up with castles which are really only a pile of boxes.

If you're going to have a castle, you have to have a dungeon. No Lord of the castle could be without a place to keep his enemies. So we have something UNDER our box. That elongates the vertical axis (our "z" in Physics 101) to include "depth" (although sailors and seafarers had long before added depth to their vertical dimension.)

Dungeons became "socially unacceptable". We changed the name to "cellar". We now had cellars to store jars of pickles and home brew and old tables and junk. When indoor heating moved from the fireplace to a massive furnace with a ton of coal, it usurped the space in the cellar. Our cellars ran out of room under our house so we added an Attic, During these ages we continued living in our comfortable house (or boat) in our 4 dimensions and measuring everything as we always had, with a tape or a yardstick or a surveyor's transit and by a 24 hour clock.

While most of us were happily plodding along in the daily grind, our more ingenious *homo sapiens* friends were over in a corner with other ingenious folks who decided to go to the Moon. POW. That was an instantly popular thought that intrigued almost everyone. It appeared that each of us had a small child inside us that always hoped the moon was made of green cheese and that a Man in the Moon was a possibility? The 5th dimension doesn't seem to have the same appeal.

The 5th Dimension is measured in relation to we have added the concepts of "Time" and "Space". These involve basic changes in ways of measurement. The yardstick, while useful on the ground, is not functional in Space. We must measure in "light years". (A light year is the distance that light can travel in a vacuum in one Julian calendar year. Let's not get into "parsecs"). We need to keep this treatise simple as the "5ᵗʰ Dimension for Dummies".

What we call 'SPACE" today should more properly be called "near-space." It is that area **above** your house and it goes a long way UP from your home. But it is NOT the Universe. It is only Earth's, our beautiful Blue Planet's universe, a truncation of time and space. That is plenty big enough to give us lots of new opportunities as well as problems in how to "measure" things and maneuver and communicate within it.

This area has many new names associated with it. Ionosphere, atmosphere, cyber space, as well as the 5ᵗʰ dimension. For our purposes we will define our 5ᵗʰ dimension measurements, equations and rules as being applicable to "near-space." Already it is a busy place. Today there is a lot of "junk" up there and more to come. Satellites and Space Stations and pieces of exploded rockets and missiles and nuts and bolts dropped off by space-walkers repairing Space Telescopes and other "stuff".

At the bottom of this "space" are aircraft on which we fly everyday. And above that, UAV's and Low Orbiting Satellites and above that are the Geostationary Satellites and more being planned to launch as we speak. And above that is Mother Nature's contribution flying around: Asteroids, Comets, other Planets and their Moons and our Moon.

Today the 5ᵗʰ dimension has entered our reality with its need for new measurements for Space/time and distance. As we try to occupy this new "attic" above our home on earth. The old measurements are not applicable. We continue to use these old ones which work so well on earth in "humanspace". While 4D concepts still apply they are not useful in the 5th dimension. They are not functional in a Space where objects (including our space shuttles) travel in orbit around the earth at stunning speeds. We need a new concept for time and distance.

This brings us to our most immediate "Catch 22."

Those same ingenious *"homo sapiens"* from our moon-walk days have gotten into the communications end of the 5th Dimension. In this sense, the 5th dimension is not merely an area for space structures and space shuttles. It has sensors and Satellites. It is better described as an "information space". Whenever someone talks through a cell phone via cyberspace, they are in effect "moving through space". In communicating with our astronauts and to the scientific probes to Mars, Jupiter and the like, we have also developed the ability to talk around the world and discovered that these transmissions travel at nearly the speed of light.

Today, communications in cyberspace interact daily with our *"humanspace"* below. These communications are nearly instantaneous. This is true regardless of the distance on earth from point to point. So the amount of "time" to calculate when our signal arrives to the desired location is not a factor – (We have designated that measurement as Zero since it is not a factor in our equations FOR SPACE.) In our calculations, the time needed for the transmission to reach its destination is essentially Zero.

What about Distance? Remember the signal is traveling at the speed of light. It IS light, and therefore it has to "see" where it is going. It cannot go through a mountain or underground, but providing that signal can "see" its destination, distance is almost instantaneous and again is not a factor. It is Zero. However we are still telling Time by Distance traveled IN SPACE as we do on Earth BUT the SCALE is totally new. It is in **light years** (ly) and trillions of "miles" in "OUTER SPACE to the stars in the Universe.

For our treatise for Dummies and the immediate future, let's focus on our closer planets. Take Planet Mars. Mars permits us to start our exploration of these interesting opportunities/problems closer to home. One advantage is we can hit Mars with sensors (robots) that can dig and move and send photographs and data back to earth. But it cannot (at present) carry enough weight for the signals to handle anything but the most rudimentary two-way communications.

Again, those smart friends over in the corner are busy figuring ways to increase the range of these robots to communicate more "intelligence" back to the scientists on Earth. One of their ideas is to plant a Space Network on orbiting asteroids to hop the earth signals to Mars via these orbiting repeaters. Why use an expensive Satellite when you have all these natural platforms? However this is not "Legos for Adults". This is NOT a simple solution.

In 1960 the CIA had our U-2 flying in near-space over Russia when Gary Powers was brought down. Then the Berlin Wall fell and we decided we didn't need "spy planes" anymore?

The Military replaced the U-2 capability with the "Blackbird" SR 71. What a plane that was. It flew at Mach 3 in near-space with a 2 man crew. Very few were produced. You can see one of those original planes in San Diego's Balboa Park in the forecourt of the Air and Space Museum.

Don't just look at it, as beautiful and sleek as it appears. Walk underneath it and see its size. It is as wide as a highway. From below it resembles a platter on which to serve a roasted dinosaur. It is immense! But it was a stealth aircraft and appears narrow and fast but not threatening. Oh yeah. It flew very few times as the Berlin Wall crumbled and reconnaissance changed from manned aircraft to Satellites. Check it out. It's a thrill to see.

Yes, we are struggling with the words for all these new opportunities and once we have the words, we must agree on their meaning. In the meantime, NIUSR and YOU, (like it or not) –are living in the new generation of Cyberspace. This "operational space/information space" is a distinct dimension <u>without</u> the attributes and features of either space or time. It is a conceptual **"place"** outside the same gravity of our earth, with new rules, new measurements, and new ways of maneuvering. You don't use physical objects to maneuver in it per se, but I guess you could say that you would use physical objects to capture, deny, delay, or manipulate information, etc. but I really think that analogy would confuse a person who has yet to be convinced that such a dimension exists. Likewise, the maneuver objective is not to gain and maintain control of key terrain because there is no "terrain". The goal is to gain understanding.

Interestingly, Secretary of Defense Robert Gates established an Oversight Committee on Cyber Security last month and this week of June 20, 2009 established a new Military "Command for CyberSpace".

Remember the 5th Dimension is a "Concept" which cannot be seen. But it is <u>there</u>. It is a conceptual **"place"** with new rules, new measurements, and new ways of information exchange. It is a "place" with challenges, which could bode both benefits and danger. It is here today, and it will be here in our foreseeable futures.

You and I live "Here". We are "Here". But look around you. Our "Here" has changed and continues to change ever more rapidly. Get into the new "Here", the New Main Stream. NIUSR is providing the transportation to what is becoming the new "normal". We're providing a "NIUSR" 5th dimension imaginary "bus". On its side it reads NIUSR and it's painted International Orange for Lifesaving. The first trip is already en route but YOUR seat is reserved. (The "bus" is a hybrid using petroleum and electricity, heh, heh.) **The destination is still somewhat unclear in detail.**

That is your job. NIUSR provides the transportation for your ideas and your smart answers for the next vision of "normal" for 2010 and up.

Get on the Ride. We promise it will be a great trip accompanied by the best people in the business, your NIUSR friends. Press On.

End Notes

[1]. Dr. Robert J. Bunker: CEO. Counter-OPFOR Corporation. "Testimony before the U.S.-China Economic and Security Review Commission". 2007.

[2]. Charles "Sid" Heal, U.S. Marine Corps Reserves (ret), "21st Century Tactics: Fighting in the Fifth Dimension". *Tactical Edge* 2003.

Section 8:
Police Operational Art for a Five-Dimensional Operational Space

John P. Sullivan and Adam Elkus

Originally published in
Small Wars Journal, 23 July 2009.

The last fifteen years have yielded a rich literature on structural dimensions of modern-day tactics and operational art, particularly on the challenge posed by information age command and control (C^2) technology, decentralized swarming, and irregular opponents.[1] The linguistic shift of "battleground" to "battlespace" recognizes the current reality of forces operating in a multidimensional battleground against complex opponents.[2] Similarly, many have recognized that in a rapidly urbanizing world, cities will be the main battlefields in fights between military/police units and "hybrid" opponents. "Global cities" such as New York, Tokyo, London, and Mumbai have become prime targets for terrorists, networked insurgents, and criminal organizations. Operations in global cities carry a special weight because of the strategic compression created by globalization, and pervasive communication networks—raising the significance of what would ordinarily be considered purely tactical counterterrorism operations.[3]

In our previous pieces "Postcard from Mumbai: Modern Urban Siege" and "Preventing Another Mumbai: Building a Police Operational Art" we've explored the operational level of police and counterterrorism response.[4] While military doctrine for operations is sophisticated and battle-tested, police operational doctrine has lagged behind. Counterterrorism response—situated in a complex operational space (opspace)—can now be considered as part of the operational level of maneuver, the midlevel point where strategic objectives are implemented on the theater level.[5] Genuinely *operational* doctrine for this unique form of engagement is underdeveloped, consisting of an ungainly mishmash of police, military, and emergency response tactical doctrine.

We propose a model for urban police operational art that has a five-dimensional view of the operational space, focusing in particular on the doctrinally neglected elements of cyberspace and temporality. [6] Our intention is to summarize and clarify a wide array of military thought, incorporating it into an operational framework for police operational response. In particular we will examine the military theories of Robert Bunker, Robert Leonhard, and William McRaven.

Understanding Cyberspace in Operations

Cyberspace is a contested—and critically misunderstood—element of the modern battlespace. The Department of Defense Dictionary of Military Terms holds that cyberspace is "A global domain within the information environment consisting of the interdependent network of information technology infrastructures, including the Internet, telecommunications networks, computer systems, and embedded processors and controllers."[7] However, many see it solely as a purely informational realm that we enter through the Internet. When we talk about cyberspace in the context of police and counterterrorism operations, we are not referring to the rather overused concept of "cyber warfare." Instead, we're talking about a wider definition of cyberspace that has bearing on command and control of operations.

The power of the Internet-oriented interpretation is not surprising, as science fiction writer William Gibson popularized the term "cyberspace" with his series of cyberpunk novels.[8] The Internet and "cyberspace" are now interchangeable in popular language, making the "humanspace" (or "meatspace" as Gibson called it) "real" world where guns fire and bombs go off. While cyberspace is certainly not the same thing as the physical world, it is contiguous with our day-to-day reality. Cyberspace permeates both the "real" and "virtual" worlds, and is thus both "everywhere and nowhere."[9] The Greek term *kyber*, (to "steer") from which the term "cyber" derives means steersman. The term "cyberspace" in this conception encompasses the "the idea of navigation through a space of electronic data, and of control which is achieved by manipulating those data."[10] As the Principia Cybernetica project argues, Gibson himself conceived cyberspace as a global computer network encompassing all people, machines, and sources of information.

[11] In the introduction to his book *The Hacker Crackdown*, Bruce Sterling elaborates further on the nature of cyberspace:

"Cyberspace is the 'place' where a telephone conversation appears to occur. Not inside your actual phone, the plastic device on your desk. Not inside the other person's phone, in some other city. The place between the phones. The indefinite place out there, where the two of you, human beings, actually meet and communicate."[12]

The Cold War was dominated by the science of *cybernetics*, which conceived physical organisms, organizations, and even whole societies as self-regulating systems optimized according to the flow of information.[13] Cybernetics is fundamentally a science of control, as it seeks to uncover how information, broadly understood as feedback, regulates systems. In *Command Concepts*, Carl H. Builder, Steven C. Bankes, and Richard Nordin argue that the concept of "control" in command and control refers to a cybernetic loop of nodes whose interactions and exchange produce operational plans. [14] Many command and control systems are predicated on the idea of the organization as an information-processing system. Of course, this doesn't mean that the correct posture for the commander is to act as a simple information- processing node. As Builder notes that a successful "command concept" originates in the cognitive processes of the commander and regulates and prioritizes the minimum amount of information that must travel through the system.[15]

Within the military or police organization, cyberspace is the totality of the communication and interaction between fielded forces. Thus, a cyber attack means an attack that manipulates the "data" that is exchanged in the process of communication. This understanding of cyberspace is in accordance with the holistic systems perspective recommended by the Army's *Commander's Appreciation and Campaign Design* pamphlet.[16] Cyber attacks are directed towards disrupting instruments of control—whether those are specific communication systems or the human mind. A cyber attack does not have to originate from a computer—it could be a bomb placed in a commander's barracks or an accumulated process of a series of swarming attacks destroying an opponent's C^2 ability to function in the battlespace. Overarching opposing force C^2 nodes are coordinated through cyberspace, as demonstrated during the Mumbai attacks.

This is not an endorsement of controversial "effects-based" operational theory. The commander rarely has enough information to determine the nature of the "effects" applied to a system, as human complex systems are not purely mechanical. They are complex adaptive systems that are very sensitive to initial conditions—and their course of future evolution cannot be scientifically predicted.[17] This is why Effects-Based Operations (EBO), a method of operational art derived from systems thinking, is widely acknowledged to have failed against Hezbollah in Lebanon.[18] Nevertheless, organizations do comprise systems between which information is spread in the form of interaction between nodes and messages sent up and down the chain.

We must also point out that the understanding of cyberspace we outlined also acknowledges the importance of the infosphere, the layer of communications that the global media comprises.[19] When many people write about cyberspace, they are thinking about the infosphere. Information effects have substantial effects on battlespace shaping, information operations, and can give tactical events strategic significance. Cyberspace comprises a part of the infosphere, but cyberspace is more of a limited and technical area whereas the infosphere by definition comprises the totality of media.[20]

As military theorist Robert J. Bunker points out, terrorist hide in a "virtual" domain that adversaries cannot reach, utilizing organic camouflage, sympathetic social spaces, or aspects of cyberspace to mask their activities until the last moment.[21] While this sounds exotic, insurgent camouflage could be something as simple as a sniper's cover in an abandoned building, an underground tunnel, or a crowd of civilians protesting in an urban center. Cyberspace is a form of camouflage, as the distributed online jihadist network in the infosphere demonstrates. While they ordinarily cannot be targeted from these areas, insurgents can fire from them. As stealth technology and advanced camouflage in First World states continues to develop, it is inevitable that it will also trickle down to insurgents.

In turn, Bunker notes, conventional forces use "data fusion" to rapidly reach hidden targets and neutralize them.[22] The adaptive information processing Bunker describes isn't necessarily technological in scope—it ranges from a technical countersniper system that pinpoints the exact location of the shot to sociological information gained through intelligence work that allows an Army patrol to locate and ambush a crew of insurgents laying Improvised Explosive Devices (IEDs) on a street corner. In the context of irregular warfare, the technological race is not necessarily as important as the social dimension of operations. IED planters and counter-IED systems will engage in a rat race to out-innovate each other. But by targeting the social networks that support IED-planting operations, the Army made the technical contest largely irrelevant.

When coordinating large-scale counterterrorism operations in urban environments, command and control often fractalizes because of the complexity of the physical terrain, the presence of the media, and the chaotic and individualized nature of the battlespace. The commander uses cyberspace to visualize his forces in a single point of space and organize and coordinate their efforts through visualization technologies, tactical radio, and other command and control systems. As previously mentioned, the commander's concept of future operations—the command concept—informs the resources allocated and the actions of subordinates, giving them the autonomy to carry out their duties and avoiding the trap of becoming a prisoner of his own cybernetic array of C^2 nodes.[23]

To summarize, the cyber dimension of the battle space consists of the infosphere, organic and cyber forms of camouflage, the cyber element of deployed forces, critical electromagnetic infrastructure in the battlespace, and C^2 networks. The cyber element of deployed forces consists of command and control (C^2), communications, the flow of information within the organization, and the distributed computational intelligence of the force itself.

What does this mean in a typical tactical setup? Sid Heal, a retired commander in the Los Angeles Sheriff's Department and a tactical theorist sketched out the implications in his essay "Fighting in the Fifth Dimension."[24] First, any commander who expects only to fight in "humanspace" will be targeted from cyberspace. Second, sensing rather than firepower will be the key to victory.

Detecting combatants in order to strike them becomes paramount, utilizing both technological and social sensors. Developing networks of human sensors is often the best means of preventing attack. Third, rules of engagement become more interlinked with issues of privacy and civil rights. Collecting both technological and social data will inevitably raise questions about rights-security tradeoffs. Fourth, sorting relevant data from noise will comprise the chief barrier to targeting hidden opposing force units. Lastly, complex situations are going to require that the commander reach across cyberspace (and geography) to utilize cross-organizational and civilian expertise needed to accomplish the goal.

Understanding Temporality and Surprise

Sustained study of operational theory shows that time is in fact a contested zone of the operational space. Opponents contest time in the same way they fight over a crucial piece of terrain. Most understand time as the general timeline, the event horizon on which opposing forces place their assets in time and space. While the linear timeline is undoubtedly one element of the temporal dimension, it ignores the fact that different sides of the engagement perceive time in vastly different ways. The divergence between Blue Force and Red Force's perception of the engagement guides operational planning, shaping their respective approaches to the central clash of forces. There are two dominant perspectives on time as an element of tactical warfare: Robert Leonhard's writings on surprise and William McRaven's theory of special operations direct action.

Robert Leonhard argues that the issue of readiness makes time is the controlling element of war. Forces are perpetually unready because they cannot always remain in a state of alert and full combat readiness. Because unready forces cannot respond at their full combat strength, opposing forces seek to strike them before they can position themselves to defend. In turn, the defender will attempt to quickly detect attacking adversaries in order to destroy them. The opposing force planning the attack will attempt to create surprise (which is simply a delayed detection of attack) by *slowing down* the adversary's detection through stealth, surprise, operational security, or deception. In turn, the defending commander will try to *hasten contact* to deny the attacking force the advantage of surprise at the point of unreadiness.[25]

Leonhard's theory of surprise was written during the era of maneuver warfare, which principally concerned itself with conventional force-on-force contests. However, it has great applicability to today's "hybrid" contests. What is most crucial to Leonhard's concept of temporal battle is his emphasis on readiness. Garrison societies can place their forces on 24-hour alert, but this still does not obviate the human need for rest, dispersion, and recovery. Only the *Terminator* robots stand perpetually alert and ready to battle.[26] The most important element of time for Leonhard is the amount of time it takes for a force to *detect* an approaching attacker, which in turn determines its ability to fight off the attacker.

William McRaven advances a complementary theory that explains how some foes attack without the benefit of general surprise. In special operations warfare operations have succeeded in spite of a lack of general surprise through the concept of relative superiority. This does not mean that surprise isn't important—rather it means catching the enemy off guard as opposed to unprepared.[27] What this semantic difference means is that targeting weaknesses and points of slackness should be valued above all else. As in Leonhard, the point is not to completely escape detection (which is impossible) but slow down detection in order to prolong your advantage. Relative superiority is the pivotal point in an engagement when the attackers have the advantage over defenders.[28]

Ideally, relative superiority is achieved early on. To do so, the operators must quickly pass through the point of vulnerability (defined as the point in the mission when the force reaches the opposing force's first line of defense). At this point the frictions of war (chance, uncertainty, the will of the opponent) have the opportunity to scuttle the mission. The longer it takes to achieve relative superiority, the greater havoc these frictions wreak on the attacker.[29] For McRaven, who undoubtedly writes from the point of view of the attacker, the most important factor is the time it takes for the special operations operator to reach the point of advantage. Time is constructed as a linear chart that shows the crossover from vulnerability to operational superiority. The operator has to get to the objective as fast as possible, as any delay widens the vulnerability window.[30]

What both Leonhard and McRaven suggest is that the attacker and defender both perceive time differently. This is especially true in contests between terrorists and other irregulars and counterterrorist/counterinsurgent groups. In counterterrorism and modern irregular warfare the adversary starts out in a state of dispersal and unreadiness to attack. He is "cloaked" beyond what Bunker calls "human-sensing" by various forms of camouflage, be it organic camouflage, technology, the vastness of the modern city, or the support of a segment of the population. In order to strike, the defender takes a series of steps that makes him vulnerable to detection. The act of "uncloaking" and building up the assemblage of the "kill chain" to strike is slow and is the terrorist's chief window of vulnerability.[31]

While formless, he has the advantage of being unseen. But he must trade his safety away for mass in order to create combat power. Time factors into his calculation of relative superiority— he has to find the right moment to strike and must minimize the period of vulnerability while he conducts pre-operational surveillance and puts the elements of the attack together. Once he has achieved relative superiority, he can kill as many as he chooses with little blowback. Time is *slow* for him because he can choose the point of attack. During the attack itself, however, he *speeds up* in order to create relative superiority and operational shock.

The defender is usually unaware of the specific nature of the plot. If he is doing dignitary protection or protecting a mass event, he has deployed assets on the field but suffers from an information asymmetry. He is also completely visible to the attacker. However, his command of resources ensures that he can act quickly to crush an attack provided he has the correct information and his command and control (C^2) and capabilities enable him to rapidly swarm forces. He must defeat the adversary before he attains relative superiority. It is preferable to prevent the attack before it happens, but once an attack is in progress it can be stopped through rapid response. Time is *fast* for the defender because he has to quickly move to neutralize the attacker before the attacker can attain relative advantage. Otherwise, the attacker accomplishes the mission and the defender's C^2 and ability to counterattack withers.

For the Blue Force commander, an intuitive notion of timing is an essential component of negotiating and influencing a complex operational setting. Timing is critical to achieving mass, selecting an opportune time to maneuver, and leveraging surprise to engage an adversary. Time is thus a significant dimension for operations. It can be exploited by both sides and is critical at all levels of engagements: tactical, operational, and strategic. Indeed, time is an integral element of all political and consequently terrorist and warfighting endeavors.

Synchronizing operations in largely dependent open the selection of optimal timing for engagement, maneuver, or counterforce operations. Intelligence is frequently geared toward understanding time. When will a group or element attack, what is the optimal timing for an operation to influence the strategic and political calculus? Indications and warning are frequently pegged to time. Understanding a terrorist "kill chain" or an event horizon is largely dependent upon discerning a phase of operations by observing key transactions and signatures. Selecting alternative courses of action to counter an attack or craft a response is also time dependent. An operational commander (and his or her staff) seeks to identify tripwires or decision points for selecting options. In this sense, time interacts with speed in forming a basis for successfully negotiating a decision cycle.[32]

The addition of the cyber-dimension interacts with time in a special way. The choice to act, the choice to temporally modulate (speed or slow) pulses in a swarming operation, the timing of convergence of physical and cyber attacks all demonstrate that time is the key to unlocking cyber potentials. The infosphere element can be used to leverage the impact of time, by allowing a message, meme, or information operation to resonate. Likewise, a maneuver operation that rapidly targets a point of weakness to target C^2 or use speed to overextend an opponent's C^2 is leveraging cyberspace.

Cyber attacks create a temporal advantage for the attacker. A cyber attack targeting a command and control (C^2) system creates a singular weakness in time and space that is quickly exploited in the operation itself. For example, in the Mumbai attack, the accumulated collapse of C^2 functions through swarming created a critical weakness in the Indian command network. Propaganda and forms of societal warfare or dislocation otherwise known as battlespace shaping put up social, political, or physical obstacles to the defender's ability to counter attacks. If no one in the population is willing to help the defender or actively assists the terrorist or insurgent, then the response to the attack is critically weakened. Likewise, if the attackers lack popular support and cannot utilize camouflage it causes them to speed up their planning and target acquisition process and take unnecessary risks.

To summarize, the temporal dimension of the operations/ battlespace consists of the general timeline (the event horizon), the moment of relative superiority, and the respective perceptions of time by the defender and attacker. The general timeline is the event horizon on which opposing forces place their assets in time and space. The moment of relative superiority is the moment in which the attacker gains a pivotal advantage over the opponent that allows him or her to complete the operation. The defender perceives time as a fast process because he must quickly response and/or detect the adversary. The attacker perceives time as slow because he can choose a target at his leisure. However, one the choice has been made the attacker must gradually speed up as he or she assembles his forces in time and space for attack.

Conclusion: A Framework for Operational Art

The implications of both cyber and temporal dimensions for operational framework may appear intuitive or commonsensical, but are not well stated in doctrine. The irregular battle is essentially a struggle situated around targeting. The attacker, situated within organic or inorganic cover, must attack before he is pinpointed by the defender and neutralized. The defender hastens contact to target and neutralize the attacker before he can assemble his weapon and employ it in the operational space. If the battle is essentially a targeting duel, then police and counterterrorism operational forces must devote the most doctrinal space and research and development time to coming up with means of speeding up data fusion and making it more comprehensive.

Improving data fusion and detecting is not merely a matter of inventing more technological tools, which only have an impact on the technical level of engagement. Rather, improving data fusion results from the harmonization of tactical level information-dispensing through both technological and command tools and higher-level strategic foresight and intelligence. The Intelligence Preparation for Operations (IPO) process and the Terrorism Early Warning (TEW) concept acts as a kind of bridge between tactical and operational levels of engagement, creating a networked intelligence system.[33] IPO, a civilian analog to the military planning system Intelligence Preparation of the Battlespace (IPB), generates operational plans and defines the parameters of engagement. The TEW is an engine for networked intelligence and meta-analysis among regions at the operational level.

However, the increasing complexity of engagement points to the necessity of strategic forecasting and futurism. Although the military employs countless analysts engaged in strategic forecasting and futurism, operational level counterterrorism limits thought about future operations to wargaming and strategic forecasting of near-term threats. Futurist workshops and long-range studies devoted to long-term trends in the evolution of the operations/battlespace, technological and geosocial change, and the capabilities of opponents are necessary in order to guide future operations planning. Without being cognizant of the future evolution of the operations/battlespace, counterterrorism professionals will continue to be caught flat-footed by opponents who must adapt in order to survive—and thus will extensively study new military theory and developments.[34]

Likewise, C^2 capabilities have to measure up to the challenge of modern operations. Recent operations like Mumbai have shown that current counterterrorism response doctrine is overwhelmingly tactically focused and is not up to the task of facing down a complex attack that can attack from multiple directions, with multiple elements. Dealing with this has both cognitive and doctrinal implications. Carl H. Builder's idea of the "command concept" holds that effective command and control is rooted not in information tools but in the cognitive processes of the leader. A well formed "command concept" of future operations intuitively guides choices about the minimum of information that should flow through command and control systems.[35]

Although it is mediated through machines, this concept *necessarily originates* in human cognitive processes. Command concepts for operations can help organizations deal with cyber attacks—technical strikes from command and control warfare, psychological warfare and deception, disruption strikes, and simultaneous attacks designed to overload C^2 networks and software. On the doctrinal end, forces must be trained to operate in a fluid environment with multiple levels of engagement. This requires written doctrinal concepts for operations that can be standardized and institutionalized into free-play wargaming exercises.

The elements of the temporal dimension sketched out in preceding sections also have implications for warning and response. By understanding surprise as merely the delayed detection of attack—and something that can occur in even the most fortified of environments, we can move away from a static and rote concept of force protection that sees layers of fortifications and personnel as the best means of preventing attack. As Leonhard argues, no force can remain at full battle rattle in perpetuity, and openings for attack occur as a result of this entirely human weakness. Rather, speeding up detection of approaching attack is more a matter of creating layered sensing networks—both human and technological—integrated closely with operational response.

As previously noted, societal warfare and operations/ battlespace shaping also has a long-range impact on the temporal dimension of operations. An opponent supported by the populace or able to shape the parameters of the operations space to his will can choose an attack with leisure. It takes longer for the defender to detect him, and response is also greatly complicated by lack of information. If police and military forces, through adaptive intelligence networks, human and technological sensors, and the support of the populace, have shaped the operations/battlespace in a manner that gives them the advantage, the opponent operates in fear of being apprehended and makes quick and hasty decisions.

A focus on understanding cyberspace in its original meaning and incorporating time as a dimension of operations may seem pedantic or perhaps overly academic. But understanding cyber and temporal dimensions of operations means synthesizing a mixture of old and new ideas to gain a better understanding of the modern operational space—and is crucial to dealing with opposing force and environmental challenges.

End Notes

[1]. See Frederick Kagan, *Finding the Target: The Transformation of American Military Policy,* San Francisco: Encounter Books, 2006, Antoine Bosquet, *The Scientific Way of Warfare,* New York: Columbia University Press, 2009, and Thomas K. Adams, *The Army after Next: The First Postindustrial Army,* Palo Alto: Stanford Security Studies, 2006 for intellectual histories of recent military thinking.

[2]. See *Joint Publication 5-0: Joint Operation Planning,* Washington D.C.: US Department of Defense, 26 December 2006, p. 17.

[3]. Charles C. Krulak, "The Strategic Corporal: Leadership in the Three-Block War," *Marines Magazine,* January 1999. http://www. au.af.mil/au/awc/awcgate/usmc/strategic_corporal.htm

[4]. See John P. Sullivan and Adam Elkus, "Postcard From Mumbai: Modern Urban Siege," *Small Wars Journal,* 16 February 2009, and John P. Sullivan and Adam Elkus, "Preventing Another Mumbai: Building a Police Operational Art," *USMA Countering Terrorism Center Sentinel,* June 2009, pp. 4-7.

[5]. Lt Gen Sir John Kisely, "Thinking About the Operational level," *Royal United Services Journal,* December 2005, p. 38.

[6]. Five-dimensional battlespace or operational space (opspac) is introduced by Robert J. Bunker in his many works, op sit.

[7]. http://www.dtic.mil/doctrine/jel/doddict/data/c/10160.html

[8]. Martin Libicki discuses "Gibson warfare" his McNair paper "What Is Information Warfare?," Washington, D.C.: National Defense University, August 1995. http://www.ndu.edu/inss/books/Books%20 %201990%20to%201995/What_is_IW_Aug_95/a003cont.html

[9]. John Perry Barlow, "A Declaration of the Independence of Cyberspace," Electronic Frontier Foundation, 8 February 1996. http:// homes.eff.org/~barlow/Declaration-Final.html.

[10]. "Cyberspace," Prinicipia Cyberntica Web, 17 October, 1994. http://pespmc1.vub.ac.be/CYBSPACE.html

[11]. Principia Cybernetica.

[12]. Bruce Sterling, *The Hacker Crackdown: Law and Disorder on the Electronic Frontier,* New York: Bantam, 1993. p. xii.

[13]. See Fred Turner, *From Counterculture to Cyberculture: Stewart Brand, the Whole Earth Network, and the Rise of Digital Utopianism,* Chicago: University of Chicago Press, 2006.

[14]. Carl H. Builder, Stevn C. Bankes, and Richard Nordin, *Command Concepts: A Theory Derived from the Practice Command and Control*, Santa Monica: RAND Corporation. p. 10.

[15]. Builder et al, p. xiv.

[16]. The United States Army Commander's Appreciation and Campaign Design, TRADOC Pamphlet 525-5-500, 28 January 2008, p. 5.

[17]. Major Ketti Davison, "From Tactical Planning to Operational Design," *Military Review*, September-October 2008, p. 33.

[18]. See James N. Mattis, "USJFCOM Commander's Guidance for Effects-based Operations," *Parameters*, Autumn 2008, pp. 18-25.

[19]. John Arquilla and David Ronfeldt, *The Emergence of Noopolitik: Toward an American Information Strategy,* Santa Monica: RAND, 1999, p. 18.

[20]. Arquilla and Ronfeldt, p. 11.

[21]. Robert J. Bunker, "Advanced Battlespace and Cybermaneuver Concepts: Implications for Force XXI," *Parameters*, Autumn 1996. http://www.carlisle.army.mil/USAWC/PARAMETERS/96autumn/bunker.htm

[22]. Ibid.

[23]. Builder et al, p. 13.

[24]. Sid Heal, "Fighting in the Fifth Dimension," *US Cavalry on Point*. (Date Unavailable) http://www.uscav.com/uscavonpoint/Feature

[25]. See Robert Leonhard, "Surprise," at http://www.jhuapl.edu/areas/warfare/papers/surprise.pdf

[26]. One might argue that even Terminators need a break, hence Arnold Schwarzenegger's famous saying "I'll be back."

[27]. William McRaven, *Case Studies in Special Operations Warfare: Theory and Practice*, New York: Ballantine Books, pp. 16-17.

[28]. McRaven, p. 4.

[29]. McRaven, pp. 6-7.

[30]. McRaven, p. 19.

[31]. Sullivan has termed this window of vulnerability the "I&W Envelope" in his many works on Intelligence Preparation for Operations (IPO); see especially John P. Sullivan and Alain Bauer (Eds.), *Terrorism Early Warning: 10 Years of Achievement in Fighting Terrorism and Crime*, Los Angeles: Los Angeles County Sheriff's Department, October 2008, pp. 147-150.

[32]. John Boyd's Observe-Orient-Decide-Act (OODA) loop is a crucial element of timing and response.

[33]. See John P. Sullivan and Alain Bauer (Eds,), *Terrorism Early Warning: 10 Years of Achievement in Fighting Terrorism and Crime*, Los Angeles: Los Angeles County Sheriff's Department, 2008, available at http://www.lasd.org/tew/TEW2009.pdf for a comprehensive history and doctrinal template of the LA TEW.

[34]. See "Bin Laden Lieutenant Admits to September 11 and Explains Al-Qa'ida's Combat Doctrine," Middle East Media Research Institute, Special Dispatch No. 344, February 10, 2002. http://www.memri.org/bin/articles.cgi?Area=sd&ID=SP3

[35]. Builder et al, p. xiv.

Section 9:
Five-Dimensional Battlespace

Charles "Sid" Heal

Originally published in
The Tactical Edge, Spring 2010: 60-62.

By nature, tactical operations unfold support of tactical operations and disaster in a multidimensional battlespace. A dimension may be best understood as a realm characterized by a specific feature and governed by its own rules. Battlespace is that domain or realm where an adversary can be acquired and engaged. Battlespace is always multidimensional and so the term replaces the more antiquated "battlefield" to broaden thought and understanding of the implications.

The most familiar dimension is *space*. Space is already three-dimensional in that it has a length, width and height/depth. Space always involves terrain of some type and so an understanding of how to identify and control terrain to gain an advantage becomes important. The maneuver elements are physical; that is, they take up space and have weight and mass. People and conveyances, like vehicles, trains, boats and aircraft, are some of the most common. Maneuver in space is measured in distance and the predominant objective is to gain and maintain control of key terrain.[1]

The fourth dimension is *time*. Time is a "nonspace continuum" where events occur in an irreversible succession from the past through the present to the future. There is no terrain in time so the rules that govern maneuver in space are irrelevant and inapplicable. Therefore time is a separate and distinct dimension but a critical component of battlespace nonetheless. Being in the right place but at the wrong time is every bit as bad as being at the wrong place anytime. Because the dimension of time is a nonspace the maneuver elements are notional; that is, they exist only as a mental image. Maneuver in time is measured in speed and the predominant objective is to identify or create and exploit opportunities.[2]

For thousands of years these four dimensions were sufficient to provide a basis for planning and decision-making in responses. As time has passed, however, this understanding of battlespace is proving increasingly inadequate. Battlespace has acquired a new dimension.

The fifth dimension is *cyberspace*. While most people think of cyberspace[3] as the online world of computer networks it is actually a much richer and deeper environment. It is better understood as a domain of information. Besides information transferred between computers (like email, file transfer protocols [FTP], web browsing and the like) it includes all types of information like that transferred from wireless cell phones, text messaging, pagers, and even electronic door locks, TV tuners or garage door openers. Understandably, the maneuver elements in cyberspace are information of all types. Maneuver is measured in knowledge and the ultimate goal is to acquire and apply understanding.[4] Conversely, when adversaries are involved the goal may be to deprive them of understanding. As USMC General Al Gray once commented, "The best tactics not only leave your enemy defeated, but confused!"[5]

Of critical importance is to understand that each of these five dimensions is fundamentally distinct from one another and rules for one dimension are completely irrelevant for another. For example, speed in space means nothing without time and there is no distance in time. Likewise, in cyberspace time and space are completely irrelevant for one simple reason; knowledge can reside in more than one place at the same time.

Despite their fundamental differences all five dimensions interact with one another with humans the common "go between" or element. Every disaster or tactical situation is a result of a unique and temporary set of circumstances. Unique because each situation is dependent only upon the peculiar situation which is present at that particular time and place, and temporary because the outcome of actions affects the next set of circumstances. Unseen but ever present is the information involved, including that of the authorities, victims, bystanders, witnesses and even suspects. It also includes information between people and things, like a suspect remotely opening or closing a garage door or setting off a bomb. Some of this information is valuable and some is even crucial. Imagine trying to manage such a situation without an ability to transfer knowledge from one person or place to another. Thus, all five dimensions are an integral part of battlespace.

In law enforcement applications, 5D battlespace can be readily understood in the stark reality of everyday examples. For example, it is not uncommon to stop a vehicle for a traffic violation and after leaving the scene to find out that the driver was just involved in a crime. It is a stark example that the suspect was trapped in both time and place during the stop but the lack of knowledge left him immune from attack. So it is with tactical operations. No good commander ignores an unprotected flank and a lack of knowledge can be every bit as devastating as being in the wrong place or at the wrong time.

It would seem prudent then to understand the implications of a multidimensional battlespace. It is important is to understand, for example, that two adversaries need not be in each other's battlespace at the same time. The officer's lack of knowledge of the driver's criminal conduct was a critical vulnerability [6] which resulted in the escape of the suspect. Conversely, the knowledge of the driver provided an ability to manipulate a situation to make getting caught even more difficult, to include the use of surprise. Tragically, this has resulted in the deaths of officers who stopped criminals unaware and were killed. As can be seen, because of a lack of knowledge the officer was in the suspect's battlespace but the suspect was not in the officer's battlespace—which provided a decisive advantage.

Likewise, attempting to impose rules for one dimension on another is a recipe for disaster. No amount of force, for example, will defeat an undetected adversary. Arriving at a location after a suspect has left is only one common example. Similarly, submachine guns and large caliber handguns are completely irrelevant in defeating an anonymous terrorist. Tactical teams must be equipped to fight in all dimensions. Retooling rather than rearming will be necessary.

Most importantly, planners and decision-makers need to recognize the existence and implications of a multidimensional battlespace. Terrorists and criminals gain a substantial, even decisive, advantage by maneuvering in all five dimensions of battlespace if a commander chooses to ignore any one of them. Well over a century ago, American Civil War General Ulysses S. Grant said, "The laws of successful war in one generation would ensure defeat in another."

Whether it is the war on crime or the war on terrorism, the surest way to lose it is to use the last one as the model for the next one. It may not be the war we want but it's the one we have.

End Notes

[1]. For more information on key terrain, see "Terrain Analysis," *The Tactical Edge*, Summer 2000, p. 73.

[2]. For more information on time, see "Maneuvering in Time," *The Tactical Edge*, Fall 2001, pp. 60-61.

[3]. "Cyberspace" was coined by science fiction author William Gibson, in his book Neuromancer, published in 1984.

[4]. For more information on cyberspace, see "Fighting in the Fifth Dimension," The *Tactical Edge*, Winter 2003, pp. 20-25.

[5]. General A.M. Gray, 29th Commandant of the Marine Corps.

[6]. For more information on critical vulnerability, see "Center of Gravity and Critical Vulnerability," *The Tactical Edge*, Winter 1997, p. 53.

Section 10:
Command, Influence and
Information in 3D Tactics

Christopher Flaherty

Originally published in
Journal of Information Warfare. Vol. 9. No. 1: 18-31. 2010 [1].
https://www.jinfowar.com. Reprinted with Permission.

Abstract

This paper has three objectives. Firstly, critically examine the triatic relationship between 'Command', 'Influence' and 'Information' in three dimensional (3D) tactics. Secondly, explain how this relationship enables the 3D *tactics of rhizome manoeuvre. Thirdly, explain the role of command, information and influence as a mechanism for achieving battle coordination, and operational supremacy. In undertaking addressing these questions, the paper reviews the current literature on* 3D *tactics, outlining how this approach has developed and its major conclusions, leading to the key question posed in this paper— How does Boyd's OODA conception actually work in circumstances illustrated by* 3D *tactics scenarios? And, how do people actually communicate information to others in this complex environment? As well, the paper looks at a group of corollary issues, as to the origin and nature of the distinction between command and control (C2), and the alternative command and influence (CI). As well, with in this context the internalisation at an individual level of information concepts and the implications of these in terms of understanding the different C2 and CI paradigms.*

Keywords: 3D Tactics, Information warfare, OODA loop, C2, Counter terrorism.

Introduction

The three dimensional (3D) tactics model presents a highly complex tactical scenario, as it is illustrating operations in a chaotic battlespace. One of the central propositions derived from the literature on 3D tactics, is that these tactics operate outside the command and control (C2) paradigm. Instead these rely on a triatic relationship between 'Command', 'Influence' and 'Information'. In order to explain how these linkages operate, the basic thesis is that at a granular or cellular level, there are sets of individual relationships operating as repetitive and patterned communications, which in semiotics and psychology are called 'microcycles'. The notion of a 'microcycle' is not well known. It is best explained as similar to Boyd's concept of an 'Observe, Orient, Decide and Act' (OODA) loop (Boyd, 1986). It is a process, whereby individuals' situational awareness is achieved through inter-personnel exchange, and intuition. The central thesis presented here is that through high level professional mastery a complex battle can be fought outside of any requirement for C2 to be present.

3D Tactics Defined

As an introduction, 3D tactics is defined—"as tactics in the third dimension which is the space above and below ground level in land and urban operations." (Flaherty, 2009a) In operation, the application of 3D tactics is a methodology, consisting of three propositions (Flaherty. 2007b), and these are summarised in table 1, below.

Table 1: Core 3D Tactics Propositions

Proposition 1	3D tactics is a set of definitions and observations about three dimensional tactics, and how these influence thinking about security, threats and consequence in an urban environment.

Proposition 2	The 3D tactics 'definitions and observations set' is intended to inform analysis of mass gathering events, including urban built structures; and enabling analysis of multiple consequences and multi-polar risks using geographical information methodologies (such as cluster modelling, and linear modelling).
Proposition 3	The 3D tactics approach can be scaled into graphic representation and geographical information systems (GIS) analysis, or it can be used intuitively as a 'definitions and observations set' intended to inform analysis of mass gathering events within complex urban environments.

A Summary of Key Themes in 3D Tactics Literature

The U.S. Army future view in 1997 developed the idea that "forces will not be able to afford linear, sequential campaigns that require discrete staging and phasing." (Deputy Chief of Staff, 1997) The alternative is the execution of near-simultaneous campaigns and application of precision fire and manoeuvre. This is developed as a "Expansive takedown operation where the enemy's will to resist collapses when he finds himself smothered by fire and surrounded everywhere by manoeuvre forces occupying positions of advantage." (Deputy Chief of Staff, 1997)

The genesis of 3D tactics has several themes. Firstly, there is recognition that "traditional security and defence operations do not transcend into an essentially peaceful environment such as crowded lunchtime shoppers, busses in transit and delivery vans." (Flaherty, 2008; Flaherty, 2009b) Secondly, 3D tactics has been used as an overarching concept to situate multi-agent modelling and analysis of group behaviours concepts, such as the complex movement (or stationary location) of many active agents within a 3D environment (Green et. al., 2009). This approach was developed to solve the counter terrorism problem presented by the 2007 Haymarket attack scenario (Flaherty, 2007a; Flaherty and Green, 2008; Green et. al., 2009). The method proposed to answer the 'Haymarket problem', was a methodology with the following characteristics:

- Random or chaotic interdiction;
- Successful identification of an opponent's approaches along lines of least resistance (where a terrorist force could effectively be ambushed at its own game); and,
- A concept of operations based on non-deterministic randomised or dynamic defence. Finally, 3D tactics has been merged with 'Command and Influence' (CI) ideas, as to how to achieve "superior battlefield command" (Flaherty 2009a).

In historical-genealogy terms the literature on 3D tactics has been poorly developed in conventional land tactical theory. Flaherty (Flaherty, 2008; 2007a; and 2007b); and Flaherty and Green (Flaherty and Green, 2008; Green et. al., 2009) elaborate most of the work in this area. Later works make the link between 3D tactics and rhizome manoeuvre tactics; as well as introducing the notion of a city operational space as completely fluid (Sullivan and Elkus, 2009; Flaherty, 2009b). As well, further back there is work of Giuseppe Fioravanzo, who defined the concept of 3D tactics in naval warfare history (Fioravanzo, 1979).

The early antecedent of 3D tactics can be found in U.S. military thinking in the 1990s. Bauer and Sullivan identify a U.S. Army definition of 3D tactics from 1999, as—"The urban environment is multi-dimensional. It includes the ground, underground and the third dimension (each building can hide enemies)." (Bauer, and Sullivan, 2008) Flaherty relates the 3D tactics concept to the notion of a three-dimensional cube which conceptually overlaid urban space (Flaherty 2009b; 2008; 2007a; 2007b). The 3D tactics cube incorporates conventional understanding of the third dimension in land combat—as the airspace above terrain—and the urban environment consisting of the three-dimensional solid forms of typical central business district (CBD) buildings and spaces formed between buildings. As well, the 3D tactics cube notionally conforms: within 300m^2, which gives coverage to most weapons effective ranges, and incorporates most CBD buildings.

The 3D tactics cube approach to urban security is also an application of the Curtis LeMay's 'combat box'. This was a tactical formation designed by U.S. Army Air Force heavy (strategic) bombers during WW2. Examining WW2 period U.S. Air Force tactical manuals, these formations were illustrated in 3D, as a means to visualize how heavy bomber formations would defend themselves against enemy interceptors in the absence of escorting fighters, by providing interlocking fire from each of the plans operating in mutual support.

The object of recent 3D tactics analysis has been to develop a methodology framework which accommodates continuous simultaneous actions (Flaherty 2007a). As well, the "phenomenon that attacks are typically unpredictable, often involve deception, and are frequently staged so that multiple vectors converge simultaneously" (Flaherty, 2009b). The issues of unpredictability and chaos have been developed in the literature on 3D tactics illustrating how a 3D tactual user gains asymmetric advantages over conventional tactical methodologies. The view is that, the 3D tactical approach allows the decision cycle to turn faster (Flaherty, 2009a). As well, an advantage is gained through erratic behavior—is another core finding in the literature (Flaherty, 2009a). It is further argued, that in a civil environment this advantage translates into force superiority and greater tactical advantage in a comparative analysis (Flaherty, 2009a). This new paper attempts to delve deeper as to why this is the case, and argues that it fundamentally has to do with the perception/ information interface at a granulated level. However, to do so require answering questions, namely:

- How does Boyd's OODA conception actually work in circumstances illustrated by 3D tactics scenarios?
- How do people actually communicate information to others in this complex environment?

Rhizome Manoeuvre

Early WW1 infiltration tactics by assault parties demonstrate the first rhizome manoeuvre, as units moved toward enemy trench lines seeking weak points to infiltrate. However, in a 3D tactics regime, figuratively speaking movement is more like "wending rhizomously through and over" geography (Kincheloe and Steinberg, 2003). The U.S. Army future view in 1997, notionally described rhizome manoeuvre (without using the phrase), as:

"Future land combat units will exploit terrain by manoeuvring for tactical advantage within the folds and undulations of the earth's surface without suffering the restrictions imposed on mobility by contact with the ground." (Deputy Chief of Staff, 1997)

A rhizome manoeuvre has close parallels with Liddell-Hart's notion of movement along the line of least resistance (Liddell-Hart, 1954). In that, it is movement through space (solid or empty) that is unforeseen. And this creates surprise and impact. However, a rhizome manoeuvre is counter intuitive to the classical understanding of manoeuvre. In 3D space a rhizome manoeuvre resembles the complex pattern of a plant root structure, as it manoeuvres through soil. Modern examples of rhizome manoeuvre have four distinctive characteristics:

- Radically departing from conventional manoeuvre—which is movement around or over terrain in order to achieve operational advantage.
- Decentralized units convergence from many different directions simultaneously, operating out of contact with the enemy.
- Aggressive move.
- Physical and open operational space is treated as having the same fluid properties.

Israeli defence forces that practice rhizome manoeuvre blast through walls and floors to reach their targets (Sullivan and Elkus, 2009). In summary, a force executing a rhizome manoeuvre move through solid as well as open space three-dimensionally. What makes this manoeuvre radical is that physical objects and the space above, or below ground can be the route through which manoeuvre takes place. In summary, the rhizome manoeuvre concept is a composite notion, incorporating simultaneous action and multidimensional manoeuvre. Simultaneous action involves multiple actions initiated by a manoeuvre force all occurring within the same timeframe. Current thinking about rhizome manoeuvre in 3D space sees the crux-point as producing an 'effect' of disorienting and offsetting the adversary's OODA cycle. In summary, implicit in the affecting of a radical rhizome manoeuvre, is achieving surprise and deception, as much as reaching at the adversary at a critical point, either in a time or materiel sense. The object is creating a simultaneous problem that an adversary cannot resolve.

Rhizome manoeuvre close ancestor is network centric warfare (NCW); sharing a common evolutionary trait, namely presenting a new paradigm that "assumes continuous change and dynamic interactions, rather than equilibrium as the norm". (Echevarria, 1997) Echevarria's other NCW observation is also apt—"more accurately reflects the dynamic and interdimensional nature of conflict in opposition to the classical paradigm's linear analytical systems nature of military thinking". (Echevarria, 1997) Problematically, the question raised by Echevarria's thesis, is what is the alternative thinking? One possible methodology is Martin Burke concept of "knowledge operations" (Burke, 2000).

Knowledge operations can be synthesised into the proposition that the foci are thoughts, thinking processes, and thought systems which are concerned with the ways and means by which meaning is assigned, derived and shared. Explaining Burke's thesis, it is based on influence theory. Hovland, Janis and Kelley ventured that factors such as expertise and trustworthiness are the main reasons convincing an audience (Hovland et al., 1966).

Corollary to which, people base decisions on the information received from others who have the status of "opinion leaders". (Katz and Lazarsfeld, 1955) In summary, Burke's knowledge operations thesis, and influence theory argue that the alternative thinking to linear analytical systems, is:

- Within groups, opinion leaders, influence audiences' minds because of characteristics such as higher or dominant social status, special competences (such as greater experience in the matter at hand);
- Group consensus emerges through these opinion leaders, and influence; and,
- Opinion leader's status may not directly correspond to effective chains of command. It may well be, that certain

individuals are recognised as opinion leaders, even though they share the same rank position as everyone else.

For instance, Katz and Lazarsfeld argue that opinion leaders tend to be limited to "being leaders with a proficiency in specific issues". (Katz and Lazarsfeld, 1955) Similarly, Burke's thesis identifies opinion leaders as selected people whose role it is to move and translate information around an organisation, thereby deriving situational awareness for the group. The notion of an opinion leader is further developed in social actor network theory, which identifies how relations between various actors/agents either work directly, or work through intermediaries. The intermediaries help articulate flows of information, and decision making.

Conventional C2 thinking posits that high level coordination would be needed to affect a rhizome manoeuvre. However, in all likelihood much of the time, there can be no formal command links in place, given the radical nature of a rhizome manoeuvre; as well as the operational difficulties encounter in complex urban space. The type of organisation to affect rhizome manoeuvre would more likely be driven by a knowledge operations process. The question remains however, how is this actually achieved?

The traditional thesis is that for manoeuvre success there has to be some type of electronic connectivity enabling C2 to overcome the human (Clausewitzian) factors of—fog and friction. If these are not overcome then a force attempting simultaneous action could be self-defeated. The main impact of the information age on contemporary operations has been ability to collect, undertake analyses, disseminate and act upon battlefield information, and thereby enable simultaneous action. Systems integration Frater and Ryan observe is the latest revolution (Frater and Ryan, 2001). Problematically, due to the speed of action there has to be an organisational medium beyond systems integration to cope in situations—such as rhizome manoeuvre where there may be no C2? The argument is that CI fills this space, and this question will be addressed in the next section.

Rhizome Manoeuvre and C2 Failure

A conventional C2 approach to archiving rhizome manoeuvre, is that in place:

- Are closely linked C2-based capabilities;
- Effective decision-making at all levels, is achieved through synchronisation of forces;
- Balanced hierarchical command responsibilities.

Problematically, in addition to the C2 elements, the notion of 'Influence' is also identified as the enabler of complex manoeuvre. However, this does not get the recognition needed, and fundamentally is treated as a sub-set to C2. Rhizome manoeuvre typically involves forces moving at speed, in a chaotic battle and in such circumstances it is foreseeable that these forces may fall out of effective communications and control of superior commanders. From a C2 perspective this would be fatal. Theoretically, circumstances where this may occur are:

- Normal C2 arrangements have been compromised;
- The need to conceal a manoeuvre force (hence, it falls out of effective communications); or,
- Normal C2 arrangements cannot give the decision agility needed to enable manoeuvre.

Where C2 failure occurs, there is little to compensate, except in the instance that an independent command decision rectifies the situation. Fundamentally, the C2 paradigm is about distributing information throughout a force. However, how important is direct communications between superior and subordinate forces? Alternatively, if we accept that effective command does not always require direct control of forces, the question becomes when do superior commanders see operational advantages in allowing his/her forces independent action? The alternative is to take an influencing approach to command, as a means to maintaining force cohesion and command direction. Explaining this argument, two issues need to be further explored, these are:

- Professional mastery, at an individual level helps overcome C2 failure.
- A revamped view of 'Influence' as an alternative to C2.

Professional Mastery

Aki-Mauri Huhtinen observes that "global networking and information exchange increase cooperation and mutual understanding but also entail challenges and threats to the traditional Western military and soldier culture." (Huhtinen, 2009) In essence, a fundamental division can be identified between C2 centralisation, and the place of the individual warrior culture which underpins Western military organisation historically. The corollary issue as Table 2, below illustrates is that the notion of 'Information' at an organisational level, has a close association with C2 systems. However, at an individual level it is more the case about modes of thinking, and how these are internalised, in individual and particular circumstances. At the individual level we are addressing the information issue in terms of the sociology/anthropology of how is this individually internalised— and, asking the question, what is that?

Table 2: Division Between Organisation and Individual

ORGANISATIONAL & SYSTEMS
INDIVIDUAL & INTERNALISED

The question remains, how do we define individual and internalised aspects of an information approach—in short, what is the individual thinking? And at that level, in a military context, are we not talking about the individual martial arts culture? Unexpectedly, we need to look at martial arts exponents such as Bruce Lee, who in Western terms historically have been influential in this particular aspect. As well, Bruce Lee's philosophical approach to martial arts arguably parallels the type of operational thinking needed to see/react/pre-empt events in complex or chaotic battle. For instance, at the heart of Bruce Lee's martial arts philosophy was the dictum— 'From form to formless and from finite to infinite' (Lee, 1975). By not having specific form, all forms can be included, as an approach at an individual level serves as an analogy with rhizome manoeuvre. As well, this dictum closely parallels the radical approach that rhizome manoeuvre requires operationally as a mindset. Similarly, we find that in most formulations of rhizome manoeuvre the approach seeks to shatter enemy cohesion through radical, unpredictable or impossible moves through space, largely creating what Bruce Lee would have called broken rhythm. Bruce Lee illustrated this concept as counterpoint movement, and radical time-shifts during sparing.

Bruce Lee taught that 'no set rules or codified techniques exist for this art' (Lee, 1975). The basis of Bruce Lee's famous dictum was to discourage preconceived notions about martial arts, and to free up use, methods and techniques from all styles. Similarly, in effecting a rhizome manoeuvre in 3D space exactly the same no-systems approach needs to be adopted.

Manoeuvrist approaches such as rhizome manoeuvre historically rely on universal professional mastery. Manoeuvre is one of the Clausewitzian two-pole strategies, representing the dominance of professional mastery, over the alternative reliance on defensive and entrenched operations to overcome command deficiency and low level professional mastery (Flaherty, 1996). Applying rhizome manoeuvre in 3D space requires a high degree of professional mastery. At an individual level rhizome manoeuvre in 3D space parallels the—Free Running—phenomenon. This is a form of urban acrobatics in which participants use the city and rural landscape to perform movements through its structures.

In summary, from a professional mastery perspective effecting rhizome manoeuvre in 3D space is more in line with the fighting philosophy of the Hong Kong martial artist—Bruce Lee. The 'no-systems' approach has fundamental implications for the way we conceptualise the informational aspects of coordinating 3D tactics, at the individual level. In part, there is need for a high degree (at the individual level) for professional mastery to overcome some of the fog and friction factors experienced in conflict. At an operational level there has to be a higher driving notion of an influencing approach to command, as a means to maintaining force cohesion and direction. However problematically, there is no real conception of 'Influence' in the C2 lexicon, and this issue will be addressed in the next section.

Current Doctrine Application of Influence

The notion of 'Influence' is definable as the effect of one person or thing on another. Influence can have both controlling and forcible aspects; as well, a guiding or persuasive element. Scott and Agoglia critically argue that "coalition forces tend to view information operations and the competition to influence as supplementing lethal operations." (Scott and Agoglia, 2008) Adapting 'Influence' to achieve operational objects is established in most Western Defence thinking. Malone observes that information operation (IO) is predicated on influence strategies:

> "A further key factor noted was the rise of the so called "CNN effect", the pervasiveness of global electronic media and the influence that it exerts on public opinion, thereby shaping political and (therefore) military decision making." (Malone, 2003)

Justifying, the utility of IO Malone notes that 'Influence' enables a wide range of operational activities throughout the spectrum of conflict:

> "Experience and observation of peace operations demonstrated the utility of influencing the information environment at all levels of conflict, not just the middle to high end of the conflict spectrum. In particular, it was noted that a technologically inferior adversary might still have the ability to influence the information environment in their own favour, by exploiting the vulnerabilities and weaknesses of high technology systems." (Malone, 2003)

Perception management is well established in IO, however problematically this example of an 'Influence' approach, largely covers circumstances where there is no relationship between opposing forces. That is, from a doctrinal view most military thinkers would be seeking influence through various IO strategies and tactics. However, there appears a clear demarcation between notions of direct control (as in C2 effective command) of one's own forces, and that of affecting an adversary's behaviour. In relation to the history of the operation of the 'U.S. National Command Authority', Bash mentions 'Influence' in relation to decision-making. However, he sees it as a "negative" in terms of service bias permeating joint force planning (Bash, 1999).

As well, problematically for modern IO thinking the notion of influence shares a common root with conventional military thinking where influence in command attaches to notions like 'direct contact or guidance across separate command hierarchies, unit or military justice' (Burrell, 2000). As well, the notion of 'Influence' has clearly negative connotations, commonly cited as typically improper affect on decision making. In particular, Cohen's model for "unequal dialogue" in supreme command decision making (Cohen, 2002).

The Cohen thesis is interesting in that he looks at the discourse aspects of the information relationship between superior and subordinates; seeking out 'privately blunt disagreement' and 'tension' inherent in these relationships during decision making. This Cohen justifies as the only reasonable mechanism to arrive at good decisions. Cohen has three requirements:

- A superior's greater qualifications and responsibility;
- A means to overcome dissenting views or uncertainties from subordinates; and,
- Subordinates lack ability at making good decisions.

Cohen's panoptic view of C2 sees influence as a subordinate function in the information process. However, problematically, in the battle situation it is improbable that C2 can have a truly panoptic view of events, and that once this is contrasted with a more decentralised philosophy of influence command, the only viable mechanism from an informational view is CI, as the central mobilising principle for overall battlefield coordination.

Simpkins' analysis of the role of WWII German Staff Command at work is typically held up as an historical example of a command structure based on influence decision making (Simpkins, 1985). A condensed illustration of Simpkins' historical description is that in WW2 German staff officers displayed a symbiotic relationship with each other, and that irrespective of position in the chain of command, there appears to have been a largely collaborative approach in terms of information flow, interpretation and decision making, that was achieved through ongoing staff meetings and telephone exchanges. According to Simpkins this enabled a highly flexible and organic decision-making process, which was seen to be more efficient at producing accurate situational awareness, helping the Germans overcome the fact that much of their coded electronic transmissions were being decoded by Allied intelligence.

The Simpkins model of WW2 German staff workings presents an alternative to more classical notions of C2, as being a one-way downward flow of decisions. This model has human-to-human interactions as manipulative, where staff officers discuss information, and consultatively make decisions. Another point that needs to be considered is that Simpkins' German staff officers made consistent decisions, because of a high level of social cohesion. Other key factors, highlighted by this example is that due to a high level of professional mastery institutionally within the German Army of the period, and the tendency to display a high level of decision consistency (largely because the staff officers tended to think along similar terms), the end affect was a highly flexible and organic decision making process, which to the outside observer had all the appearances of effective centralised C2. However, in actual fact this whole system relied more on influence relationships. And, from this perspective Burke's knowledge operations thesis, and influence theory actually explains much of the process in terms of the role of opinion leaders.

Effective Command

Conventionally, the notion of command is the authority, responsibility and accountability vested in an individual for the direction, coordination, control and administration of military forces. Sproles' thesis is that traditionally 'Command' is treated as inseparable from 'Control', and the two—'Command and Control'—have, "metamorphosed historically from being a phrase to being a compound word". (Sproles, 2002) Problematically, this relegates effective command as only possible through a C2 paradigm. As well, sees operational success as only possible, based on Builder's idea of the "command concept", which holds that effective command and control is rooted not in information tools but in the cognitive processes of the leader (Builder, et al, 1999). The contra-argument is that this hierarchical model is at odds with network based organisation, as these routinely employ non-hierarchical based decision structures (Arquilla and Ronfeldt, 1996). A condensed view of Arquilla and Ronfeldt operation of network based forces has four elements:

- An archetypal netwar actor consists of a web (or network) of disperse, interconnected 'nodes' (or activity centres).
- A network based organisation is structurally flat, meaning there is no single central leader or commander, and with little or no hierarchy.
- Decision making and operations are decentralised and depend on consultative consensus-building that allow for local initiative and autonomy.
- A mobilising factor for decision making depends on a powerful doctrine, ideology, or narrative.

Point four, of the Arquilla and Ronfeldt thesis, is best expressed in the dictum that—netwar actors be of all one mind. This dictum clearly identifies 'Influence' as the enabling mechanism allowing actors/agents to disperse, devote to different tasks, as well as coordinate from a ground level up emulating operational centrality. Arquilla and Ronfeldt coordination provides the structure, without resort to a hierarchy, thus giving actors/agents capacity to know what they have to do. Massive information flow gives individual elements embedded within a network sufficient ability to act— without reference to each other, or some leadership. Problematically, we are left with a question:

- How can individual or groups of devolved/decentralised commands utilise 'Influence' as a mechanism for battle coordination, and achieving operational supremacy?
- And corollary, is it still possible to affect rhizome manoeuvre in 3D space, given all its complexities, relying on devolved, de-centralised or 'no'-controls?

OODA Microcycling

Taking a very simple biological approach to Boyd's OODA loop, it can be argued each of the segments—observe, orient, decide and act—operate at a granular or cellular level. In other words, embedded in each segment is a microcycle operating as sub-process emphasizing a feed-back pattern of individuals' perception/recognition. In simple discourse theory terms, this connective link is a microcycle process of 'validation/observation/belief'. This would also require people spread throughout a force capable of leading or reinforcing other acting elements, without being directed to do so, and acting on pure initiative and intuition. Thus, embedded within Boyd's OODA loop conception we can further situate Burke's concept of knowledge operations, working as myriad individual-level microcycles processing and disseminating sense, information, intelligence as product of the 'validation/observation/belief' process. The operational centrality proposed by Arquilla and Ronfeldt comes into play at this point where doctrine, ideology, or narrative intent 'Influence' forces.

Implicitly for the 'Influence' approach to replace C2 the underlying assumptions are that: the force is well trained; highly professional; and self-organising. Conventionally Western military decentralised command doctrine advocates training that fosters initiative and mission command. Under this doctrine, a commander maintains personal contact with subordinate commanders during all stages of an operation and can moderate the battle plan to accommodate the unforeseen, on the back of cultivated referent power—that is trust-based relationships between commanders and subordinates. Even where devolved/decentralised command is utilised, a defacto C2 emerges, with referent power playing an important cohesive role. Comparatively, 'Influence' in a CI model flows both ways. The qualitative difference between utilising CI (or not utilising C2 approaches) is that it advocates commanders release control to the point, that subordinate actions are independent and actions are coordinated collaboratively and consultatively (without commanders existing), and operating as syndicalist operatives. Thus, 'Influence' in a CI model actively dismantles hierarchy, through a process of microcycling knowledge operations. This in effect flattens the organisational structure, as was predicted by Arquilla and Ronfeldt. This factor marks CI fundamentally different from C2 models.

The key features of CI approaches are that 'Influence' would operate as the attractor and motivator for human-to-human organisation. The key functional question is how far can the 'Influence' model be taken? Classically, the Napoleonic precept—marching to the sound of the guns, has clear CI underpinnings; largely to overcome information deprivation experienced in early 19th century armies. In more contemporary circumstances terrorist cells separated by ethnic, religious and national differences nevertheless operate as transnational confederacies without (or do not appear to have) any supra-command links. In which case, typical of network based inter-relationships, these tend to rely on broad ideologies to motivate and direct, which operate as unifying and directing precepts, which is largely explained by the Arquilla and Ronfeldt thesis. The end process flattens and dismantles hierarchy, replacing it with multiple devolved and decentralised individualised 'non-commands'.

Asymmetric Advantages of the CI Approach

As a final point for discussion, thought out this paper the issue of asymmetric advantage has been eluded. There are two aspects, which will be briefly covered. Firstly, a key advantage offered by the CI approach is that it enables fighting asymmetrically. Adopting a non-C2 approach, such as CI could represent an asymmetric response to a C2 based command. The logic being, if the object was to attack an opponent's C2 arrangements in order to break his/her capacity to fight, a CI-led force would not have a structure to attack, let alone any designated commanders, to attack as well.

The second asymmetric advantage arises by way of increased capacity to execute a rhizome manoeuvre, which represents—it can be argued—an exploitation of irrational logic, which gains asymmetric operational advantages. The identification of non-linearity-logic (which is a requirement for chaotic behaviour) has been shown to produce a defence which effectively counters erratic terrorist tactics in urban battle (Flaherty, 2009a). Theoretically, achieving asymmetric advantages comes from 'doing the unexpected' to adopting organisation or force types, which are unknown to the adversary, equally applies in the attack or the defence.

Conclusion

The CI approach underpins successful execution of 3D rhizome manoeuvre. In answering the questions posed at the onset—how can 'Influence' be effectively utilised as a mechanism for battle coordination, and for achieving operational supremacy? The flow of information within a system, organisation or battlespace for instance occurs in circumstances of a wide range of dynamic interactions between influencers and influences. We find that, a continuous process of microcycling between individuals achieves sufficient speed in individual/group perception and response to achieve combat effect in an urban battlespace, all of which are nested within Boyd's OODA loop. The complexity, however is that when viewed from effecting rhizome manoeuvre in 3D space, we need to explicate the informational issues. Thus, it is worthy of consideration, in future simulations, what contribution CI makes to an asymmetric force?

End Notes

[1] Updated information by the author: This 2010 article was based on a 2003 work—Flaherty, C.J. (2003) 'The Role of Command and Influence in Australian Multidimensional Manoeuvre Theory', *Defence Force Journal*. (September/October 2003). (162): 31-38.

The 2003 article 'The Role of Command and Influence' is listed along with several of Chris Flaherty's articles on the UK Shrivenham Index (URL: http://naca.central.cranfield.ac.uk/si/index.php?m=r&q=theory&page=10), to defence journal literature - produced by indexing significant articles from the current defence, management, engineering and applied science journals holdings of the Library at the College of Management and Technology at Shrivenham.

The 2003 article 'The Role of Command and Influence', is an examination of the multidimensional manoeuvre approach to warfare and its relationship to manoeuvre theory. The article argues that command and influence based command should be utilised as well as command and control (C2) based command when using a multidimensional approach. This basic thesis was re-evaluated in 2010, for 'Command, Influence and Information in 3D Tactics'. The focus of this new paper had three objectives:

- Firstly, critically examine the triatic relationship between 'Command', 'Influence' and 'Information' in three dimensional (3D) tactics.
- Secondly, explain how this relationship enables the 3D tactics of rhizome manoeuvre.
- Thirdly, explain the role of command, information and influence as a mechanism for achieving battle coordination, and operational supremacy.

Addressing these questions, the paper undertook a review of the current literature on 3D tactics, outlining how this approach has developed and its major conclusions, leading to the key question posed in this paper –

- How does Boyd's OODA conception actually work in circumstances illustrated by 3D tactics scenarios?
- And, how do people actually communicate information to others in this complex environment?

As well, the paper looked at a group of corollary issues, as to the origin and nature of the distinction between command and control (C2), and the alternative command and influence (CI). As well, with in this context the internalisation at an individual level of information concepts and the implications of these in terms of understanding the different C2 and CI paradigms.

In the paper, it should be noted that there is a reference, to "social actor network theory, which identifies how relations between various actors/agents either work directly, or work through intermediaries. The intermediaries help articulate flows of information, and decision making". This was actually based on Chris Flaherty's PhD thesis – Flaherty, C.J. (2002) *Australian-Chinese Business Networks: A Case Study of the Role of Networks Used to Organise Trade Between*

Firms in Melbourne (Adelaide) and Shanghai. Thesis (Ph.D.)-University of Melbourne, School of Anthropology, Geography, and Environmental Studies, 2002. UniM Bail T. Call No. FLAHERT. At time of writing the 2003 paper (Flaherty, C.J. (2003) 'The Role of Command and Influence in Australian Multidimensional Manoeuvre Theory', *Defence Force Journal* (September/October 2003). (162): 31-38), he had held appointments in the Australian Department of Defence since 2000 (and received his doctorate from the University of Melbourne in 2002, while still in Defence). His thesis of work on social actor network theory was translated into this early defence–related research on CI and C2.

Additionally, the fundamental basis of the CI approach can be traced to Chris Flaherty's 1996 essay—'The doctrine of waging war':

"To cap, our object is to progress beyond Keegan's criticism of text. The aim is to define what should be our military thinking. This theory is based on the rejection of the didactic use of military history. We will follow in step with the Clausewitzian position that the basis of military thinking rests on the making of a guess as to the course of future events. In short, our theory will be to reject the use of the guess as the cogent basis of future action; we will reject yesterday, start afresh now (and forget about tomorrow). In conclusion, our only interest will be in describing the world as it is-now. The result will be to establish the attitude that change and uncertainty are positive influences in war." (Flaherty, C.J. (1996) *Australian Manoeuverist Strategy*, Seaview Press. ISBN 1876070110: 91-92).

References

Arquilla, J. Ronfeldt, D.F. (1996) *The Advent of Netwar*. RAND, Santa Monica, CA: 9.

Bash, B.L. (1999) Leadership and Parochialism: An Enduring Reality. *Joint Force Quarterly*, 22: 65.

Bauer, A. Sullivan, J.P. (eds.) (2008) *Terrorism Early Warning:* 10 *Years of Achievement Fighting Terrorism and Crime.* Published by the Los Angeles County Sheriff's Department, Los Angeles, California, October 2008: 12.

Boyd, J. (1986) Patterns of Conflict. Presentation, unpublished collection of diagrams by John Boyd, dated December 1986. URL: http://www.d-n-i.net/boyd/pdf/poc.pdf [Accessed: 15th October, 2009]: Presentation 5.

Builder, C.H. Bankes, S.C. Nordin, R. (1999) *Command Concepts: A Theory Derived from the Practice of Command and Control,* Santa Monica: RAND Corporation: xiv.

Burke M. (2000) Knowledge Operations: above and beyond Information Operations. 6th_ICCRTS. URL: http://www.dodccrp. org/events/6th JCCRTS/TracksIPapers/Track7/022 tr7.pdf [Accessed: 21st July, 2009].

Burrell, R.A. (2000) Recent Developments in Appellate Review of Unlawful Command Influence. *The Army Lawyer.* URL: http://www. loc.gov/rr/frd/Military Law/pdf/05-2000.pdf [Accessed: 21st July; 2009].

Cohen, B.A. (2002) Supreme Command in the 21st Century. *Joint Force Quarterly,* 31: 51. Policy Guidance and Analysis Division (December 2002) *ADDP-D.3 Future Warfighting Concept,* Australian Commonwealth Department of Defence: National Capital Printing: 18.

Deputy Chief of Staff (1997) Knowledge and Speed: Annual Report for the Army After Next Project to the Chief of Staff of the Army. Deputy Chief of Staff for Doctrine Headquarters, Training and Doctrine Command Fort Monroe, Virginia (July, 1997): 18, 20.

Echevarria, A.J. (1997) Dynamic Inter-Dimensionality: A Revolution in Military Theory. *Joint Force Quarterly,* 15: 33.

Fioravanzo, G. (1979) *History of Naval Tactical Thought.* Trans. A. Holst. Annapolis, Md.: United States Naval Institute Press.

Flaherty, C. (2009a) 2D Verses 3D Tactical Supremacy in Urban Operations. *Journal of Information Warfare,* 8(2): 13-24.

Flaherty, C. (2009b) A New Approach to Mass Space. *Red Team Journal.* URL: http://www.redteamjournal.com [Accessed: 21st July, 2009].

Flaherty, C. (2008) 3D Tactics and Information Deception. *Journal of Information Warfare,* 7(2): 49-58.

Flaherty, C. Green, A.R. (2008) 3D Tactics, Interdiction and Multiagent Modelling. International Crime Science Conference, University College London, Centre for Security and Crime Science, 17/18 July, 2008. Proceedings on CD-ROM format.

Flaherty, C. (2007a) Mass Space Vulnerabilities Analysis in 3-D Tactics, International Crime Science Conference. University College London, Centre for Security and Crime Science. Proceedings on CD-ROM format.

Flaherty, C. (2007b) 3D Tactics: An Advanced Warfare Concept in Critical Infrastructure Protection, *International Journal of Emergency Management,* 4(1): 33-44.

Flaherty, C.J. (2003) The Role of Command and Influence in Australian Multidimensional Manoeuvre Theory. *Defence Force Journal,* 162: 31-38.

Flaherty, C.J. (1996) *Australian Manoeuverist Strategy,* Seaview Press. ISBN 1876070110. Frater, M. Ryan, M. (2001) Communications Electronic Warfare and the Digitalised. Battlefield, Land Warfare Studies Centre: Working Paper, 116: 9.

Green, A Piper, R. Keep, D. Flaherty, C. (15 - 18 June, 2009) Simulations in 3D Tactics, Interdiction and Multi-Agent Modelling.

SimTect 2009 *Simulation Conference: Simulation Concepts, Capability and Technology* (Adelaide). Proceedings on CD-ROM format.

Hovland, C.R. Janis, I.L. Kelley, H.H. (1966) *Communication and Persuasion: Psychological Studies of Opinion Change,* New Haven: Yale University Press.

Huhtinen, Aki-M. (2009) The Changing Nature of Leadership in Finnish Military Organisational Culture: The Melting of Mechanistic Command and Control in Media Networked Circumstances. 4th International Conference on Information Warfare and Security. Cape Town, South Africa, 26-27 March 2009. Proceedings of ICIW 2009: 19.

Katz, E. Lazarsfeld, P.F. (1955) *Personal Influence: The Part Played by People in the Flow of Mass Communications,* Free Press.

Kincheloe, L. Steinberg, S.R. (2003) Curriculum Visions, *International Journal of Education & the Arts,*4(1).

Lee, L. (1975) *Tao of Jeet Kune Do,* Ohara Publications, Inc. ISBN 0-89750-048-2.

Liddell-Hart, B.H. (1954) *Strategy: the Indirect Approach,* London: Faber and Faber.

Malone, J. (2003) Introduction to I0 in Australian Defence Force. Kuehl, D. (ed.) *Information Operations: The Hard. Reality o f Soft Power,* National Defense University: Washington, DC: 109.

Scott, T, Agoglia, J. (2008) Getting the Basics Right: A Discussion on Tactical Actions for Strategic Impact in Afghanistan. URL: hnp://www.smallwarsjournal.com [Accessed: 21st July, 2009].

Simpkins, R.E. (1985) *The Race to the Swift: Thoughts on Twenty-First Century Warfare,* London: Brassey's.

Sproles, N. (2002) Dissecting Command and Control with Occam's Razor or Ask not what 'Command' and 'Control' means to you but what you mean by 'Command and Control'. *Australian Defence Force Journal,* 155: 19-26.

Sullivan, J.P. Elkus, A. (2009) Postcard from Mumbai: Modern Urban Siege. URL: http://www.smallwarsjournal.com [Accessed: 21st July, 2009].

Section 11:
The Growing Mexican Cartel and Vigilante War in Cyberspace: Information Offensives and Counter-Offensives

Robert J. Bunker

Originally published in
Small Wars Journal, 3 November 2011.

This short essay blends traditional Mexican cartel analysis indicative of earlier S*mall Wars Journal* writings by this author with advanced (5th dimensional) warfighting concepts. These concepts have utility for engagement with non-state (new warmaking) entities. They are being increasingly discussed now that cyberspace and 'dual dimensional' operations are more frequently breaking out in the Mexican conflict.

The criminal insurgencies in Mexico are rapidly evolving with regard to media (informational) based conflict [1]. This is an outcome of an action-reaction (offensive and defensive) dynamic of the conflict that has transcended older forms of media (newspaper, radio, film, and television) into new media forms (websites, blogs, texts, tweets, et al.).

Earlier analysis of elements of this theme—focusing on cartel use of instrumental and symbolic violence to shape the conflict environment and two concepts of communications theory—can be found in John Sullivan's November 2010 "Cartel Info Ops: Power and Counter-power in Mexico's Drug War" *MountainRunner* and April 2011 "Attacks on Journalists and 'New Media' in Mexico's Drug War" A Power and Counter Power Assessment" *Small Wars Journal* essays [2].

For a comparison of the components relating to this conflict refer to Table 1. Old Media vs New Media. That table provides a general overview of the difference between older and newer media forms. Overall the newer cyber-media form is far superior to the older media form as would be expected of a more networked, dynamic, and entrepreneurial set of informational technologies. However, it is still considered inferior to the 'industrial media' by much of the status quo and older aged cohorts due to its anonymity of reporting, lack of accountability, and more illegitimate nature (e.g. most of the blogs post pictures with no concern over copyright issues).

Table 1. Old Media vs New Media

Component	Old Media	New Media
Examples	Newspaper Radio Film Television Car Radio/Theater/TV	Website/Blog Text/Tweet Social Networking Email/Newsgroup Laptop/Smart Phone
Dimensionality	4th (Space + Time)	5th Dimension (Space + Time + Cyber)
Temporal	Static/Historical	Real Time/Dynamic
Transmutability	Physical/Non-Malleable	Digital/Malleable
Organization	Hierarchical	Networked
Reporting Value	Legitimate	Illegitimate
Accountability	High	Low
Identification	Known/Places Identified	Anonymous/Spaces Unidentified
Cost	Increasingly Expensive	Increasingly Free
Maturity	Institutionalized/Ritualized	Experimental/Entrepreneurial

The Mexican cartels and, more recently, cyber-vigilantes (both bloggers and hackers), have been involved in a number of identified information offensives/counter-offensives. It should be noted that these engagements are increasingly taking place in both human (4th dimensional) and cyber (5th dimensional) space. The hybrid expression of this is 'dual-dimensional' operations—ones that have both forms of dimensionality present [3]. These more complex operations are also now taking place in the conflict with the cartels. In addition, disruptive targeting—also known as 'Bond-Relationship Targeting (BRT)'—is being widely utilized by the cartels and directed against Mexican society [4]. The basic timelines in this information-based conflict are as follows:

Time 1: The First Cartel Information Offensive

The initial cartel information offensive sought to establish a climate of fear and compliance in their areas of operation. Tortured and brutalized victims were left out in public areas with graffiti scrawls, body writing/carving, and signs/banners attached to their lifeless bodies. This leveraged traditional media forms and helped to create turf/drug market control and initially establish cartel/gang reputations as deadly killers [5]. This was combined with a 'dual-dimensional' initiative to utilize new forms of media and merge them with ghastly images of 'on camera' torture and killing. YouTube and other social media platforms were then utilized from about 2005-2006 on as a conduit for the transmission of this information [6]. The disruptive effects on Mexican society are readily apparent and have resulted in an assault on the bonds and relationships that hold that nation together—the relations between the people, the government, and law enforcement/the military are becoming increasingly frayed. It has been combined with unrelenting corruption to graft cartel and gang influence, authority, and elements of narcoculture (narcocultura) throughout that country.

Time 2: The Second Cartel Information Offensive

The cartels then sought in the various towns and cities to suppress and co-opt information produced and distributed by journalists/ reporters and their employers. This has resulted in the targeting of media personnel, their families, and their places of work via threats, beatings/torture, kidnappings, killings, and workplace drive-bys/ bombings. At least thirty Mexican journalists have either been killed or kidnapped and remain missing since 1992 [7]. The targeted killings have been recently increasing with eleven killed in 2011 alone [8]. As a result, the freedom of the press has been severely compromised in Mexico. Old media forms of reporting on narco-violence has virtually ceased in many of the cartel controlled cities or is being manipulated by the cartels for propaganda and psychological warfare purposes directed at opposing cartels, the Federal government, and the Mexican public.

Time 3: The First Vigilante Information Counter-Offensive

A response, or counter, to the second cartel information offensive was implemented by concerned Mexican citizens. They established social media networks—derived from websites, such as *Blog del Narco* that came online in March 2010, texting, and tweeting—that bypassed the cartel assault on press freedoms in Mexico. Many of these networks are city based and allow for real time reports to be filed in order to alert others to cartel violence, roadblocks, and patrols taking place in specific locations [9]. While the concerned citizens engaging in these social networks typically viewed themselves as non-combatants, they could also be interpreted as 'passive combatants' (they reported on cartel activities only to protect other citizens) or even, and probably more accurately, as 'active combatants' or 'cyber-vigilantes' (who reported on cartel activities which may then allow Mexican authorities to arrest or kill cartel operatives) [10]. Still, because of the anonymity of reporting and complex nature of the social media networks (which could be hosted outside of Mexico and whose location/ownership could remain hidden), they posed a significantly 'harder media target' for the cartels to contend with.

Time 4: The First Cartel Information Counter-Offensive

In September 2011, two incidents occurred that represented the initial cartel counter-offensive against the Mexican citizen/cyber-vigilante social networks. The first incident took place on the 13th and is linked to Los Zetas:

> The mutilated bodies of two bloggers were hung from a passenger overpass in the Mexican border town of Nuevo Laredo last month, with a sign attached saying, "This will happen to all Internet busy bodies." [11].

> "This happened for snitching on Frontera Al Rojo Vivo," read a note attached to the man's leg. Another, on the overpass, said: "This will happen to all the Internet snitches (Frontera al Rojo Vivo, Blog Del Narco, or Denuncia Ciudadano). Be warned, we've got our eye on you. Signed, Z." [12]

The next incident involved "La 'nena' de Laredo" ("Girl from Laredo") whose severed head wearing headphones was found next to a computer keyboard on 24 September. Her death is also attributed to the Los Zetas cartel [13]. The intent of this new counter-offensive is to attack the perceived weak point of the social networks—the actual blogger physically in a cartel area of operations. The rationale is that, if enough of them are identified and tortured/killed, the bloggers too can be intimidated and neutralized just as have mainstream journalists and reporters.

Time 5: The First Vigilante Information Offensive [or a Cartel-on-Cartel Information Offensive]

In what mirrors the initial "Time 1: The First Cartel Information Offensive": "...two pick-up trucks were left abandoned on 20 September 2011 in broad daylight on a busy Veracruz boulevard with 35 bodies in their beds and on the ground..." [14]. A few weeks later 46 more bodies were found in stash houses in Veracruz. Five hooded men dressed in black then appeared in a social media video distributed on 25 September and claimed to be "'Mata Zetas' ('Kill Zetas') [who] are the 'armed wing of the people' and that their 'only objective is to wipe out the Los Zetas cartel'" [15]. These vigilantes ('anonymous warriors...proudly Mexican') are suspected of being linked to the Sinaloa cartel—blood feud rivals to Los Zetas—and, for that reason, it is unknown how to characterize this operation. It can be viewed either as a 'vigilante information offensive' or a 'cartel-on-cartel information offensive'. Federal Mexican complicity and indirect support of the Sinaloa cartel has also been suggested in this matter, but no definitive proof has as of yet surfaced to support these allegations. Further, eight of these 'vigilantes' were said to be captured and tied to the New Generation cartel who are known Sinaloan allies [16].

Time 6: The Second Vigilante Information Counter-Offensive

In a strange twist in October 2011 the hacker group Anonymous then threatened the Los Zetas cartel for kidnapping one of its members from a street protest in Mexico. It did so via an online video [17] of one of its members wearing a Guy Fawkes mask as seen in the 2006 movie V for Vendetta. He further "...underlines the group's international ties by speaking Spanish with the accent of a Spaniard while using Mexican slang." [18] If the member is not released, Anonymous intends to start hacking into secure websites/protected accounts and release sensitive information pertaining to the members of the Los Zetas cartel and those who work with them such as co-opted journalists, police officers, and taxi drivers. This counter-offensive escalates the war in cyberspace by moving away from licit information reporting to illicit information acquisition. To give it more credence:

> ....Anonymous followed up its threat to the Zetas by defacing the website of former Tabasco state prosecutor Gustavo Rosario Torres, accused by anti-crime activists three years ago of discussing a $200,000 cocaine deal with a deputy on audio tape. With a Halloween background, a message splashed above the group's signature on Rosario's homepage read: "Gustavo Rosario is Zeta." [19]

How this engagement will further develop is unknown but a 5 November ultimatum was given to Los Zetas. It is quite likely the initial pretext for the counter-offensive, the kidnapping of an Anonymous member, was fabricated and meant to cause initial ambiguity and discord within the ranks of Los Zetas. See this from a twitter thread:

> @Sm0k34n0nStarting today #OpCartel begins. Heads up #Zetas! Love, @Sm0k34n0n @anonkitsu @ AnonSyndiv cc @AnonymousIRC @YourAnonNews @MotormouthNews
>
> @AnonKitsuCountless people live in fear everyday because they fear #Zetas. There was no kidnapped #anonymous member but this one still has targets set
>
> @Sm0k34n0nLos #Zetas are the most dangerous drug cartel in Mexico. We dont take kindly to this is my crew #OpCartel [20].

Thus, it is far more plausible that Anonymous has simply come into this conflict, due to the new cartel policy of torturing and killing Mexican bloggers—as an offensive cyber-vigilante force. The other possibility is that the hacker collective is simply toying with Los Zetas and seeking media attention but this would potentially be a very dangerous game to play. Individuals identified as working with Los Zetas, and the Anonymous hackers involved, all potentially risk being killed.

Given the economic resources of Los Zetas and the other cartels, a future counter-move—regardless of Anonymous' intentions—may be that of hiring additional cyber-mercenaries to bolster their defensive and offensive information operations capabilities [21]. Blowback on Mexican bloggers may also take place. A near term incident in which someone turns up headless wearing a Guy Fawkes mask, as a warning to Anonymous, is not beyond the realm of possibility.

Conclusions

What is noticeably missing from the ongoing cartel and vigilante information offensives and counter-offensives is any meaningful form of participation from the Mexican Federal government. Creating laws—notably enacted only at the state level—to punish the malicious spreading of rumors and fear via social networking messaging (the "#twitterroristas") is not however meaningful participation [22]. While the Mexican government is quite comfortable with the 'industrial media' of the 20th century—it appears incapable of engaging in information operations leveraging social networking. At best it may be able to provide 'journalist/reporter protection' but even this appears problematic given the silencing of much of the free press in Mexico.

The Mexican state is increasingly falling behind the action-reaction dynamic of the conflict as the criminal insurgencies migrate into 5th dimensional (cyber) space. This is somewhat perplexing given Mexican military operations against Los Zetas telecommunications networks in ten cities in the state of Veracruz in September 2011, although once again such networks represent old media (communications) based systems used for operational control of the Los Zetas insurgent forces [23]. Earlier though, from a December 2007 Naval Post Graduate school thesis, it was recognized that:

> In summary, Mexico has significantly increased its efforts to counter drug trafficking activities, as well as, insurgent and paramilitary groups within the country. Nevertheless, Mexico's military and law enforcement agencies have not established an Information Operations-based capability. Instead, Mexican government agencies communicate with the population primarily through the public affairs offices of each department. While this is a useful means to inform the public of government projects and military operations, it does not sufficiently strengthen the government's relationship with the population. As a result, some efforts of government agencies are inadequate, thus overlooking an opportunity to positively influence public opinion...[24].

The Mexican Federal government would thus be well advised to either stand up its own internal new media/social networking capability and/or immediately contract out to a specialized group or corporation in order to do so. Rather than create an overly centralized and hierarchical response coming out of Mexico City—which simply will not work—it should look to build a networked and distributed capability that would leverage the Mexican citizen/cyber-vigilante social networks already in existence. The intent would be to foster bottom up operational early warning and response, promote media flows necessary for Democratic governance, and, ultimately, rebuild trust across Mexican society by repairing the bonds and relationships being targeted by cartel activity.

Further, Mexico, as well as the United States, is going to have to learn how to appropriately operate in 21st century conflicts against non-state threats. Many of the old rules and underlying assumptions concerning both warfare and policing—such as dimensionality— are no longer valid. According to John Sullivan and Adam Elkus:

A focus on understanding cyberspace in its original meaning and incorporating time as a dimension of operations may seem pedantic or perhaps overly academic. But understanding cyber and temporal dimensions of operations means synthesizing a mixture of old and new ideas to gain a better understanding of the modern operational space— and is crucial to dealing with opposing force and environmental challenges [25].

This proposed approach may sound like a radical plan, but given the realities of 21st century conflict, it is far more sound than the current Mexican state trajectory of a) either ignoring cartel information operations altogether or b) responding to them from an 'industrial media' perspective. War and conflict are dramatically changing as witnessed by the criminal insurgencies being waged across Mexico. For the Mexican Federal government to remain relevant in this evolving conflict, it must develop a 5th dimensional (cyberspace) capability. Further, it must implement its own counter-informational operations leveraging the older media forms and then attempt to quickly learn how to engage in 'dual-dimensional' operations drawing upon the newer media forms to achieve synergistic effects.

Developing Stories

As this essay was being concluded, two stories were developing. The first dealt with the ongoing Anonymous vs Los Zetas conflict. Conflicting reports have been circulating that initially Anonymous had called off their targeting of this cartel [26] and later that it was still a "go" [27]. These reports were derived from Twitter feeds and social networking statements made by individuals said to be members of this hacker collective. The true status of the Anonymous 'OpCartel' counter-offensive is currently highly ambiguous.

The second story concerns the present status *of Blog del Narco*. Since about 24 October 2011, viewers have been having trouble accessing the site:

> "The government and some individuals want to censor us, they've denounced us to Blogger, where the site is hosted for security reasons and because we do not have the resources for a dedicated server," replied an anonymous representative via e-mail when the Knight Center asked what caused the site's technical problems [28].

The new site is MilCincuenta.com but technical issues appear to also exist. This development follows the earlier Los Zetas threats against a number of blogs in the Nuevo Laredo incident on 13 September 2011. Since that time, two of the blogs have been shut down after threatening messages appeared on them. The user was worried because the blog accounts had personal information in them [29]. This marks two more victories for Los Zetas in the 'Time 4: The First Cartel Information Counter-Offensive'. What the future status of *Blog del Narco* will now be is unknown, however, those behind it have shown no intention of shutting it down.

End Notes

[1]. For an early example of social netwar breaking out in Chiapas Mexico in the mid-to-late 1990s and lessons learned, see David Ronfeldt and John Arquilla, "Emergence and Influence of the Zapatista Social Netwar." David Ronfeldt and John Arquilla, eds., *Networks and Netwars*. Santa Monica: RAND, 2001: 171-199.
[2]. Access via http://mountainrunner.us/2010/11/cartel_info_ops_power_and_counter-power_in_Mexico_drug_war.html and smallwarsjournal.com/blog/journal/docs-temp/730-sullivan1.pdf respectively. See also the earlier *MountainRunner* publication by Matt Armstrong, "Mexican narcos step up the information war." 6 November 2010, http://mountainrunner.us/2010/11/mexican_narcos_step_up_information_war.html.
[3]. These concepts date to the 1990s. See Robert J. Bunker, "Advanced Battlespace and Cybermaneuver Concepts." *Parameters*. Autumn 1996: 108-120 and Five-Dimensional (Cyber) Warfighting. Carlisle Barracks: Strategic Studies Institute, US Army War College, 10 March 1998: 1-42 and "Higher Dimensional Warfighting." Military

Review. September-October 1999: 52-62. They have since been applied to policing and SWAT operations. See Sid Heal, "Fighting in the Fifth Dimension". *OnPoint: A Counterterrorism Journal for Military and Law Enforcement Professionals.* April 2005; John P. Sullivan and Adam Elkus, "Police Operational Art for a Five-Dimensional Operational Space." *Small Wars Journal.* 23 July 2009, http://smallwarsjournal.com/blog/journal/docs-temp/274-sullivan.pdf; and Sid Heal, "Five-Dimensional Battlespace." *The Tactical Edge.* Spring 2010, http://www.ntoa.org/site/images/TEArticles/Five-dimensional.pdf.

[4]. The environmental modification discussed in previous writings is one outcome of the application of bond-relationship targeting (BRT). This is implicit in works such as Robert J. Bunker and John P. Sullivan, "Societal Warfare South of the Border?" *Small Wars Journal.* 22 May 2011, http://smallwarsjournal.com/jrnl/art/societal-warfare-south-of-the-border. Also see the work of Dr. Gordon McCormick—his "Magic Diamond" counter-insurgency model focuses on the relationships between the insurgent force, the counterinsurgency force, the population, and the international community.

[5]. The earliest *Borderland Beat* (http://www.borderlandbeat.com/) postings date to mid-2009. These postings provide one of the best depositories of cartel violence imagery from the streets of Mexico.

[6]. For an initial analysis of cartel use of social networking, see Sarah Womer and Robert J. Bunker, "Sureños gangs and Mexican cartel use of social networking sites." Robert J. Bunker, ed., *Narcos Over the Border.* London: Routledge, 2011: 81-94.

[7]. "27 Journalists Killed in Mexico since 1992/Motive Confirmed." *Committee to Protect Journalists,* http://www.cpj.org/killed/americas/mexico/.

[8]. Jose Luis Sierra, "Dark September: Journalist' Deaths Mount in Mexico." *New American Media.* 28 September 2011, http://newamericamedia.org/2011/09/dark-september-journalists-deaths-mount-in-mexico.php.

[9]. Damien Cave, "Mexico Turns to Social Media for Information and Survival." *New York Times.* 24 September 2011, http://www.nytimes.com/2011/09/25/world/americas/mexico-turns-to-twitter-and-facebook-for-information-and-survival.html.

[10]. For the rise of vigilantism in Mexico, see George W. Grayson, *Threat Posed by Mounting Vigilantism in Mexico.* Carlisle Barracks: Strategic Studies Institute, US Army War College, 15 September 2011, www.strategicstudiesinstitute.army.mil/pdffiles/PUB1082.pdf.
[11]. Larisa Epatko, "Mexican Drug Cartels' New Target: Bloggers." *PBS Newshour.* 13 October 2011, http://www.pbs.org/newshour/rundown/2011/10/mexico-bloggers.html.
[12]. J. David Goodman, "In Mexico, Social Media Become a Battleground in the Drug War." *New York Times.* 15 September 2011, http://thelede.blogs.nytimes.com/2011/09/15/in-mexico-social-media-becomes-a-battleground-in-the-drug-war/.
[13]. Her name is Maria Elizabeth Macias. She worked as an advertising supervisor at Prima Hora and moonlighted as a blogger. See "Bloggers and press freedom groups vow to fight on." *Borderland Beat.* 29 September 2011, http://www.borderlandbeat.com/2011/09/bloggers-and-press-freedom-groups-vow.html. See *Borderland Beat* for other stories on this incident.
[14]. "Mexican Government Examines Videos from Anti-Cartel Vigilantes." *Borderland Beat.* 28 September 2011, http://www.borderlandbeat.com/2011/09/mexican-government-examines-videos-from.html. The source is EFE. See the embedded Mata-Killers video. Even earlier videos predate that one proclaiming the rise of the Mata-Killers. See "Mata-Zetas Release Video Accusing Officials as Supporters of Los Zetas, Mexico." *Latin America: Current Events & News.* 19 July 2011, http://latinamericacurrentevents.com/mata-zetas-release-video-accusing-officials-as-supporters-of-los-zetas-mexico/10781/ and "Video en internet confirma existencia de grupo 'mata zetas.'" *Terra.* 2 de julio de 2009, http://www.terra.com.mx/articulo.aspx?articuloId=842793&ref=1.
[15]. Ibid.
[16]. José de Córdoba, "Mexico Captures Alleged 'Zeta Killers'." *The Wall Street Journal.* 8 October 2011, http://online.wsj.com/article/SB10001424052970203388804576616884152273092.html. See also Tracy Wilkinson, "Some welcome violence against cartel." *Los Angeles Times.* 20 October 2011: A1, A6-A7.
[17]. Access via http://www.borderlandbeat.com/2011/10/online-hackers-threaten-to-expose.html. This link also provides a translation of the video. "Online Hackers Threaten to Expose Cartel's Secrets".

Borderland Beat. 29 October 2011. Mirror/synopsis to Dane Schiller Note 18.

[18]. Dane Schiller, "Online hackers threaten to expose cartel's secrets: Group called Anonymous demands release of one of their own who was kidnapped." *Houston Chronicle.* 29 October 2011, http://www.chron.com/news/houston-texas/article/Online-hackers-threaten-to-expose-cartel-s-secrets-2242068.php.

[19]. Robert Beckhusen, "Anonymous Threatens Mexico's Murderous Drug Lords." *Wired: Danger Room.* 30 October 2011, http://www.wired.com/dangerroom/2011/10/anonymous-vs-zetas/.

[20]. "Hacking Grp Anon IRC-Gives 1st Zeta Name." *Borderland Beat.* 30 October 2011, http://www.borderlandbeat.com/2011/10/hacking-grp-anon-irc-gives-1st-zeta.html.

[21]. According to STRATFOR "Since we have seen evidence of cartels employing their own computer scientists to engage in cybercrime, it is logical to conclude that the cartels likely have individuals working to track anti-cartel bloggers and hackers." Ben West, "Dispatch: Anonymous' Online Tactics Against Mexican Cartels." *STRATFOR.* 1 November 2011, http://www.stratfor.com/analysis/20111101-dispatch-implications-online-tactics-against-mexican-cartels.

[22]. Tania Lara, "Mexicans accused of terrorism for spreading rumors on Twitter spark new law to limit expression on social networks." *Journalism in the Americas Blog.* 26 September 2011, http://knightcenter.utexas.edu/blog/mexicans-accused-terrorism-spreading-rumors-twitter-spark-new-law-limit-expression-social-netwo.

[23]. EFE, "Soldiers dismantle telecom network used by Mexican traffickers." *Fox News Latino.* 31 October 2011, http://latino.foxnews.com/latino/news/2011/10/31/soldiers-dismantle-telecom-network-used-by-mexican-traffickers/.

[24]. Saul Hiram Bandala-Garza and David Vargas Schulz, *Information Operations, an evolutionary step for the Mexican Armed Forces.* Thesis. Monterey: Naval Post Graduate School, December 2007, www.worldcat.org/wcpa/ow/214110691. The authors later provided suggestions for information operations capabilities to be developed by the Mexican navy.

[25]. John P. Sullivan and Adam Elkus, "Police Operational Art for a Five-Dimensional Operational Space." *Small Wars Journal*. 23 July 2009, http://smallwarsjournal.com/blog/journal/docs-temp/274-sullivan.pdf.

[26]. Buela Chivis, "Anonymous Cancels Crackdown on Mexican Drug Cartel (ZETAS)." *Borderland Beat*. 1 November 2011, www.borderlandbeat.com/.../anonymous-cancels-crackdown-on-mexican.html.

[27]. "News/Anonymous to drug cartels: 'The dice are already rolling'". *Dailydot*. Via Twitter. 31 October 2011, http://www.dailydot.com/news/anonymous-latin-america-opcartel-names/. Note—even though this source has an earlier publication date than note 26 it is responding to claims made in it. Another video was also purported to be released by hacker group: *Anonymous NO suspende #OpCartel*, http://www.youtube.com/watch?v=eiFW3see2Ec&feature=youtu.be&a.

[28]. Tania Lara, "Mexico's Blog del Narco denounces attempts at censorship as website access hindered." *Journalism in the Americas Blog*. 27 October 2011, http://knightcenter.utexas.edu/blog/mexicos-blog-del-narco-denounces-attempts-censorship-website-access-hindered.

[29]. Ibid. The original blogger message is "Mi blog lo elimine pero están usando mi dominio por métodos hacker para difundir un mensaje de un grupo delictivo." *Blogger*. 23 September 2011, http://www.google.es/support/forum/p/blogger/thread?tid=663c508a4751f3f0&hl=es. See also 'The Knight Center's recommended 15 steps to help guarantee privacy and anonymity online when reporting on dangerous subjects' at the end of the article in note 28.

Section 12:
Cyberspace

Charles "Sid" Heal

This is an excerpt from an essay that was
originally published as Section 5 of
Field Command, Lantern Books: New York, 2012: 267-275.

> *We lack dominance in cyberspace and could grow
> increasingly vulnerable if we do not fundamentally
> change how we view this battlespace.*
> —General James Cartwright [1]

No one willingly takes a beating. Lacking an effective means of resisting, flight is the natural and understandable alternative. This reveals an axiom that holds true in all conflicts; the weaker adversary always seeks refuge. Escape in the realm of space is usually accomplished by either moving beyond the range of the offending force or seeking protective cover which shields from injury. Escape in the realm of time is almost always some type of avoidance. There are other sanctuaries, however. For example, criminals (and terrorists) depend on remaining undetected. Once identified and located they are virtually powerless to continue their anti-social behaviors and are extremely vulnerable to arrest and prosecution. This concept is called the **sanctuary of anonymity**. What is revealing here, however, is that anonymity is dependent on neither time nor space. It lies in an entirely different dimension altogether.

The fifth dimension is cyberspace.[2] **Cyberspace** is an intangible information space where people interact with one another and with machines. While most people think of cyberspace as the online world of computer networks it is actually a much richer and deeper environment. It is better understood as a domain of information. Besides information transferred between computers; such as email, file transfer protocols (FTP), web browsing and the like; it includes all types of information like that transferred from wireless cell phones, text messaging, pagers, and even electronic door locks, TV tuners or garage door openers.

Like all dimensions, the rules for one are completely irrelevant for another. Neither space nor time is applicable in cyberspace for one simple reason; information can reside in more than one place at the same time. For example, a mother purchases a combination padlock for her young son's school locker because when he inevitably loses the key she can unlock it over the telephone by giving him the combination. When that happens the information needed to unlock the padlock is simultaneously at home with the mother and at school with the son. So it is with all information. Only the medium used to store and transmit it occupies space.

In law enforcement applications, five-dimensional battlespace can be readily understood in the stark reality of every day examples. For instance, it is not an uncommon occurrence to stop a vehicle for a traffic violation only to discover after leaving the scene that the driver was just involved in a crime. It is a vivid example that the suspect was trapped in both time and place during the stop but the lack of knowledge left him immune from arrest and prosecution. So it is with tactical operations. No good commander ignores an unprotected flank and a lack of knowledge can be every bit as devastating as being in the wrong place or at the wrong time. It would seem prudent then to understand the implications of a multidimensional battlespace.

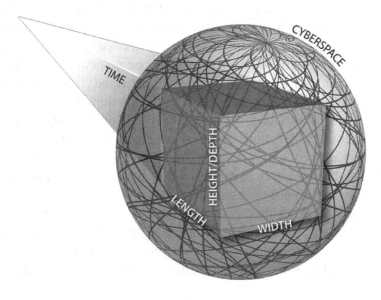

If it were possible to see battlespace, it might look something like this. Length, width and depth/height comprise the dimension of space. In space the maneuver elements are physical in that they take up space, have weight and volume. The fourth dimension is time. Time is a notional dimension in that the maneuver elements are conceptional and exist only as a mental image. Each tactical situation is a temporary and unique combination of circumstances and as such, is dissimilar at different times. Together, space and time comprise humanspace. Humanspace is where humans move and fight. The fifth dimension is cyberspace. Like time, in cyberspace the maneuver elements are intangible and the maneuver elements are informational in nature, often as a means of communication between people and other people or people and their machines. Information has one critical aspect that distinguishes it from others in that it can reside in more than one place at the same time. Thus, both time and space become irrelevant. An adversary in cyberspace is thus immune from attack because his identity and/or location are unknown. Commanders who ignore the vagaries of multi-dimensional battlespace surrender the advantage to their adversary.

Maneuvering in Cyberspace

Maneuver in cyberspace requires a new paradigm because the defining characteristic is information. Whether it is needed to locate a criminal hiding in darkness or to identify a terrorist concealed by anonymity, it is information that is necessary to acquire and effectively engage him. Consequently, the maneuver elements in cyberspace are informational, often obtained as the "fruits" of devices designed to allow humans to interact in this dimension. Examples include the information obtained from cell phone conversations, pager messages, location reports from global positioning systems, or that taken from email, web sites and other on-line transactions. It also includes the information gleaned from sensors, such as motion detectors, surveillance cameras, thermal imaging devices and night vision goggles. This interaction not only includes humans interacting with each other, but with machines. Examples include television tuners, garage door openers and even remotely operated automobile alarms and locks. No law enforcement officer is likely to miss the tactical significance of being able to remotely open a garage door, lock a criminal out of his car or prevent him from watching a live TV broadcast.

Despite their fundamental differences all five dimensions interact with one another with humans as the common "go between" or element. Every disaster or tactical situation is a result of a unique and temporary set of circumstances unfolding in space. Unseen, but ever present, is the intrinsic information, including that of the authorities, victims, bystanders, witnesses, and even suspects. It also includes information between people and things, like a suspect remotely opening or closing a garage door or setting off a bomb. For actions in time and space, some of this information is valuable, and some is even crucial. Thus, all five dimensions are an integral part of battlespace.

When attempting to gain an advantage it is important to understand that two adversaries need not be in each other's battlespace at the same time. In the previous example of the traffic stop the officer's lack of knowledge of the driver's criminal conduct was a critical vulnerability which resulted in the suspect's escape. Conversely, the knowledge possessed by the suspect provided him with an ability to manipulate a situation to make getting caught even more difficult, to include the use of surprise. Tragically, this has resulted in the deaths of officers who stopped criminals unaware of the danger and were attacked, and even killed. As can be seen, because of a lack of knowledge the officer was in the suspect's battlespace but the suspect was not in the officer's battlespace—which provided a decisive advantage.

Understandably, maneuver in cyberspace is measured in knowledge, and the ability to acquire, deprive and manipulate information is critical. The two most commonly sought after facts in law enforcement are usually the identify of culprits and their location. Similarly, an ability to manipulate information is of great value. Many a fugitive has been arrested as part of a sting operation after having been lured to a location with false information.

While the maneuver objective in space is gaining and controlling key terrain and in time it is identifying, creating and exploiting opportunities; in cyberspace the goal is gaining understanding. Information is only useful if it contributes to identifying and comprehending the factors and influences involved. Information that does not provide better understanding is distracting. In some cases this necessitates acquiring new information but in many cases the same thing can be accomplished by rearranging and interpreting information that is already available. Once a fact has been determined to be relevant to some concern, a second fact can not only be used to corroborate the first but also to extrapolate a wealth of information. Just two sightings of a fleeing suspect, for example, provide such things as a direction of travel, approximate speed and may even indicate intentions with a potential destination.[3]

Multi-dimensional Battlespace

Dimensio	Maneuver Element	Measured in	Objective
Space	Physical	Distance	Gain and maintain control of key terrain
Time	Notional	Speed	Identify, create and exploit opportunities
Cyberspace	Informational	Knowledge	Acquire and apply understanding

Multi-dimensional battlespace is not as complex as it might seem. In fact, adversaries with no understanding whatsoever move seamlessly between them. A commander with a thorough understanding of the nature of battlespace can understand and anticipate actions and counteractions. The matrix above compares each of the five dimensions with the major factors that differentiate each of them.

Nature of Knowledge

The maneuver elements in cyberspace are informational; meaning that they are related to the nature of information. Gains and losses are measured in knowledge and the objective is to acquire and apply understanding. Accordingly, it is of great benefit to have some understanding of the nature of knowledge and comprehension.

The rawest form of information is **data**. Each datum refers to a single fact, statistic or code that exists without context. Data, in and of itself, is not information because it provides no ability to inform. It only becomes information when a context is added, either with circumstances or from other data. Data comes in any number of varieties and formats and can range from the binary code of a computer to the oscillations in a radio frequency wave. In tactical operations data may appear as a discrete event, fact, observation, message, or statement. In order to be useful, data must be collected, organized and interpreted.

Information may be best understood as a collection of facts or data from which conclusions may be drawn.[4] Information is the first step toward understanding and where meaning is attached. It is intended to provide substance and shape to a person's perspective and provide a basis for judgment. Unlike data, information is always enclosed in context and needs to be organized to be useful. Information that is jumbled, confusing, or ambiguous requires a decision maker to make a personal investment of effort and attention. Accordingly, the value of information is determined by the recipient. When the expected effort exceeds the perceived value the information is likely to be glossed over or ignored entirely.

Knowledge refers to a state of awareness of facts and circumstances accompanied with a personal assessment. Consequently, all knowledge is based on interpreted information. While data and information may be captured and stored on paper or a hard drive, knowledge belongs to people. While information is derived from data, knowledge is derived from information. The four most common ways that humans transform information to knowledge is through the use of:

- Comparison—how does one piece of information compare with another?
- Consequences—what are the implications of a particular piece of information in regards to forming a judgment?
- Connections—how does a particular piece of information relate to others?
- Conversation—what do other people think about a particular piece of information?[5]

Like information, knowledge can be shared. The knowledge belonging to a group is usually referred to as "corporate knowledge." **Corporate knowledge** is the collective knowledge of all participants in any plan or decision. It is invaluable in dealing with complex situations and is what makes units like explosive ordnance disposal, gang enforcement, SWAT, and narcotics teams so formidable.

The maneuver objective in cyberspace is gaining and applying understanding. **Understanding** identifies a person's thorough comprehension of the nature of something. It surpasses simply knowing something and provides insight for probabilities, expectations, opportunities, creativity and resourcefulness. True understanding enables intuition and so subtle factors and influences are more easily detected and reliable inferences can be formed. The difference between knowledge and understanding may seem subtle because they are so similar. The differentiating feature is that knowledge refers to a mental comprehension about something while understanding refers to the comprehension of something. As such, understanding includes an ability to interpret and extrapolate. That's why understanding, not knowledge or information, is the maneuver objective.

To better understand how these function and interact, imagine running a license plate while on patrol. The numbers and letters on the license plate are data. By themselves they have no meaning but when compared with other data, as that in the database of the department of motor vehicles, it provides the registered and legal owner of the vehicle, the vehicle description, the address, and even traffic accidents and offenses. Likewise, the officer notes that the license plate frame identifies a car sales agency from another state. The combined data is now information. The officer remembers a briefing concerning guns being transferred to a local gang from the distant state and begins following the vehicle. He soon realizes it is headed toward a local gang hangout. His personal awareness of facts, coupled with the circumstances, has now transformed the data and information into knowledge. The officer is a seasoned veteran who has not only had much instruction on the nature of gangs but has personally had experience with this particular gang. He knows that when moving contraband gangs routinely use counter-surveillance and support vehicles and quickly identifies a likely possibility. He rapidly formulates a plan and relays his instructions to responding units. Because of his understanding of the situation as a whole both vehicles are stopped well away from the gang area with sufficient support to ensure a decisive action should a confrontation occur. When guns are indeed discovered, the officer's increasing understanding provides even more insight and so everything from the identity of the recipients of the guns to information for obtaining a search warrant and even the expectation of a gang war can be reliably intuited.[6]

While the maneuver objective in cyberspace is understanding, maneuver is actually measured in knowledge. This is because while knowledge can exist without understanding, the reverse is not true. When seeking knowledge it is important to understand that it is not evenly distributed. In tactical operations it tends to accumulate according to two attractors. The first is by locale. There is more knowledge of the unfolding events at a crime or disaster scene, for instance, than at an emergency operations center. It also tends to be clumped by type. Experts are able to harvest more knowledge from the same information than are novices. Consequently, knowledge related to a particular event or activity is greater with technicians who specialize in that particular area. Furthermore, these specialists themselves tend to be grouped in specialized units like SWAT, canine, explosives ordnance disposal, narcotics, gangs, and so forth. With this in mind, some priorities begin to emerge in that efforts need to be made to make this knowledge available for decision makers. The extensive use of versatile and reliable communications is one the best methods of propagating knowledge from various locales. The use of liaisons and advisors for harvesting knowledge from subject matter experts is another.

Figure 17-3 Creating Understanding: Whether baking a cake, making an omelet or brewing coffee a process is involved. So it is with creating understanding. If one were to compare the process of gaining understanding with brewing coffee it might appear as the graphic above. The coffee beans represent the raw data and incapable of being used in their present form. After being ground and blended with other coffee beans they constitute a substance that provides a pleasant aroma but are still of no benefit. When placed in a coffee press with boiling water they create the first substance that would be readily recognizable as coffee. If the process were stopped here, however, the coffee is still undrinkable. Only after it is poured into a cup do the coffee beans fulfill their purpose. So it is with data, information, knowledge and understanding.

The process begins with the identification of facts, statistics or codes. These are called data and constitute the raw material from which understanding is ultimately drawn. As these data are gathered they create information. This is the first step in the process where meaning is attached. When information is gathered it can be analyzed to ascertain its relevance, reliability and accuracy. This is where knowledge is gained. Even so, only when a person uses knowledge to comprehend the nature of something does understanding result.

End Notes

[1]. USMC General James E. Cartwright, Vice Chairman of the Joint Chiefs of Staff. General Cartwright is a pilot who, as he rose through the ranks, became known for his exceptional understanding of the changing nature of threats. The comment was made on March 21, 2007 as a statement to the House Armed Services Committee while General Cartwright was the Commander of the United States Strategic Command. He was not only explaining some of the challenges of cyberspace but why it was appealing to adversaries unable and unwilling to fight a conventional war. He also emphasized the need for an offensive capability in cyberspace. Even more poignant for the purposes of this chapter was a statement in which he pointed out that the principles of warfare also apply to cyberspace. "If we apply the principles of warfare to the cyber domain, as we do to sea, air, and land, we realize the defense of the nation is better served by capabilities enabling us to take the fight to our adversaries, when necessary to deter actions detrimental to our interests."

[2]. "Cyberspace" was coined by science fiction author William Gibson, in his book *Neuromancer*, published in 1984. The book is essentially a science fiction crime novel. While Gibson had used the term in a magazine article two years earlier, it wasn't until the book became popular that it gained widespread recognition.

[3]. The combination of two or more pieces of information to gain some new insight is called "information fusion" and is discussed in more detail in Chapter 9—Intelligence.

[4]. For a more thorough discussion of information, see Chapter 9—Intelligence.

[5]. Many of the ideas on generating knowledge and understanding for this chapter come from two seminal books on the subject. For further exploration and understanding see: *Working Knowledge: How Organizations Manage What They Know*, by Thomas H. Davenport and Laurence Prusak, Harvard Business School Press, Boston, MA, 2000 and *Information Anxiety 2*, by Richard Saul Wurman, Que Publishing, Indianapolis, IN, 2001.

[6]. As the example illustrates, humans do not acquire understanding in a linear process but rather a highly complex and interactive process that includes gathering, organizing and testing data and assumptions, drawing inferences, making comparisons and mentally "explaining" the outcome. Experts are particular adept at making sense in situations where the available information is unreliable, confusing, incomplete and even conflicting because they have a larger repertoire of experiences for comparison. Moreover, they are just as likely to notice something that should be present but is not as something that is present but out of place. They also engage in mental simulation of what has occurred and is transpiring, as well as what it means and what is likely to occur in the near future. One of the premier researchers in this area is Dr. Gary Klein (author of *Sources of Power, Power of Intuition, Intuition at Work* and *Streetlights and Shadows*) who coined the term "sensemaking" to describe this phenomenon.

Section 13:
Dimensional Bubbles and Future Army Warfighting

Robert J. Bunker

Any sufficiently advanced technology is indistinguishable from magic.
— Arthur C. Clarke

Introduction

Movies about sentient and hostile alien lifeforms invading Earth are common science fiction themes. From a dimensionality perspective, the more plausible movies, such as *Predator* (1987) and the more recent *The Darkest Hour* (2011), portray storylines in which alien forces enjoy superior land warfare capabilities—such as active stealthing and energy weaponry effects—derived from advanced space-time capabilities. The conventional military forces of the besieged humans are typically at a great disadvantage in their engagements with the invading aliens. In fact, in these sagas they take on the role of industrialized primitives whose circa late 20th and early 21st militaries are inconsequential in the face of the superior warfighting abilities of their technological alien betters.

In many ways, such a scenario is no different than the empires of the Western Europeans overrunning the new world, as well as many regions of the old, from the early 16th through the late 19th centuries. This is due to the simple truth that significantly advanced civilizations are deadly for those less advanced ones they come into contact with. They are built upon higher levels of dimensionality—*an advanced understanding of space-time and the capability to exploit that higher level of knowledge.*[1] While that knowledge translates into peaceful civilizational pursuits, it also translates into advanced warfighting capabilities. Against such superior technologies, and the accompanying organizational and logistical means to effectively implement them, the militaries fielded by inferior civilizations have gone down in defeat as did the army of the feathered soldiers of the

Aztecs at the hands of a smaller group of invading Conquistadors in the early 16th century.

While an appreciation for tesseracts and hypercubes will never rival a senior officer's affinity for basic terrain maps and the implements of war, an elementary understanding of higher dimensional space-time is now a military imperative. History is replete with battlefield disasters and failures—few are worse than getting the battlefield wrong and thus preparing for the wrong fight such as the French who found this out with their Maginot line in the early years of World War II. The French, who plowed their resources into a very limited four-dimensional defensive construct against the German Blitzkrieg in 1940, whose battlespace vision included the breath and depth of that nation, failed to recognize that warfare had evolved beyond their limited and woefully obsolete doctrines. The space-time phenomena highlighted in this work, however, has the potential to be even worse for the vanquished than that suffered by the French in their defeat some seventy odd years ago.

As a result, the intent of this essay is to educate the U.S. Army strategic community concerning the need to grasp the importance of dimensionality for the purposes of fielding an effective early-to-mid-21st century fighting force.[2] To do so, it will first provide a theoretical discussion of 'dimensionality.' Second, it will explain how it and the dimensional symmetries and asymmetries that emerge have a direct impact on warfighting. Third, it will explore the 'dimensional bubbles' construct and highlight how it has historically portended the new capabilities offered by a higher order of emergent battlespace. Fourth, it will discuss just a few of the new capabilities offered by today's dimensionally disruptive technologies. These capabilities are derived from, in many cases, nascent technologies significantly advanced that, when fielded, will allow the U.S. Army to create its own 'dimensional bubbles' for warfighting advantage.

Dimensionality

The concept of dimensionality is important for warfighting because it literally defines the boundaries in which organized political violence conducted between states and state challengers (e.g. proto and new warmaking entities) takes place. These dimensional boundaries in which war is waged mirror the prevailing techno-military level of development of the civilization in question (See Fig. 1.).[3] For example at the most basic level early Western civilizations waged war in 2 dimensions—the 'x' of linearity and the 't' of temporality. They are, for want of a better term, 'line fighters'—'x + t' —whose infantry based formations clashed head on with each other. Even then, early Greek phalanx's were plagued by the 'drunken man syndrome'—unable to walk a straight line—with a tendency to drift to the right stemming from a soldier's need for self preservation by seeking protection behind the shield of his comrade on his right flank. The vaunted Romans, whose more versatile legions eventually ruled the Mediterranean world and a goodly chunk of Europe itself, even remained limited by the 2 dimensional nature of Classical civilization.

Medieval civilization, built upon the smoldering ruins of the Western Roman Empire and the resiliency of the Byzantine Empire of the East, in turn, waged war in 3 dimensions—the 'x' of linearity and the 't' of temporality with the addition of 'y' to allow for 'x + y + t' geometric plane fighting to be conducted. This civilization effectively incorporated mounted forces into its military forces, unlike the earlier Romans, and utilized better metallurgical techniques than the preceding eras resulting in the better armoring of its soldiers. From a defensive perspective, the development of the castle resulted in a hardened patchwork defense system throughout Europe and the lands seized on the frontiers of Christendom. Still, this civilization posed limited scientific knowledge with no understanding of ballistics, the curvature of the Earth, the circulatory system of the human body, or the heliocentric nature of the solar system.

Modern civilization, with which we find presently find ourselves in the waning years, wages war in 4 dimensions—the 'x + y' geometric plane and the 't' of temporality with the addition 'z' to allow for 'x + y + z + t' cube fighting to be conducted. This civilization effectively wages war with missile weapons (broadly defined) whose European origins extend back to 14th century *hand gonnes*—primitive infernal devices that spewed sulfur and death and whose users were initially thought to be in league with the devil. Hand-in-hand with modern civilization arose industrialization and mechanization and the ongoing exploitation over the course of centuries of the battlespace cube with the development of war machines that could operate on the land, on and under the sea, and in the skies. As a testament, to the longevity of the dominance of this cube based approach to warfighting the mercenary companies of the early modern period and the coalition forces participating in *Operation Iraqi Freedom* a little over a decade ago operated within the same space-time dimensionality. Of course, in the latter engagement, the U.S. armed forces achieved complete mastery of the battlespace cube acquiring and killing—practically at will—all Iraqi conventional forces operating within the confines of 4 dimensional space.

Cyber civilization, which increasingly represents a likely successor to our modern civilization, appears to be following the same historical developmental pattern of gaining an additional level of dimensionality beyond that of its predecessor civilization. This would mean that it will ultimately engage in war in 5 dimensions—the 'x + y + z' cube and the 't' of temporality with the addition of 'c' for cyberspace (an informational construct) to allow for 'x + y + z + t + c' based tesseract fighting.[4] A number of 5 dimensional warfighting capabilities have been theorized and even documented. [5] Components of this still forming civilizational approach to warfare—while hazy—include networked organizational forms, disruptive targeting, directed energy projection and manipulation, and materiel resiliency derived from organic self-healing capabilities.

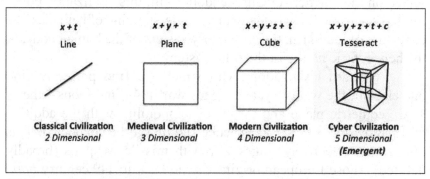

x + t	x + y + t	x + y + z + t	x + y + z + t + c
Line	Plane	Cube	Tesseract
Classical Civilization *2 Dimensional*	Medieval Civilization *3 Dimensional*	Modern Civilization *4 Dimensional*	Cyber Civilization *5 Dimensional (Emergent)*

Figure 1. Dimensionality Examples

The reason that dimensionality is so important is that it thus defines what a civilization's military force *can do* and *cannot do* in terms of its warfighting capabilities and potentials.[6] A Greek hoplite army composed of heavy infantry is very much limited to basic 2 dimensional activities. Positioning it in on a small open field with the flanks secured or in a narrow pass (ala the Thermopylae example) maximizes its combat potentials but anything beyond that is too dimensionally sophisticated for such a military force on its own. [7] In turn, a more advanced Medieval 3 dimensional host has no capability to reign death down upon opposing troops 'in defilade'— such as behind a sturdy protective embankment or wall. This capability does not exist until the English development of shrapnel shells which did not become common until the mid-1800s—many centuries and one level of dimensionality higher in sophistication than that found with armored knights and their men-at-arms. On the same note, the airmobile infantry concept, based first on the use of gliders and later on the helicopter transport of troops, was not even conceivable to pre-20th century military forces—even those whose native dimensionality was lesser battlespace cube based.

Dimensional Symmetry and Asymmetry

The second insight pertaining to dimensionality in warfighting is that two different space-time types of wars may be fought. Such wars are dependent on the basic symmetries or asymmetries of the opposing forces involved. Dimensionally symmetrical wars are derived from opposing military forces that have a parity of capabilities within the dimensional boundaries of a civilization. This means similar line, plane, or cube based militaries engaging each other, respectively. Trench warfare indicative of the First World War and the blitzkrieg operations in the later phases of the Second World War are both examples of such a dimensionally symmetrical conflict.

Dimensionally asymmetric wars, on the other hand, come in two variants—lesser and greater. The lesser asymmetrical conflicts take place intra-dimensionally within a civilization level. The lesser conflicts are reminiscent of the 1990s debates derived from the precursor Military Technical Revolution (MTR) and more mature Revolution in Military Affairs (RMA) that raged in this and other strategic and defense journals. Those debates ultimately addressed operational level changes in warfare such as that brought forth by military advances in the 1920s and 1930s. These advances were juxtaposed with precision targeting and similar military innovations that performed so well during the first Gulf War of the early 1990s.

Intra-dimensional asymmetries can clearly be seen with the previously mentioned 1940 French Maginot line vs. German blitzkrieg example as an expression of a techno-military revolution in land warfare. Another clear example would be a comparison of the 1916 Jutland battleship engagement between the British and German navies against that of the 1942 Battle of Midway between the opposing American and Japanese carrier fleets. Those engagements portray a techno-military revolution in naval warfare had taken place even though the Japanese Imperial Navy still operated under the belief, even after their success at Pearl Harbor, that the climatic battle of that war would still be fought Jutland style with their *Yamato* class super battleships holding the center of the line. In both the land and naval warfare examples, the expanse of 4 dimensional space delineating the battlefield dramatically increased in volume as did the speed of operations even though the underlying nature of that space remained constant (See Fig. 2).

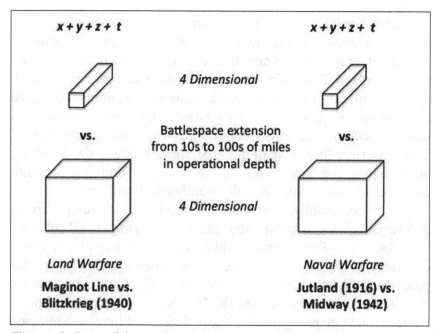

Figure 2. Intra-Dimensional Asymmetry Examples

Greater asymmetrical conflicts, on the other hand, are even more militarily significant as they take place inter-dimensionally between civilization levels. Wars of this type are recognized at the epochal level of change.[8] Two historical examples and one contemporary example of these greater asymmetrical conflicts exist (See Fig 3.). In the first instance, the transition from Classical to Medieval civilization saw the eventual downfall of the dominant Roman 2 dimensional line based military at the hands of successive waves of 3 dimensional plane based raiders on horseback. Eventually, the European empires recovered and adapted their military forces to the requirements of mounted combat centered on the knight in the West and cataphract cavalry of the Byzantines of the East. In the second instance, the transition from Medieval to Modern civilization saw the demise of the Empires of Christendom and the rise of secular states in the West and the Ottoman Turks in the East. This asymmetric struggle was between the older civilizational form of 3 dimensional plane based knights on horseback, and their castle (and larger fortress) articulations, against early 4 dimensional based cube military forces with increasingly sophisticated firearms and field and siege artillery pieces.

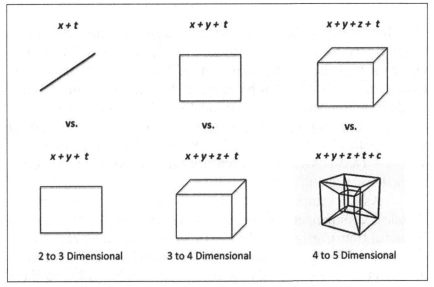

Figure 3. Inter-Dimensional Asymmetry Examples

The contemporary dimensional struggle now pits our Modern civilization against the rise of an emergent Cyber (or Hyper) civilization. Legacy 4 dimensional based cube military forces are increasingly coming into conflict with early forms of 5 dimensional tesseract based forces. The 9-11 attack by al-Qa'ida is representative of an early military engagement in this struggle. The attack conceptually bypassed the strongest conventional military forces on the face of the Globe by using stealth-masked forces that relied upon a cheat (e.g. they wore no uniforms). In the process, they dropped two World Trade Towers, damaged the Pentagon, slaughtered roughly 3,000 U.S. nationals, and caused untold hundreds-of-billions in dollars in direct and indirect economic damage to the United States. In both of the historical and in the present inter-dimensional asymmetric conflict, the threatened legacy civilizational form initially considered such attackers to be anathema; be they bow-legged Huns, lowly Landsknechte arquebusiers, or wild-eyed suicide bombers. These heinous criminals and vulgar barbarians essentially blur the conventional wisdom concerning the separation of the conditions of crime and war, public and private, sovereign and non-sovereign.

Dimensional Bubbles

The 'dimensional bubbles' construct is meant to portray the ability of a military force, both legitimate and criminal-military such as terrorists, to transcend the limitations of its own dimensionality and operate in a higher level of battlespace. The reason a military force would seek to open up a dimensional bubble is so that it can gain advanced warfighting capabilities. This allows it to gain a combat advantage that it otherwise would not possess. To open such a bubble, a cheat—a technological or organizational innovation, or some other method—may be utilized.

As an example, the superior use of cavalry by the celebrated Classical commanders Alexander the Great from Macedonia and Hannibal from Carthage strike us as anomalies for those eras. In this civilizational epoch dominated by 2 dimensional line infantry forces, the effective use of cavalry by these commanders allowed them to create a dimensional bubble that provided them an asymmetric advantage as 3 dimensional plane fighters over their opponents (See

Fig. 4). Likewise, as a result of colonial traders providing firearms to some of the American Indian tribes that they came in contact with, those tribes also gained a dimensional bubble advantage. In that instance, what had been essentially point based 1 dimensional ('t' only) band of warriors were now able to engage in basic 4 dimensional cube based activities against competing tribes not so armed. This resulted in some of the Indian tribes 'punching above their weight' militarily and created a dependency over time for them on the European traders, much like armament addicts who needed their ongoing fixes of powder and shot, to stay competitive with more and more tribes increasingly so armed.

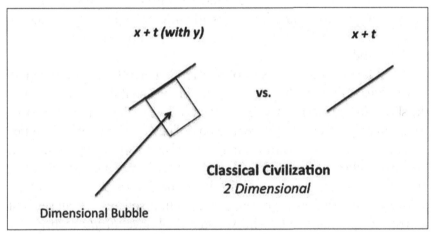

Figure 4. Two Dimensional Force with Dimensional Bubble Against Contemporary Opposing Force

As can be imagined, such bubbles are at times difficult to sustain because they represent a discontinuity within the prevailing space-time dimensionality of the contemporary military forces fielded. Those military forces are a product of the underlying civilization in which they exist. Such civilizations are essentially too technologically primitive to keep the bubbles from eventually collapsing. As an example, the cavalry forces of Alexander and Hannibal were always more entrepreneurial than institutionalized and were dependent on the great commanders unlike the Roman legions which over time had undergone a normal developmental process and became institutionalized by a society that that could field and sustain them.

We suffered a classic setback—and a hard lesson learned—in this same regard with the demise of the Los Angeles Terrorism Early Warning (TEW) Group that had emerged back in 1996 and finally stood down in 2009. This mother cell created the fledging TEW network— established via cellular replication in a couple of dozen domestic operational areas throughout the United States— with the intent of providing tesseract based (eg 5th dimensional) intelligence fusion capabilities.[9] In hindsight, we can now say that this network of TEW Groups existed for a time in one of those bubbles. It ultimately fell victim to a federally mandated fusion center program whose retrograde views on intelligence, while inferior, better represented a bureaucratic expression of our traditionalist cube based approaches to homeland security.

These historical examples offer but a glimpse of the new capabilities offered by higher forms of dimensionality. As we undergo the shift from Modern to Cyber civilization, every day that goes by now means that we are one step closer to a host of new warfighting capabilities that are increasingly within our grasp. These will be highlighted in the next section of this article, though it should be cautioned that our present understanding is still somewhat limited; possibly no better than a square's description of his encounter with a sphere and subsequent journey to spaceland in Edwin Abbott's 1884 novel *Flatland*.[10]

New Capabilities Offered by Dimensionally Disruptive Technologies

Disruptive technologies are defined as technologies that unexpectedly replace established or sustaining technologies in business.[11] In our usage, we will refer to dimensionally disruptive technologies as ones that challenge the theoretical understanding of the present civilizational level and the capabilities of its space-time artifacts—in this instance, the performance of its implements of war. A listing of six new such capabilities below are illustrative of such potentials. They are representative of how the warfighting limitations of traditional 4 dimensional space-time can be transcended by a higher level of dimensionality.

Overcoming ballistic limitations: For well over three hundred years, the weaponry of our dominant Modern civilization has been plagued by gravitational limitations influencing the performance of our projected bullets, shells, missiles, and bombs. Directed energy weapons (DEWs) are finally being fielded after many decades of research—initially as vehicular based point-defense systems against rockets and on our warships and military aircraft as a defense against precision guided munitions. These new weapons do not follow ballistic trajectories and for the purposes of warfighting (except in the case of directed energy counter counter measures) do not have a time of flight—the effect is instantaneous. In the case of infantry weapons, this will eventually greatly simplify the targeting of these weapons against opposing soldiers because these targets do not have to be led, wind does not have to be accounted for, and ballistic trajectories do not have to be factored in. For good or for bad, every laser-armed soldier with the proper optics will gain the accuracy of a highly trained sniper (See Fig. 5).

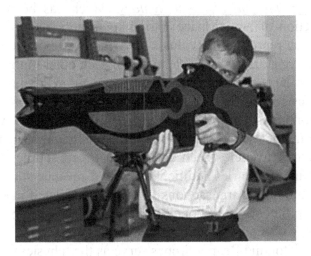

Figure 5. *U.S. Air Force Capt. Drew F. Goettler, of the Air Force Research Laboratory' Directed Energy Directorate, demonstrates the Personnel Halting and Stimulation Response, or PHaSR, a non-lethal illumination technology developed by the laboratory's ScorpWorks team. (U.S. Air Force Photo. November 2005. For Public Release)*

Overcoming industrial logistics: 3D printers have increasingly made the news with the creation of functioning small arms and now a unmanned aerial vehicle (UAV) with a two meter wingspan and a speed of 100 miles per hour being reported.[12] 4D printers—whose whole creations exist in one state but can change into another over time (and thus form the basis of self-assembly robots)—are also being developed.[13] While portending a manufacturing revolution, these printers—in essence early 'replicators'—will also significantly change the way military logistics are carried out. With enough energy and stocks of goo (the basic materials to construct objects), these replicators will replace stockpiles of spare parts—in some cases even weaponry or vehicles (like the UAV example)—in forward operating bases and aboard warships. Further, since DEW have different ammunition requirements—benefitting from the 'deep clip' phenomena of being able to fire as long as energy exists—logistical needs will further be lessened for the fielding of these weapons.

Fielding virtual and physical avatars: Much has been made of the projection of humanspace into cyberspace via the creation of 'avatars' that represent individuals in virtual worlds such as Second Life. These avatars directly interact with each other in these virtual realms that have witnessed acts of protest and symbolic terrorism via the destruction of national and corporate edifices. Further, cyber economies are developing that are interacting with real world economies with cyber money, such as game currencies and independent currencies such as BitCoin (open source P2P), that offer criminal-militaries additional forms of revenue streams and a means to hide illicit transactions from U.S. mandated international reporting protocols. Additionally, a humanspace to cyberspace to humanspace phenomena is emerging where unmanned UAVs such as armed Predator and Reaper drones serve as the 'physical avatars' of their operators safely out of harm's way. This extension of self—that of a combatant—is no different that that of a game participant in a virtual world except that it is taking place in our physical world with an easily replaceable avatar. As an outcome, drone pilots represent 'immortal warriors' that cannot be killed in combat. Moral implications aside, this provides them a psychological warfighting advantage against organic human combatants who once killed are gone forever. It is only a matter of time before this capability is extended to armed ground robotic units.

Fielding invisible and dimensionally shifted forces: While the camouflaging of ranger-type forces has been going on for centuries and the use of camouflage has become standard for conventional military forces since at least the First World War, this capability goes way beyond such traditional means of not being identified by an opposing force. An array of technologies are being explored from biomorphic materials through research on the bending of light and the suppression of sound and heat signatures in an attempt to render friendly military forces undetectable. Documented U.S. and British R&D military programs have been in effect for some time now that seek to provide their ground military forces with such capabilities. This research exists in a similar vein to that of stealth technology that reduces the radar cross section (RCS) of aircraft making them practically invisible to modern air defense systems. More mature variations of these stealthing technologies will eventually be energized which will allow for our soldiers and their fighting platforms to be slightly out-of-phase with their physical surroundings. As a result, they will much harder to detect than legacy 4 dimensional based military forces.

Creating transgenic & cyborg soldiers: Disruptive bio-medical and bio-technical advances will result in the increasing augmentation of stock human beings unless bio-ethics preclude such modifications. Lesser forms of enhancement already exist and include gene therapies to treat diseases and the replacement of minor body parts such as hips and knee joints and the implantation of wetware such as pacemakers and hearing implants. Transgenic augmentation will import foreign species DNA into the human body while cybernetic augmentation will begin to see organic and machine hybrids. Both of these forms of augmentation would provide enhanced warfighting capabilities for our soldiers. While we still may be many decades away from actual cyborg emergence—even if they ever are allowed to be constructed— the removal of an eyeball and in its place the eventual implantation of an enhanced vision device for infrared vision capability has clear military implications. Even more significant are the potentials

193

represented by Google Glass linked to cloud computing and the likely evolution of this technology from glasses, to contacts, to an optical interface. At some point, our soldiers will not only being sensing within our physical reality—possibly via organic multispectral imaging—but also with an organic virtual informational overlay.

Creating energy barriers: Primitive energy barriers to protect soldiers through pre-detonating incoming mortar and artillery shells by spoofing their fuzing have been in existence for some time now. This capability also exists to detonate improvised explosive devices (IEDs) targeting VIPs and/or being built in bomb factories in villages and towns via vehicular mounted countermeasure suites. More specific energy barriers are developing for vehicles—via energized armor and shielding projection—that will pre-detonate conventional munitions and counter the wavelengths of opposing directed energy devices. Additionally, less-lethal anti-personnel millimeter wave systems have been deployed such as the ADS (Active Denial System) that create invisible energy barriers that cannot be penetrated by humans due to the increasing levels of physical pain that they generate as one goes deeper into the projected energy field (See Fig. 6).

Figure 6. *Active Denial System (ADS) mounted on U.S. Military Humvee (U.S. DOD Photo. For Public Release)*

Conclusion

The dimensionality of our Modern civilization now appears on the cusp of the transition to Cyber civilization. If lessons learned are any guide, what took place over the course of centuries with the transition from Classical 2 dimensional to Medieval 3 dimensional civilization and Medieval 3 dimensional to Modern 4 dimensional civilization will now take place in the span of decades due to historical compression.

During this epochal transition, blended 4th and 5th dimensional warfighting capabilities will increasingly be possessed by both military and military-criminal forces. In fact, various criminal-military forces have already been straying into 5th dimensionality—not because of scientific prowess or superior knowledge—but because of the simple rules of Darwinism. This is due to the U.S. war machine having effectively mastered 4 dimensional operations—we own the battlespace cube—and any military force, be it state or non-state fielded, that fights us in that space will be annihilated. Further, since non-state military forces are already organically network configured, they already partially exist in Cyber civilization. That simple fact on its own makes them an increasing asymmetric threat to the United States.[14]

Opposing state fielded military forces do not as of yet appear as adaptive as the non-state forces in regards to new forms of dimensionality but they can be expected at some point to more competently respond to our present dimensional dominance. Our concerns over their use of advanced anti-access technologies against our entry forces are representative of such a trend. Still, a rising China, whom we would prefer to engage rather than contain, may well represent a wild card with regard to emergent state based dimensionality. This concern is due to its conceptual advances in building architecture and artwork—a reflection of its perspective of reality—that is possibly now more sophisticated than our own and hence better in tune with the new civilization upon us.

Given the grand strategic context in which dimensionality is changing, our U.S. Army forces, and those of the sister services, now have an imperative to increasingly gain new warfighting capabilities derived from the dimensionally disruptive technologies that have emerged. To do so, we must begin to create as many 5th dimensional bubbles as feasible and determine how to stabilize them. In the process, we must recognize that not only will this forever change the nature of our military forces but the underlying society of which they are an extension. In this matter we have no choice—only those states that possess an advanced understanding of space-time and the capability to exploit that higher level of knowledge will triumph in early-to-mid-21st century warfighting.

End Notes

[1]. For an overview of works on this subject, see Robert J. Bunker and Daniel Musa, *5th Dimensional Law Enforcement Operations.* FBI Library: Bibliographies and Subject Guides. 12 December 2012, http://fbilibrary.libguides.com/content.php?pid=330445.

[2]. Early essays on this topic are Robert J. Bunker, "Advanced Battlespace and Cybermaneuver Concepts." *Parameters.* Autumn 1996, pp. 108-120, http://www.carlisle.army.mil/USAWC/parameters/Articles/96autumn/bunker.htm; Robert J. Bunker, *Five-Dimensional (Cyber) Warfighting.* Carlisle: Strategic Studies Institute, U.S Army War College. March 1998, http://www.strategicstudiesinstitute.army.mil/pubs/display.cfm?PubID=233; and Robert J. Bunker, "Higher Dimensional Warfighting." *Military Review.* September-October 1999, pp. 53-62, http://cgsc.contentdm.oclc.org/cdm/singleitem/collection/p124201coll1/id/317/rec/2.

[3]. Pre-civilizations with no effective state or warmaking ability exist in point based dimensionality. Their warriors engage in ritualistic 1 dimensional—'t' temporal—activities devoid of any form of organized political violence component.

[4]. The use of 'h' for hyperspace, a geometric expression of this dimension of space, is probably a far more accurate term to utilize than 'c' for cyberspace which is a informational expression. The use of the term cyberspace, however, quickly gained dominance in the military literature due to the early recognition of the increasing importance of information warfare and operations.

[5]. A number of these capabilities will be highlighted at the end of this essay. For other capabilities, see the earlier works listed in note 2.

[6]. For state-of-the-art special law enforcement operational thinking on dimensionality, see 'Section 5: Multi-Dimensional Battlespace' in Charles 'Sid' Heal, *Field Command*. Herndon: Lantern Books, 2012.

[7]. Still, heavy infantry armed with pikes, were later utilized as a maneuver base for cavalry that engaged in 3 dimensional operations or as protective formation when combined with arquebusiers (via the concept of 'Pike and Shot') who engaged in early 4 dimensional operations.

[8]. Also known as the RPMA (Revolution in Politico-Military Affairs) which corresponds with social and political organizational form (*eg.* state type) civilizational shifts.

[9]. John P. Sullivan and Alain Bauer, eds. *Terrorism Early Warning: 10 Years of Achievement in Fighting Terrorism and Crime*. Los Angeles: Los Angeles County Sheriff's Department, October 2008, http://file.lacounty.gov/lasd/cms1_144939.pdf.

[10]. See Edwin Abbott Abbot, *Flatland: A Romance of Many Dimensions*. London: Seeley, 1884.

[11]. See Clayton M. Christensen, *The Innovator's Dilemma*. New York: HarperBusiness, 2011 (Reprint of 1997 work).

[12]. "World's first 3D printer-made aircraft flies in the UK." *domain-b.com*, 19 April 2013, http://www.domain-b.com/technology/engineering/20130419_southampton.html.

[13]. "3D printing is yesterday's news—time for 4D?" *GCN.com*, 12 April 2013, http://gcn.com/blogs/emerging-tech/2013/04/4d-printing.aspx.

[14]. For early thinking on this form of asymmetric conflict, see John Arquilla and David Ronfeldt, *The Advent of Netwar*. MR-789-OSD. Santa Monica: RAND, 1996, http://www.rand.org/pubs/monograph_reports/MR789.html.

Section 14:
Dimensional Bubbles: A Short Critique and Response

T. Lindsay Moore and Robert J. Bunker

A Short Critique

Dr. Robert Bunker has offered a framework for exploring the impact of cyber-weapons on war in a paper entitled "Dimensional Bubbles and Future Army Warfighting."[1] He introduces the concept of a dimensional bubble and asserts,

> The concept of dimensionality is important for warfighting because it literally defines the boundaries in which organized political violence conducted between states and state challengers... takes place. These dimensional boundaries in which war is waged mirror the prevailing techno-military level of development of the civilization in question.

He goes on to note that the history of the West reveals four such bubbles. A fifth bubble, labeled, "cyber," is emerging today. The first four dimensional bubbles are identified as: the x for linearity, the t for temporality, y as the geometric plane, and z representing fighting within the dimensions of a cube. Each bubble replaces the one preceding it and is regarded as existing at a higher level of techno-military dimensionality than the one preceding it. Forces waging combat in the x + t dimensional bubble will have a distinct advantage over those fighting only in the x level, etc. In addition, more developed forces within the same dimensional bubble will be advantaged over those at a lesser developed level. In the final analysis, Bunker's arguments are prelude to introducing the concept of a new dimensional bubble—cyber—which he finds superior to the other four.

While I find Bunker's fundamental ideas of dimensional bubbles and the contemporary dawn of a new dimension in warfighting initially attractive, his exposition is, for me, ultimately unsatisfactory. I believe his framework is confusing and needs considerable reformulation if it is to be employed as a way of conceiving and understanding warfighting and the battlefield of tomorrow.

It is difficult to see the underlying logic of the techno-military level of development. How, for example, does the incorporation of mounted forces, better metallurgy, and the castle convert *linearity* (x) into *geometrical* (y) plane fighting? Are linear forces not fighting in a geometrical plane; is not the geometrical plane an expression of linearity? The z dimension is equally confusing, introducing missile weapons thereby converting geometrical (y) fighting into *cube* (z) fighting. Battles have always occurred in the dimensions of space. There have always been missile weapons (slings, spears, bows and arrows, catapults, rifles, artillery, ICBMs, etc.). Time has always figured in operations and tactics. Accordingly, warfighting has always occurred within the four dimensions of the space-time continuum, so just precisely how does one dimensional bubble become superior to another?

It is also equally true that one civilization may exist at a more advanced "techno-military" level than another. But what precisely does this mean? Bunker seems to be asserting that a civilization takes better advantage of the space-time continuum than another in order to gain a more advanced techno-military level. What is missing is an explanation of what techno-military level means in terms of how that conveys an advantage in space-time. The examples he provides are clear and convincing, but something is missing in the analysis of just how the process signifies and how it works.

The concept of cyber, for which Dr. Bunker also gives several examples is not defined in a sufficiently precise way. We are simply left to 'sense its meaning' from the several examples which he provides. "Cyber civilization, which increasingly represents a likely successor to our modern civilization," he asserts, "appears to be following the same historical developmental pattern of gaining an additional level of dimensionality beyond that of its predecessor civilization." But what is a "cyber dimension," what is its distinctive constituents, and precisely how does its' historical development occur? Unlike many other writers in the cyber discussion, Bunker, to his credit, regards the cyber-dimension as involving far more than operations over the internet. But, in Bunker's exposition, they are examples, not analysis. And it is analysis that is needed.

The problems noted above are especially acute when considering policy level issues raised by the evolution of a fifth dimensional bubble. Without a more precise understanding of the processes involved, it is difficult to plan at a policy and strategic level. How, for example, does the fifth dimensional bubble interact with a policy of deterrence? Does it?

T. Lindsay Moore

A Short Response

I welcome Dr. T. Lindsay Moore's short critique of the dimensional bubbles construct. Dr. Moore is eminently qualified to provide his dissenting view points on this component of Epochal Warfare theory given that he is the co-founder of this area of inquiry with me back in the late 1980s. In the spirit of this constructive debate on an extremely important component of future U.S. warfighting and counter-terrorism activities, I will respond to his theoretical and policy level critique on a point-by-point basis:

Critique 1. "….his exposition is, ultimately unsatisfactory. I believe his framework is confusing and needs considerable reformulation if it is to be employed as a way of convincing and understanding warfighting and the battlefield of tomorrow."

Response 1. Given Dr. Moore's expertise on the strategic and policy levels—rather than on the tactical and operational levels—it does not surprise me that he takes exception to the dimensional bubbles construct. The intent of the construct is to provide an initial bottom up approach (via the tactical) rather than a top down approach (via policy) to the issue of civilizational dimensionality. Components of 5th dimensional battlespace have in the past been employed at the tactical level by SWAT teams, at the operational level in counter-narcotics activities, and in Terrorism Early Warning Group planning.

This construct has not been applied at the U.S. strategic or policy level and, in fact, is still being worked out at much lower levels of tactical and operational application.

Critique 2. "It is difficult to see the underlying logic of the techno-military level of development. How, for example, does the incorporation of mounted forces, better metallurgy, and the castle convert *linearity (x)* into *geometrical (y)* plane fighting? Are linear forces not fighting in a geometrical plane; is not the geometrical plane an expression of linearity?"

Response 2. See Response 5 concerning techno-military levels of development. Castles represented the state of the art defense against plane (x, y) forces by drawing upon an additional dimension (z) to counter cavalry warfighting dominance. Turning to the other question, I would argue that densely packed infantry forces—such as Classical spearmen and pikemen—only fight along a line segment (x). They do not possess enough tactical mobility at ~.01 hp per fighter to maneuver within plane space (x + y) as do cavalry forces with ~.05-1.0 hp per mounted rider. For this reason, the cavalry forces— drawing upon greater energy potentials—enjoy a 'geometrical plane' asymmetry advantage over linear infantry forces.

Critique 3. "The z dimension is equally confusing, introducing missile weapons thereby converting geometrical (y) fighting into *cube* (z) fighting. Battles have always occurred in the dimension of space."

Response 3. In Western Warfare, there had long been a ban on the use of the bow (missile weapons) prejudiced by the cowardice of Paris in The Illiad. *Missile weapons were long considered not to be heroic arms with their use and effectiveness having a very spotty record until the deployment of the crossbow and English longbow. Prior to this time, Western battles were not determined by the dimension of space (x, y, z) but rather by line (x) and plane (x, y) engagements with, of course, the addition of the temporal (t) dimension. Cube fighting took on paramount importance with the advent of firearms and cannon which helped to usher in Modern civilization.*

Critique 4. "There have always been missile weapons (slings, spears, bows and arrows, catapults, rifles, artillery, ICBMs, etc). Time has always figured into operations and tactics. Accordingly, warfighting has always occurred within the four dimensions of the space-time continuum, so just precisely how does one dimensional bubble become superior to another?"

Response 4. While warfighting has always occurred in the four dimensions of the space-time continuum— exemplified by humanspace which is defined as x+y+z+t — the combatants have not always exploited all of these dimensions as components of their 'techno-military' level of development. Early Hellenic spearmen, for example, have mastery over the x, questionable expertise with the t, and no mastery of the y and z dimensions. A dimensional bubble becomes superior to a lesser one via exploitation and eventual mastery of an additional dimension in conflict and war. Modern civilization can effectively utilize the z dimension to identify, target, and destroy opposing forces in the battlespace box—the military forces of Medieval civilization possessed no such advanced warfighting capability.

Critique 5. "It is also equally true that one civilization may exist at a more advanced 'techno-military' level than another. But what does that precisely mean? Bunker seems to be asserting that a civilization takes better advantage of the space-time continuum than another in order to gain a more advanced techno-military level. What is missing is an explanation of what techno-military level means in terms of how that conveys an advantage in space-time. The examples he provides are clear and convincing, but something is missing in the analysis of just how the process signifies and how it works."

Response 5. A civilization at a more advanced 'techno-military' level draws upon greater levels of energy in its peaceful and warlike pursuits. Based on the early Epochal energy models, the energy sequences identified within Western Civilization are human (experimental), human (institutionalized), animal (experimental), animal (institutionalized), early mechanical (machine experimental), early mechanical (machine institutionalized), mature mechanical (engine experimental), mature mechanical (engine institutionalized), and the present transition which will be derived from some sort of fuel cell/direct electrical (experimental) sequence.[2] *This translates into fielded military forces with ever-greater mastery of dimensional manipulation in conflict and war, stemming from their more advanced techno-military capacity. Early Hellenic bodies of spearmen, indicative of the emergent human (experimental) sequence, could not even walk a straight line (they veered right due to personnel seeking the protection of the shield held by the man on their right) and once set on a somewhat forward course were able to engage in only elementary C² (Command and Control) activities. Such a primitive techno-military level can in no way be compared to the landpower forces of World War II era indicative of the mature mechanical (engine institutionalized) sequence utilizing blitzkrieg operations based on armored formations, supporting combat arms, and far better developed C² capabilities.*

Critique 6. "The concept of cyber, for which Dr. Bunker also gives several examples is not defined in a sufficiently precise way. We are simply left to 'sense its meaning' from the several examples which he provides. 'Cyber civilization, which increasingly represents a likely successor to our modern civilization,' he asserts, 'appears to be following the same historical developmental pattern of gaining an additional level of dimensionality beyond that of its predecessor civilization.' But what is a 'cyber dimension,' what is its distinctive constituents, and precisely how does its' historical development occur? Unlike many other writers in the cyber discussion, Bunker, to his credit, regards the cyber-dimension as involving far more than operations over the internet. But, in Bunker's exposition, they are examples, not analysis. And it is analysis that is needed."

Response 6. The basis of my articulation of the cyber dimension is derived from my 1996 U.S. Army War College journal essay on the topic (see Section 1 of this this work). If the human dimension—humanspace (x+y+z+t)—can be said to be "That aspect of battlespace composed of the traditional physical dimension of the human senses in which humans and their machines move and fight; the killing ground of future warfare" then the cyber dimension—cyberspace (c)—can be said to be "That aspect of the battlespace composed of the electromagnetic spectrum and the non-human sensing dimension in which stealth-masked forces seek refuge from attack." Humans use stealthing to gain defensive access to cyberspace and offensively use data fusion to deny such access. Cyberspace (c) represents that new dimension to be exploited by post-modern civilization just as modern civilization exploited the (z) spatial dimension. The present definition of cyberspace is truthfully tactically and operationally focused—it was meant to solve the dilemma of not being able to theoretically account for a terrorist (who is essentially invisible) on the modern four dimensional battlefield. As the post-modern epoch matures, virtual overlays of cyberspace over humanspace which humans (and likely cyborgs) will peer through will undoubtedly result in a more refined dual dimensional definition of cyber civilization that Dr. Moore seeks.

Critique 7. "The problems noted above are especially acute when considering policy level issues raised by the evolution of a fifth dimensional bubble. Without a more precise understanding of the processes involved, it is difficult to plan at a policy and strategic level. How, for example, does the fifth dimensional bubble interact with a policy of deterrence? Does it?"

Response 7. I do not think that our understanding of fifth dimensional space—building from the tactical and operational levels—is anywhere near mature enough to fully understand the strategic and policy impacts. I know Dr. Moore, on the other hand, posits otherwise—or at least is attempting to do some initial theoretical exploration into the subject matter. For this reason, he has contributed 'Appendix 1: Cyber and the Future of War' to this work in order to focus on the policy and strategic implications of what he terms "dimensional domains"—essentially his own reconceptualized variation of the dimensional bubble construct.

Robert J. Bunker

End Notes

[1]. Robert J. Bunker, "Dimensional Bubbles and Future Army Warfighting," Section 13 of this work.
[2]. See Robert J. Bunker, "The Transition to Fourth Epoch War." *Marine Corps Gazette*. Vol. 78. No. 9. September 1994: 20-32.

Postscript:
Teaching the Tactical Exploitation of Cyberspace

Charles "Sid" Heal

I am often an instructor teaching a forty-hour course on tactical science to law enforcement officers of which one module deals specifically with battlespace. The module begins with space and the students are introduced to the concepts related to terrain and weather. This physical realm is easily understood and takes no great stretch of the imagination to recognize how terrain features affect movement and why some provide advantages. The second class deals with time and so they quickly grasp the significance of the temporal aspects of battlespace. Without exception, every student has personally experienced the frustration of searching an empty building after a suspect has left and so the right tactics at the wrong time is a pretty incontrovertible concept. It would seem, then, that introducing cyberspace as an extension of battlespace would also be intuitive. This is not often the case, however, and so I have had to develop exercises that expand conventional mindsets to grasp the possibilities.

The hardest thing in teaching multi-dimensional battlespace is recognizing that, like space and time, cyberspace is actually a separate dimension, complete with its own maneuver elements and objectives. Once this mental block is overcome, most of the rest quickly falls into place and makes sense. The best method I've found for introducing these concepts is with an exercise that begins with a scenario to stimulate thinking and concludes with a moderated discussion to summarize and highlight the critical aspects. The exercise begins with the following scenario:

> *"Working late one night you are suddenly confronted by two burglars. One is armed with a knife and the other with a gun. A shot narrowly misses as you flee from the well-lit office area to a darkened and vacant large warehouse at the rear of the building. While*

hiding in the darkness, you find a short pipe. Your only other equipment is a cell phone and a bright flashlight. As the suspect armed with the knife slips through the door and out of sight, following you into the darkness, you hear him say he's looking for the light switch. You can see that the suspect armed with the gun is guarding the only exit. Beyond the exit is absolute safety.

What should you do?"

As the participants begin offering suggestions, I record them on an ink board or large chart so that they can actually see the suggested courses of action. As you might suppose, the diversity of responses is limited only by imagination but the vast majority include variations of a few things like:

- Call for help on the cell phone
- Sneak up on the suspect near the door and hit him with the pipe
- Use the flashlight or cell phone as a distraction and attack the guy at the door

The moderated discussion usually begins by my asking why they chose the options they did. Some, like calling for help on the cell phone, are so obvious that they are self-evident. Likewise, the tradeoff is equally apparent, in that even a normal response time cannot assure your survival or prevent the escape of the suspects. This makes other options, albeit somewhat desperate, more appealing. Thus, an attack of some sort is almost always suggested. What is particularly revealing, however, is that the suggested courses of action that involve an attack are almost always centered on the suspect with the gun rather than the more lightly armed suspect with the knife.

When asked why they chose to attack the more heavily armed suspect, the responses are typically that his location and attention could be readily determined and exploited. When asked why not attack the more lightly armed suspect, the responses are always something to the effect of, "We didn't know where he was."

As I continue questioning their rationale for the various suggestions, I eventually ask, "What is it that is keeping you alive?" The obvious answer and the one most often cited is, "the darkness." It is then I lead into highlighting some of the critical aspects of cyberspace that are now demonstrable. For example, it is not the darkness, per se, but rather the lack of knowledge of your whereabouts that is the deciding factor. Once this is agreed upon, it is easy to extrapolate that darkness is only an enabling objective and, in other circumstances, might be provided by smoke, dust, fog, or snow. Likewise, what makes the more lightly armed adversary the most formidable is also knowledge, but in this case, the lack of it. Likewise, it is what empowers the victim. In fact, it is such a powerful factor that it makes attacking an armed suspect with only a pipe not only feasible, but promising.

Given that this class is the third in a series focused on battlespace, I then ask the students to identify the critical factors based upon their newly acquired perception. This is also revealing by the commonality of the responses as they recognize that, when considering space and time, all the adversaries occupied the same physical battlespace at the same time but, because one adversary was vulnerable while another was not, they could not technically meet the requirements of the definition of acquiring and engaging him.[1] Obviously, some other factor has to be in play besides space and time.

I continue the moderated discussion by pointing out that the victim's center of gravity[2] is the ability to maneuver without being detected and the critical vulnerability[3] is the victim's inability to continually sustain operations before the lights eventually came on. This is also revealing in that the action that would most likely prove decisive for the outcome does not involve a weapon at all, but rather who gains some essential knowledge necessary to effectively attack the other. Moreover, who first understands the significance gains an advantage of such import that it can easily prove decisive regardless of the amount of force. In fact, virtually every suggestion involves gaining, providing, depriving or manipulating information in some fashion. By now the operational aspects of knowledge are becoming clear to the students and so when I point out that these same factors are what makes terrorists so formidable it requires no great leap of intuition. Instead of darkness, anonymity will work just fine. This single factor leaves a deadly adversary free to maneuver and attack with impunity. Just like the "victim" in the scenario.

Using this mental exercise so often, it was inevitable, I suppose, not to wonder whether other attributes in conventional battlespace could be extrapolated into cyberspace. And so I'm going to continue this monologue by examining cyberspace as if I was still teaching it. Because conventional battlespace is composed of both the space and time dimensions, any extension must also be inextricably linked. Thus, any comprehensive understanding must include all five dimensions.[4]

In space, the maneuver elements are physical. They are people and vehicles and things. They take up space and have weight. Maneuver in space is measured in distance and the objective is to gain and maintain control of key terrain. In the dimension of time, however, the maneuver elements are notional. While every bit as real, they lie entirely within the confines of the human mind. In this dimension, maneuver is measured in speed and the objective is to identify or create opportunities for exploitation. In cyberspace, the maneuver elements are informational, often in some form of communication. Accordingly, maneuver is measured in knowledge and the maneuver objective is to acquire and apply understanding. Unique to cyberspace, however, is that both the maneuver elements and the objectives defy conventional understandings of battlespace because they can be in more than one place at the same time. This fact is compelling for the expansion of our conventional perceptions of battlespace.

Multi-dimensional Battlespace

Dimension	Maneuver Elements	Measured in	Objective
Space	Physical	Distance	Gain and maintain control of key terrain
Time	Notional	Speed	Identify, create and exploit opportunities
Cyberspace	Informational	Knowledge	Acquire and apply understanding

Like our scenario, the first adversary to gain understanding acquires an advantage that is sometimes powerful enough to be decisive in nature. Thus, even though armed with only a makeshift weapon (pipe), the realization that he is impervious to attack until discovered puts our victim in parity with the armed suspect. Exploiting this still further, it provides an opportunity (in time) to maneuver (in space) to strike an unsuspecting and unprepared adversary (via cyberspace). This realization opens up all kinds of options that were heretofore inconceivable.

Looking for attributes in cyberspace that are similar in nature with space and time, we also note that there are different densities. In space, density is measured by the number of people and things per given unit of space. In time, density is measured by the amount of activity in a given period. In cyberspace, knowledge is also not evenly distributed. Density in cyberspace occurs when some "attractor" consolidates knowledge. For example, there are both times and places where we can expect more knowledge than others. In space, we know that there are also natural "attractors" where knowledge is more prevalent. Those actually involved in a particular situation are often more aware and better informed than those at a command post or emergency operations center, for one example. Likewise, experts are better able to detect and interpret subtle clues and gain knowledge that eludes others. Logically then, knowledge accumulates where they are gathered. In the dimension of time, we can be more certain of the consequences of our actions in the near term future than the distant future. Likewise, we can be more certain of those that are closer to norms than for those that are more absurd. This knowledge is better understood as existing outside the conventional comprehension of a battlespace comprised solely of space and time given that both the maneuver elements and tactical objective can exist in more than one place at the same time.

This understanding of density in cyberspace is particularly important in that it can be used to identify "high value targets." A high value target in space is often commanding terrain; that is, terrain that is so critical to success that the control of it is decisive in nature. In time, exploiting a leverage point[5] can provide the same advantages. Because the maneuver elements in cyberspace are informational; where information accumulates or is exchanged becomes concentrated provide similar high value targets. These are often in the form of storage nodes or communication links. Moreover, aspects like relevance and timeliness make some information more valuable than others at different times and for different purposes. Thus, disrupting informational services immediately prior to, or in conjunction with, an attack in conventional battlespace creates a competing interest that diminishes an adversary's ability to mount effective countermeasures in all dimensions. Once identified, these high value targets can be attacked in cyberspace with tactics such as denial of service, or in conventional battlespace by physical damage or destruction. Using cyberspace alone, manipulating data so as to make it unreliable diminishes or negates its value without necessitating physical attacks. The critical takeaway, however, is that only after these high value targets are identified do they present opportunities for attack in any dimension.

In carrying the analogy still further, the fire support coordination measures that are used in space and time are also analogous in cyberspace. For instance, there are "areas" in cyberspace where information is available but searches are not allowed. Probably the best example would be voting records. This is the tantamount of a "no fire area" in space and has the equivalent effects. Similarly, there are also areas in cyberspace where searches are allowed but only under the most stringent conditions. These are the functional equivalent of "restricted fire areas." Examples include personal health records, financial transactions, arrest records and welfare records. Continuing further, there are areas in which no privacy is attached and anyone can search for pretty much anything at any time. Crowdsourcing and internet searches are good examples and would be the functional equivalent of "free fire areas." While they operate fundamentally the same, the crucial difference between the fire support coordination measures in conventional battlespace and those in cyberspace is that in conventional battlespace, force is the predominate element, while in cyberspace it is privacy.

When considering cyberspace as an extension of battlespace, several imperatives emerge. The first is that both the existence and implications of cyberspace become a tactical imperative. An adversary who recognizes and exploits this domain while the opponent does not gains an advantage which could easily prove decisive.

Second, because force is not a factor in cyberspace, retooling not rearming will be required to effectively compete. No amount of firepower is relevant in a domain in which force is irrelevant. In cyberspace, "firepower" is measured in terabytes. Instead, tactical commanders need abilities to see in the dark, track in the electromagnetic spectrum, see through walls, shut down cell phones, open electronic garage doors, lock electronic car doors—not to mention the more strategic implications of signals intelligence.

Third, rules of engagement in cyberspace will be based on privacy rather than force. This is already occurring and dictates not only who is authorized to look, but where and under what conditions.

Fourth, tactics in cyberspace will be focused on gaining knowledge and understanding, or depriving an adversary of the same. Strategies, however, will be focused on separating the relevant from the volume.

Finally, cherished practices will be challenged, especially the command and control functions. This is because the advancement of technologies has enabled a far greater dissemination of information and knowledge than ever before possible. Because situational awareness of a specific incident is nearly always greater at the scene than a command post, deployed unit commanders are better able to make quicker and more effective decisions than ever before. To exploit this factor, decision making authority, traditionally vested in higher echelons of command, can be more confidently entrusted to subordinates.

For sure, tactical pundits will decry adding complexity to an already complicated understanding of battlespace. But then history is replete with tactical failures when one adversary failed to recognize a vulnerability that was exploited by the other. Regardless of how battlespace is defined, no good commander ignores an unprotected flank.

End Notes

[1]. Battlespace is typically defined as, "The area, dimension or environment determined by the maximum capabilities to acquire and engage an adversary."

[2]. Center of Gravity (COG) is defined as, "Something for which an opponent is dependent upon for success, and which, if eliminated, damaged, diminished or destroyed, will severely impact his opportunities for success.

[3]. Critical Vulnerability is defined as, "A weakness which, if exploited, will create failure."

[4]. Space, in and of itself, is comprised of the three dimensions of length, width, and height or depth; or in other words, two horizontal (x and y) and one vertical dimension (z).

[5]. In the simplest terms, a leverage point is an opportunity where force can be applied to make a change and provides advantages disproportionate to the effort needed to exploit them.

Symbol Key and Glossary

$x =$	*1st dimension; x axis*
$y =$	*2nd dimension; y axis*
$z =$	*3rd dimension; z axis*
$t =$	*4th dimension; time*
$c =$	*5th dimension; cyber; informational [Also h; hyper; geometric]*

$x =$	*1 dimension; x axis; line*
$x + y =$	*2 dimensions; x & y axes; plane*
$x + y + z =$	*3 dimensions; x & y & z axes; cube*
$x + y + z + t =$	*4 dimensions; x & y & z axes & t; cube with point in time*
$x + y + z + t + c =$	*5 dimensions; x & y & z axes & t & c; hypercube with point in time*

$x + t =$	*2 dimensional battleline; x axis & t; linear combat*
$x + y + t =$	*3 dimensional battlefield; x & y axes & t; plane combat*
$x + y + z + t =$	*4 dimensional battlespace; x & y & z axes & t; cube combat*
$x + y + z + t + c =$	*5 dimensional battlespace; x & y & z axes & t & c; hypercube combat*

Acoustic Curtain	*The biophysical effects generated by these curtains could range from nausea and loss of bowel control at their edges to more severe effects closer to their centers. To mark these barriers, specially designed holograms could be projected within their confines with either wording or symbols to designate their danger levels; 1999.*

Advanced Battlespace	*5 Dimensional Battlespace; 1998. Initially 4 dimensional Battlespace; x + y + z + c since time was not factored in; 1996.*
Asymmetry	*Also Dimensional Asymmetry. A force-on-force relationship in which advanced cyberspace residing forces engage humanspace residing forces; 1996.*
Bond-Relationship Targeting	*Rather than gross physical destruction or death, the desired end state is tailored disruption within a thing, between it and other things or between it and its environment by degrading, severing or altering the bonds and relationships which define its existence; 1998.*
Cross-System Effects	*System targeting based on linkages between points, rather than the point themselves, offer a means to provide cross-system effects such as cascading breakdowns. Engineering techniques known as nodal analyses offer the ability to understand the impact of destroying certain nodes within a network; 1998.*
Cyber	*Informational; as relating to 5th Dimensional space.*

Cyber-Command
Post

Much like a teleconference, a cyber-command post does not rely on a physical location, but incorporates technology to provide the insight of subject matter experts wherever they are through the use of remote video viewing, the World wide Web, e-mail, cell phones, and the like. Thus, the tactical decision-making process is immensely enriched with knowledge that far exceeds the capabilities of any tactical organization alone; 2003.

Cybermaneuver

The movement of stealth-masked forces (safe from attack) in Cyberspace; 1996.

Cybershielding

The capability of defeating a precision strike by means of generating an invisible shield around a force which has been stripped of its stealthing and acquired in time and space. The shield could either prematurely detonate a precision-guided munition via electronic impulses, or potentially project a semisolid 'phase state' as a physical barrier. This secondary form of defense is derived from advanced nonlethal weaponry with dimensional-shifting capability. 1998. Also can be created by an optical wall or acoustic curtain; 1999.

Cyberspace

That aspect of battlespace composed of the electromagnetic spectrum and the non-human sensing dimension in which stealth-masked forces seek refuge from attack; 1996. The term was first coined in the work <u>Neuromancer</u> by William Gibson in 1984.

Cyberspace Shifting *The shifting of forces and other national security assets outside the boundaries of traditional humanspace; 1996.*

Data fusion *The application of adaptive information processes to stealth-masked forces for target detection, identification, and location; 1996.*

Defensive Premise *Stealth > Data Fusion = Cyberspace; 1996.*

Density *The quantity of activities per unit of time; 2003.*

Dimensional Asymmetry *It has been proposed that advanced forces gain an asymmetrical battlefield advantage over traditional forces by means of techniques and processes such as cloaking, blending into civilian populations, concealment and deception—all of which allow them to avoid detection by entering a realm which is frequently called cyberspace; 1996.*

Dimensionally Shifted Attack *A weapon with dimensionally shifted capabilities can overcome traditional defenses such as vehicular armor by passing through its physical seams and even its molecular bonds unimpeded. By traveling though the structural matrix of the armor, it is thus able to avoid its defensive physical properties; 1998.*

Dimensionally Shifted Defense	*A dimensionally shifted defense could be created by projecting a force shield around a physical object. This invisible field would not be able to affect a conventional munition passing through it, however, that is not the intent. The field would be configured to dampen or negate dimensionally shifted attacks and those conventional weapons [with electronic fuzing]; 1998.*
Extra Human-Sensing Abilities	*A capability possessed by soldiers that allows them to peer into cyberspace by means of technology or organic capabilities; 1996.*
Human-Sensing Dimensional Barrier	*Based upon this tension between stealth and data fusion, the "human-sensing dimensional barrier" separating humanspace and cyberspace will represent a dynamic and contested frontier, a transdimensional forward edge of the battle area (FEBA) between opposing forces; 1996.*
Humanspace	*That aspect of battlespace composed of the traditional physical dimension of the human senses in which humans and their machines move and fight; the killing ground of future war; 1996.*
Hyper	*Geometric; as relating to 5th Dimensional space.*
Lower Tier Cyberspace	*That component of cyberspace derived from the stealthing of military forces; 1999.*

Meatspace   *The world of flesh and blood—the opposite of cyberspace; from cyberpunk works. Later called humanspace.*

Offensive Premise   *Stealth ≤ Data Fusion = Humanspace; 1996.*

Optical Wall   *This eye-safe laser-baton [The Laser Dazzler] generates an "optical war" out to over 500 meters that causes most individuals to turn away from the light source. In addition, a "strobe" effect is built into the laser's programmable power supply, increasing the disorientation effects. Such an optical wall not only provides a time cushion to US soldiers but could potentially distract, disorient and temporarily immobilize an approaching group of rioters; 1999.*

Phase Shielding   *Shielding based upon a "phase state" found in the void between humanspace and cyberspace. Since it retains some physical properties it might not only be able to defeat five-dimensional attacks but also four-dimensional ones based upon projectiles; 1998.*

Phase Weaponry   *As a counter to this defense, "phase weaponry" would conceivably be developed which would alter its structure to pass through the "phase shielding" modulations it encounters. One delivery method could be based on a hollowed laser beam filled with an ionized substance whose frequency could be tuned as it senses the modulation of the shielding it comes in contact with; 1998.*

Rhizome Manoeuvre   *Movement through space (solid or empty) that is unforeseen; A force executing rhizome manoeurve moves thorough solid as well as open-space three-dimensionally. What makes this manoeuvre radical is that physical objects and the space above, or below ground can be the route through which manoeuvre takes place; 2010.*

Sanctuary of Anonymity   *Criminals (and terrorists) depend on remaining undetected. Once identified and located they are virtually powerless to continue their anti-social behaviors and are extremely vulnerable to arrest and prosecution. This concept is called the sanctuary of anonymity. What is revealing here, however, is that anonymity is dependent on neither time nor space. It lies in an entirely different dimension altogether; cyberspace; 2012.*

Shielding   *A combat function that 'is achieved by means that include avoiding detection, and [ensuring] protection against physical or electronic attack'; 2002.*

Spatial Contraction   *Spatial contraction takes two distant points in time and space and brings them together. This principal provides the underlying basis of telemedicine. A military doctor separated by thousands of kilometers from a wounded Blue soldier is able to directly interact with that soldier and, if need be, conduct surgery; 1998.*

Spatial Expansion	*Spatial expansion takes two immediate points in time and space and distances them from one another. The principle can be understood by thinking about a Black warrior in civilian garb. This combatant can be standing five meters from a Blue soldier but, for all intents and purposes, could be standing thousands of kilometers away because he or she has exited four-dimensional space via stealth-masking; 1998.*
Spatial Warping	*Derived from spatial contraction and spatial expansion; 1998.*
Spatial Transcendents	*Stealth and data fusion; 1996. Note—should be 'dimensional transcendents' between 4th and 5th dimensional battlespace; 2014 revision.*
Stealth	*The application of sensory defeating procedures and technologies which allow military forces to enter cyberspace; 1996.*
Synergistic Attack	*This is an attack based on the nonlinear premise that a certain amount of input can provide a disproportionate amount of output; 1998.*
Tempo	*The speed, rhythm or rate of moment of something; 2003.*
Upper Tier Cyberspace	*That component of cyberspace derived from the electromagnetic spectrum; 1999.*

Appendix I:
Cyber and the Future of War

T. Lindsay Moore [1]

The point is not to predict the future but to shape it.
—Anonymous

Introduction

The temper of our time is charged by an ever increasing excitement when anticipating the future. Driven by new possibilities in science, economic life, security, and cultural possibilities, eagerness abounds. Simultaneously entwined with this excitement are collapsing expectations for some, pervasive low-level violence for many, extensive environmental degradation for all, and a rising antagonism between cultural identities. A haunting fear that contemporary institutions may be inadequate to simultaneously reap the abundant harvest of prospects while coping with its attendant adversities underlies this excitement. This is not atypical. It is the underlying nature of the human condition.

The human condition is this: *tomorrow is unknown*. The future is ambiguous, indeterminate, and complex. This makes tomorrow unclear concerning its character, uncertain as to which of many possible tomorrows will actually transpire, and complex in the underlying forces propelling the emergence of a specific tomorrow. To cope with this "blooming, buzzing confusion" we construct a set of *narratives*.[2] A narrative establishes a set of expectations that allows us to make sense of daily living, to anticipate and rehearse a possible tomorrow. The most common of these narratives is to assume that tomorrow will be much like today. Our daily activities are planned on this foundation.

Yet there are events which render tomorrow very unlike today. [3] To cope with this possibility we investigate the past: history. We seek to identify a class of events which can remake tomorrow in unanticipated ways. Upon this historical foundation we create a *narrative of change*, an understanding of what might make tomorrow different from today and in what way. We believe that by doing so we might foresee and prepare for an otherwise unknown future. The study of history has no more *useful* purpose.[4] Fail to study history and we stumble blindly into a future not of our own making—and very likely not much to our own taste. It is time to once again consult history for tomorrow *Western civilization is in for the time of its life.*[5]

Even a cursory review of the history of the West reveals our time as not unique. What is transpiring today has occurred twice before. Classical civilization, the first epic narrative[6] of Western Civilization, was sustained by human energy. Classical life collapsed under the onslaught of the barbarians as the development of animal energy (horses, oxen) overran Rome. Mount Olympus gave way to Valhalla and, eventually, Heaven. The Medieval Age, the second epoch, blossomed. A second transformation occurred when the Christian empire of the medieval world was swept aside in the explosions of the Machiavellian ambitions of princes. On that occasion, Heaven and Earth changed places. The combustion of fossil fuels provided the energy from which the modern industrial age burst forth. On each of these occasions Western civilization launched itself onto a turbulent sea. Life became, in Hobbes' pungent phrase, "solitary, poor, nasty, brutish, and short"—and remained so until Western civilization created itself anew. How did such transformations arise?

All action, whether farming, making, building, playing, loving, or fighting, requires energy and, if action is to continue, must constantly be renewed. Civilization is a process of mobilizing existing sources of energy for the purposes of providing security, productive well-being, and cultural continuity for its membership. In so doing relationships are established together with a narrative that provides a justification for the prevailing network of relationships. Different energy mobilization networks together with the narrative sustaining them constitute the different epics of Western Civilization.

One lesson we might draw from this brief review is that a major harbinger of a different tomorrow is *a change in the fundamental source of energy available to human beings*. A change in the fundamental system of energy brings profound change in the possibilities for human action. A new energy system creates new sciences together with innovative technologies for ensuring security, designing, fabricating, and assembling new products. Novel transportation and communication systems emerge. It offers the possibility for new cultural identities irreconcilable with existing patterns of living. The result is a *clash in civilization*[7] the outcome of which is an extraordinary transformation in how the West understands and reconstructs the possibilities for living, working, fighting, loving, and playing.[8] A new network of relationships is established, a new justification created.

The transformation from one epoch to another might be characterized, after Schumpeter, as *creative destruction*.[9] Under the circumstances of creative destruction institutional relics and operational artifacts are destroyed and replaced by "something new and completely different." Old ways survive—if at all—as folk art and sport. [10] There is also change *within* each epoch and may take one of two forms. Progress occurs either as an increasingly efficient use of a given energy source or in the transference of a given energy source from one technological suite to another.[11] Initially progress is slow as experiments with the new energy source and the network it requires abound. Eventually a "take-off" point is reached and technological innovations explode, economies of scale are achieved, new networks are constructed, and a new civilization is born. Nevertheless, as John Bodnar has observed, "[A]ll technology is ultimately limited by some physical law; while performance improves in successive generations of hardware the rate of increase slows as the technology approaches its physical limits."[12] That limit is the fundamental source of energy.

Today, in order to escape the physical limits imposed by the contemporary reliance upon combustion energy and its employment in mechanical technology, many are turning toward a system of *electromagnetic* energy. Electromagnetism has transformed the foundations of knowledge from the classical science of Newton's $F = ma$ into the relativity of Einstein's $E = mc^2$ and the biochemistry of life unraveled by Franklin, Watson, and Crick. It has underpinned a suite of technologies never before possible. Developments in the use of electronic weapons are profoundly affecting the relations of nations by waging war, *cyberwar*, with an entirely new weapons suite in a region called *cyberspace*. The processes of manual labor and skilled craftsmanship employed on an assembly line are being replaced by automation, artificial intelligence, robots, 3D/4D printing, and other production technologies previously unimagined. Electronically based communication transmits information around the globe virtually instantaneously, enabling logistic chains, stimulating new ideas, and creating possibilities for new cultural identities. Electronic life is reaching into regions of the world heretofore denied access to what the West regards as a modern, civilized existence.[13] New visions are on the horizon.[14] *Those who look to contemporary research and see the cutting edge of civilized life are looking to the past; those who see in the contemporary explorations of science bubblings in the primordial soup have their sights fixed keenly and firmly on the future. A new sphere of human action is just visible on the horizon.*

Our focus here is upon new weapons for waging war and their impact upon security and strategic policies of Western civilization. Technologies such as remotely piloted vehicles, robotics, beam weapons (strategic defense initiative/electromagnetic pulse/lasers, etc.), 3-D/4-D printing, and operations over the Internet together with other forms of cyber-conflict are under development and experimental testing. The central issue for military organizations today is how they can best be used effectively in combat.

Our primary difficulty in approaching the issues generated by this dawning age of warfighting is that we do so with frameworks and concepts derived from the kinetic warfare of the past. The scary thought is that this may be all that can be done at our current level of experience and knowledge. For example, the sense of cyberspace has little if any specific meaning, varying as it does from writer to writer, from case study to case study. Indeed, if taken as a whole the literature seems to suggest that cyberwar means activity over the Internet, cyberspace is taken to be the World Wide Web. This is too narrow an approach to the issues involved. If we are to shape our future as we would choose we must move beyond the examples and case studies currently dominating the literature. The remainder of this essay is designed to provide a specific meaning for cyberspace and suggest some of the policy questions faced by our current forms of security organization.

Operational Domains and Cyber Conflict

All combat is fought in an *operational domain* defined by the primary form of energy (human, animal, or combustion) and bounded by the space-time continuum. An operational domain is characterized by the dominant *weapons system* employed in combat.[15] Weapons systems are of two types: missile and shock.[16] Both types have existed simultaneously on battlefields throughout history. Typically, missile weapons are superior to shock weapons,[17] and a given type of weapon, shock or missile, can be superior in range, precision, or destructive power to another of the same type.[18]

These considerations give rise to two general types of combat environments. The first is inter-domain war involving combat between weapons systems driven by different forms of energy as when cavalry confronts infantry[19] or artillery confronts cavalry/infantry.[20] The second is intra-domain war where forces employing the same weapons systems confront one another with weapons of equal or unequal range, precision, and destructive power. The former occurs during periods of transformation in Western civilization.[21] The latter are typical of war within a given epoch.

In order to escape the limits of contemporary combustion driven weapons systems, many nations are turning toward the use of electronic weapons in an attempt to develop a way of waging war in a region called "cyberspace." "Military" operations over the Internet have already taken place. The question is whether a cyber dominated operational domain will be the successor to the contemporary operational domain of kinetic weapons.

The conventional use of the concept *cyber* tends to focus on operations over the Internet. This is too narrow a framework to capture the consequences arising from the broad range of electronic technologies currently available and on the horizon.[22] The Internet may be a major avenue of approach, but it is not the only path available.[23] It should not be the only source of disquiet in the minds of national security policy-makers. Attention should be focused upon electronics generally.

Accordingly, *Cyberspace* is here defined as the electromagnetic spectrum extending from and radio waves to Gamma rays and perhaps beyond. Cyberlife exists wherever and whenever electrical energy is present. Cyber weapons are those making use of the electromagnetic spectrum whether as a way of transmitting (telegraph/radio) or gathering information (night vision goggles/espionage) or as a means of destruction (electromagnetic pulse). Just as electrical energy marks the rise of a fourth epic in Western civilization, electromagnetism represents a fourth operational domain in the waging of war. Electromagnetism may serve as an enhancement of kinetic weapons as is the case with a drone, or it may itself be the means of destruction as was the case with the Stuxnet worm.[24] Whether it will serve merely as an amplifier of kinetic weapons or replace them altogether is as yet indeterminate. Whichever may be the case, they are here to stay and we must make an effort to understand their impact if we are to create the tomorrow we wish.[25]

The possibility for war in cyberspace has engendered both cyber "Band Wagoners"[26] and cyber "Ho Hummers."[27] In the first category are those who point toward the possibility of operations aimed at damaging a nation's critical infrastructure and/or the operational and tactical capabilities of military forces as constituting national security dangers that must be addressed. Espionage conducted through the Internet is a major concern of civilian corporations as well as the Defense Department. Propaganda delivered through the Internet in support of political policies coupled with the ability to mobilize mass movements and demonstrations is clearly a factor in many contemporary revolts.[28] Yet there is as yet no agreement that such operations even constitute acts of war.

Cyber-Ho-Hummers argue (with the exception of espionage) that only extensive and long-term physical damage is of major concern to governments with respect to their international security policies. Lacking the characteristics of kinetic destruction coupled with a nation's capacity to recover rapidly from cyber-attacks, cyber Ho Hummers argue that cyber weapons cannot be used either to compel or deter the behavior of nation-states. Fear of long-term physical damage wrought by kinetic weapons systems is required to force a nation into a pattern of international behavior it would not otherwise choose for itself.

So far the attempts to understand cyberlife occur within existing categories of thought and analysis. But these may provide an inadequate framework, pose the wrong questions, arrive at irrelevant answers. They are proving simply too narrow a framework for adequate analysis. As a result the arguments of Band Wagoners and Ho-Hummers cannot be evaluated with any degree of confidence.

Understanding Cyber Conflict

What are the national security policy issues generated by this new system of electromagnetic technology? To say the least, they are legion. They comprise a vast spider web with electromagnetism at the center. They span the spectrum of national life from the games children play to the relations of nations. Computers and the Internet are only among the most recent of the technologies provided by electricity. Their applications are only just out of the toy stage but already their uses in international conflict are apparent. The attacks on Estonia, North Georgia, and Iran (Stuxnet) together with the ongoing espionage and covet attacks carried out by many nations and private individuals are only the more obvious examples of their use in international conflict. Others will follow.

What questions must be addressed? Is cyber-conflict war? What constitutes a cyber-attack? How can a defense against cyber-attacks be mounted? Can the answer to these and other questions like them be found within the traditional frameworks with which we have approached the study of violent conflict in the past?

Historically the West has approached violence in one of two ways: either it is a crime to be dealt with as a juridical matter or it is regarded as war and confronted as such. Events in recent years are challenging this framework. The depredations of terrorists operating outside the framework of the nation-state or the activities of hackers working from their basements are much like the pirates of old for whom, like spies, a special legal category was created. Their activities are more than mere crime; but do they amount to war? Do cyber-terrorists rate their own category? In short, how do we characterize cyber-conflict for policy development?

If cyber-conflict is to be regarded as war, do our models of war provide an adequate framework for understanding war in the cyber-age?[29] What about the various models of international relations? Our standard models all involve or threaten physical destruction inflicted by kinetic violence. The new technologies of today make possible—but not necessary—the instantaneous destruction of integrated electronic systems that operate and control a nation's critical infrastructure of power, finance, communication, and transportation. Certainly there is destruction in a cyber-attack[30] but unless we are willing to say destruction itself is violence, where is the physical destruction and death characteristic of war? Moreover significant damage can be inflicted on an economy without physically destroying the infrastructure facilities of a nation. Is the destruction of the computer program operating robots on a factory assembly line an act of war? If not, how is that different than the kinetic destruction of the factory?

What constitutes an act of war? Historically an act of war occurred when one nation's military crossed a border into the territory of another without permission to enter. The crossing could be clearly observed and depicted on a map. But what does a cyber-map look like? When everything is potentially connected to everything else, how do we depict a cyber-boundary?[31] In short, cyber-space is not at all like ordinary geographic space. Without a boundary what constitutes a cyber-crossing? Given these difficulties, what do we regard as a cyber-attack?

Once we have determined that a cyber-attack has occurred, how do we determine who is to be held responsible? Traditional military forces display all types of identification tags—including a chemical tag if all we have is an explosion. Not so an electron; one electron is pretty much like another. Nevertheless, they originate from some physical source that has a physical presence somewhere. Determining sources is a significant part the new field of cyber-forensics.

Assuming the source of the attack is identified, how do we determine if the attack was launched at the direction of the government or on an individual's own initiative? The use of mercenaries makes this problem especially acute. Some have suggested application of the principle of a nation's duty to assist. Failure to do so would entail various types of international consequences including the right of the nation attacked to enter and destroy the source of the attack.[32] However, this approach has all the symptoms of the policies that precipitated World War I.

How do we respond to an attack launched from our own soil or by an American citizen abroad? In the first instance, the constraints imposed by *Posse Comitatis* creates jurisdictional problems as to whether this is a matter for the police or the military. Relaxation of *Posse Comitatis* restrictions would permit closer cooperation between police and military and is bound to stimulate controversy. A major debate is already underway in the case of targeted assignations of American citizens who go abroad and aid an enemy. Is judicial due process required or will administrative due process suffice in the decision to kill?

If cyber-space is a problem, what about cyber-time? When is a cyber-attack? Attacks with kinetic weapons are obvious. So, too, are the preparations for an attack: military formations take time to mobilize and move into place and they can be detected doing so. But cyber-time is not like "ordinary" time. Electrons move at the speed of light. There is no warning of an impending cyber-attack such as is available with kinetic forces. Indeed, the attack may well not be known until the damage is done. Moreover, as was the case with Stuxnet, computer systems can be infected with logic bombs and worms long before they are activated. Does such an infection constitute an attack amounting to an act of war or must activation be awaited and the damage inflicted? If the latter the danger is that we will come to regard ourselves as being in a constant state of war—a distinctly unhealthy climate for a nation.

The answer to these sorts of questions and others like them will be determinative of the legal and policy framework to which cyber-conflict will be subject—that is, to the laws of war or domestic criminal law. It will also impact the development of tactical and operational doctrine. Given that we have at least a hint of the answers to these policy questions, how, then, do we proceed to protect ourselves?

Cyber Deterrence

Deterrence, however characterized and presented in various national security documents, is the strategic defense policy of the United States. However, as a consequence of the Cold War, deterrence tends to be identified almost exclusively with nuclear retaliation after suffering a first strike. Cold War deterrence was a policy of Mutually Assured Destruction (MAD) the sole object of which was to face an enemy with total and utter destruction should it launch an attack against the United States. The question arises as to whether deterrence is a viable defense policy in the cyber-age.

Deterrence can be regarded as a far broader policy than possessing an invulnerable retaliatory capacity. The object of deterrence is to prevent damage to the United States and its interests. Consider a time line in the relations between nations. There are two critical points on that line. The first is when an adversary obtains the capacity to inflict damage. That is the *acquisition* point. The second is when the capacity to inflict damage is actively employed. That is the *use* point. Actions taken prior to acquisition are *preventive.* [33] Actions taken between the points of acquisition and use are *preemptive.*[34] Actions taken after use are *retaliatory.* A nation prepares to *defend* itself throughout its entire historical life and acts defensively after an attack. All of these are aspects of deterrence for they are designed to prevent a damaging attack on the United States and, should one occur, to fight and prevail on terms acceptable to ourselves and our allies. To these I would suggest adding one additional objective: *rapid recovery* from an attack should one occur. How, then, do cyber-conflict and deterrence interact in cyberspace?

Prevention. Prevention also aims at stopping the acquisition of a capability for inflicting damage, for example, the ban on the development and spread of nuclear weapons. Although negotiations are underway,[35] it is not at all clear just what such a treaty would prohibit. It is difficult to imagine any nation viewing a ban on electronic technologies as within their national interests. They are "dual use" technologies essential in the conduct of finance, production, research, and ordinary life as well as a means for inflicting damage on anther nation. Moreover such a treaty would probably be unverifiable as compliance would require such an extensive and intrusive inspection regime as to be unacceptable to any nation and, given the existence of "hacktivists," probably unworkable even if it were acceptable.

Preemption. The object of preemption is to prevent the use of a weapon once acquired. Nations might agree that they would not be the first to launch a cyber-attack but retain the capacity to and will respond should an attack be launched against them. Such a policy would not require a treaty but could be announced by a nation as a matter of policy. Another possibility is to limit the legitimate targets of a cyber-attack. The electric grid, transportation, communication, and finance are all candidates for such a proposal.

Both no-first use and target limitations are diplomatic programs designed to prevent damage in war. In the event of a violation, what types of effective sanctions could be imposed? Diplomatic, economic, informational, and military sanctions would all be available. But what combinations of what sanctions would be effective, to what degree, and how soon is not at all clear. Would it be possible to isolate a nation from the net? That would require the cooperation of ALL the nations—an extremely unlikely possibility.

One of the key issues haunting strategic planners during the Cold War was that of "crisis instability." A surprise attack, getting there "fustest with the mostest," confers tactical and operational advantages. In a crisis tension between adversaries and the fear of either "using them [available weapons system] or losing them" mounts. The difficulty not only persists into the cyber-age it is intensified. The Cold War difficulty was theoretically settled by the concept and development of an early warning system and an "invulnerable second strike" capacity. Various stages of nuclear mobilization can be ascertained and there is a time lapse between launch and impact. But how do we anticipate a cyber-attack? Launch preparations cannot be ascertained[36] and there is virtually no time between launch and impact. If we cannot ascertain an anticipated launch time, what event or stage in a crisis would signal the necessity to launch a preemptive strike? Can this, in the cyber age, ever be more than a state of mind?

Yet another issue with which decision-makers had to cope in the nuclear age was an attack that opened with destruction of the command and control structure of the US retaliatory forces. This also increased the instability involved in a crisis situation. The various schemes developed never proved entirely satisfactory. [37] A cyber-attack on C^2 facilities increases the difficulty of the problem. If C^2 communication facilities are destroyed, how would an order to retaliate be issued? The urge to shoot first would increase enormously. A cyber-attack on C^2 systems increases the tension. Given such a circumstance are we not faced with a new version of the crisis instability conundrum?

If so, how do we solve it? Would it be possible to create an "invulnerable second strike" capacity in the cyber age? Dispersal, hardening, and hiding a nuclear force were all explored. Just what does invulnerability in cyberspace look like? Would a duplicate system off-line suffice? How long would it take to bring such a system on-line? What would it take to "harden" a cyber-site? What does "dispersal" mean in the cyber-age? In short, what constitutes an invulnerable second strike cyber-force? If a second strike force can be made invulnerable, why not the system itself?

Defense. How is defense conducted in a cyber-war? Let me begin by rephrasing a warning delivered by the British Prime Minister Stanley Baldwin to Parliament in 1936: *the electron will always get through.* Even a cursory look at military history reveals that whatever wall we human beings construct can and will eventually be penetrated by other human beings – in this case using the electron. That much is clear. The United States has not fought a war against a foreign nation on its own soil since 1815. The Monroe Doctrine (1823) originated the policy of "defending forward."[38] The possibility of cyber-conflict threatens the continuation of that policy and with it foreshadows a major alteration in civil-military relations. Given conflict in the cyber age does it follow that the only way to protect ourselves is by destroying more computers and systems more quickly than the enemy?

Defensive measures can be active or passive, overt or covert. During the Cold War certain active and overt defensive measures (e.g., anti-ballistic missiles missiles) were deliberately banned.[39] Overt passive measures (e.g., civil defense) were undertaken in a halfhearted manner as many considered them irrelevant in a nuclear age anyway. Does the US pursue a policy of "no defense" in an effort, like the Cold War, to demonstrate it has no offensive intentions? How could such a system be verified? Passive measures are obvious in the standard attempts to secure computer networks (limited access and the like). What do active measures look like?

How does the Defense Department cope with potential cyber-attacks on production facilities on US soil? There are several stumbling blocks all of which hinge on the relationship between government and the economic institutions of the nation. Business strives to keep itself free of government interference. Laws requiring a business to take steps to protect itself are often resisted on several grounds. First, the cost to the business of a cyber-attack may be less than the costs of simply absorbing the damage. Second, business fears the loss of trade secrets, patents, copyrights, future business plans, etc. if the government attempts to set up security measures itself. Third, the doctrine and laws of *Posse Comitatis* make cooperation between the military and the private sector for purposes of law enforcement difficult. Finally, there is simply the ideological resistance stemming from the belief that government has no right to interfere with business practices. How then does the United States military go about protecting the nation's privatized infrastructure against cyber-attacks? How does the United States fight a war on its own soil?

Retaliation. Assuming we determine that a cyber-attack has taken place and can ascertain who perpetrated it, how shall we respond—kinetically or electronically? What level of cyber or kinetic response would be sufficient to deter a cyber-attack? In either case what would be the appropriate level of response? When John F. Kennedy took office in 1961 he discovered that the United States could respond in only one of two ways to a Soviet move on Western Europe: either we had to accede to Soviet demands or launch an all-out nuclear strike irrespective of the degree of Soviet mischief (e.g., "massive retaliation"). Of what does a system of fine-tuned cyber retaliation responses consist and how do we construct it?

If we can tweak our level of our response, what are the available and appropriate steps in the ladder of escalation? The law of war imposes a rule of proportionality in response to an attack. But the question of proportionality has never been satisfactorily resolved. For example: should the response be proportional to the attack that just occurred or designed to prevent the next attack through signaling through a graduated escalation an intent to escalate to even greater levels of destruction should a second attack occur? Proportionality is a difficult enough concept to adhere to in a kinetic war.

Just as there was the difficulty of limiting a conventional war short of a nuclear conflagration, there will be the difficulty of halting escalation in a cyber-war short of a shooting war even though the threshold between kinetic and cyber is more pronounced. These problems were difficult enough to solve in the age of kinetic war. I doubt they are going to be any easier of resolution in the cyber-age.

What would a cyber Cold War look like?

Recovery. The real measure of damage in war is the length of time it takes for recovery and the loss of production as it impacts national defense. World War II demonstrates why it has always been better to fight on the enemys' soil.

A robust and rapid recovery effort could reduce the threat of a cyber-attack to the level of a nuisance. How difficult would it be to achieve such a condition? Would it be possible to create duplicate systems? If so, just how expensive will that task be? Moreover, if the damage also includes physical as well as electronic system damage rapid recovery may be impossible. This could lead to further secondary and tertiary damage extending the time required for recovery. Nevertheless, whatever the extent of the damage, it will certainly be less than that wrought by strategic bombing and recovery time will be correspondingly shortened. What steps can and should we take now in anticipation of the necessity to recover rapidly later?

These are some of the security questions with which the military must cope. But they do not exhaust the national security issues confronting the United States. What they do suggest is that the framework with which kinetic security policies were approached may be fundamentally inadequate for approaching security policies in the cyber-age.

Conclusion

Just as the structure and dynamics of government changed from the classical to the medieval to the modern age, government—and security—in the cyber-age will be different. There is extant in the world today an experiment in governmental change. This experiment has to do with the obligations government and the governed owe one another. The Greeks and Romans had no obligations to their slaves. The medieval serf owed allegiance to the lord of the manor who in turn governed in terms of the noble obligation. The social contract underlay the development of democratic forms of governance in the modern age. China, the United States, and Europe are all moving toward new forms of governance: China from a position of authoritarianism, the United States from democratic capitalism, and Europe from various forms of social democracy. The result will not be a blend of existing forms of government, economics, and society but something new and completely different.[40] And with it what is meant by security in the first place.

The US has both an advantage and a disadvantage in the dawning of the cyber age. Our advantage is that we are producing an organic military, one whose military skills, like World War II, are essentially the same as the civilian skills existing in society. Only adaptation to the military environment will be necessary. Our disadvantage is our recent military (if not our political) victories in war (Iraq I and II, Afghanistan). The disadvantage has created a military establishment wedded to the tools of those wars. We will suffer from the disadvantage of entrenched interests.

I have attempted to place the issues of cyberspace in an historical context in order to understand today what may be coming tomorrow. I have also attempted to outline some of the questions confronting security in cyberspace. These are far from all the questions that can and must be asked. But the most difficult problem we face is that these may not even be the right questions. The framework from which we start sets the questions we ask and defines the relevance of the answers we provide. For the moment the questions and answers we have generated are based upon analogies to war as we have known it. But, as I have tried to indicate, war in the cyber-age will produce a structure and dynamic vastly different from the industrial age. The danger is that the analogies may be false analogies. Even more basic are the concepts with which we approach them. Space and time are fundamental concepts in our conceptual models. Just as they changed with the Renaissance, so, too, will our concepts of space and time change in the cyber-age. And with them our understanding of how the world works. Just what will security in the cyber age look like? That all depends upon how we shape it.

End Notes

[1]. Paper delivered before the Army Cyber Center, United States Military Academy, February 20, 2014.

[2]. By narrative I mean philosophical essays, scientific textbooks, laws, doctrinal manuals, literature, films, songs, myths, fairy tales and all other forms by which a community communicates ideas, values, norms, and standard operating procedures to itself.

[3]. December 7, 1941, November 20, 1963, and September 11, 2001 are such events.

[4]. This is not intended to denigrate the study of history for its own sake but only to call attention to its usefulness.

[5]. A word of caution is in order: history is as light refracted through a prism, historical analogy a seductive Lorelei.

[6]. Selection of the term "epic narrative" warrants explanation. To be sure, the epics of Western civilization are not narratives in the style of Homer, *Beowulf,* the *Epic of Gilgamesh* or the Arthurian legends. Historical style changes with the intellectual currents of the time. Thucydides introduced a "rational" reconstruction to the study of history. Nevertheless, just as those heroic narratives that preceded him were historical reconstructions, his historical reconstruction of the Peloponnesian Wars is likewise a narrative, albeit a rational rather than heroic one.

[7]. Cite Samuel Huntington, *Clash of Civilization.*

[8]. A new energy system does not *cause* change in Western Civilization; it merely makes it possible. Human vision and choice are essential as well.

[9]. Joseph Schumpeter, *Capitalism, Socialism and Democracy* (New York: Harper, 1942).

[10]. Fighting with swords became fencing; horseback riding dressage; javelin throwing and archery Olympic sports.

[11]. The first is exemplified by the ever increasing mileage obtained from a gallon of gasoline. Redeploying the combustion engine from automobiles to aircraft is an example of the second.

[12]. John Bodnar, "The Military Technology Revolution," *Naval War College Review* 46:7-21 (Summer 1993). In economic terms this is known as a declining return on investment and is described by a logistic or "S" curve. It marks that point where the epoch is reaching its horizon.

[13]. The global demand for electricity is enormous – and growing exponentially. By the year 2030 the population of the Earth is predicted to expand by 2 billion, most of which will be concentrated

in the developing already highly populated regions of the world. Over the same period the corresponding demand for electricity is expected to grow by 45% over the current demand level.

[14]. See for example, Michio Kaku, *Physics of the Impossible: A Scientific Exploration into the World of Phasers, Force Fields, Teleportation, and Time Travel* (New York: Doubleday, 2008). The quantum world of the microscopic once thought irrelevant to the macroscopic appearance of everyday life is now taken to extend throughout the universe. *Scientific American* (June, 2011).

[15]. Heavy infantry (Greek phalanx, Roman legion) dominated the Classical epoch; heavy cavalry dominated the medieval epoch; and artillery dominates the Modern epoch. By artillery is here meant everything from the harquebus to the ICBM.

[16]. A weapons system has three components: launcher, warhead, and target. With respect to shock weapons all three components are in contact simultaneously. Only two of the three components of a missile weapons system are in contact at any point in time— launcher/warhead or warhead/target.

[17]. David and Goliath is a classic example. Missile weapons allow destruction of the enemy prior to actual physical contact as required by shock weapons.

[18]. In World War II Allied bombers were superior to those of the Axis in range and destructive power (e.g., bomb load).

[19]. Barbarian cavalry confronting Roman legions (6th and 7th centuries AD) provides numerous examples.

[20]. Consider here the English longbow confronting French cavalry at Agincourt (1415).

[21]. They also occurred during periods of European imperialism. See, for example, the Italians in Ethiopia (1935).

[22]. Technological developments trace a developmental path from the laboratory to entertainment to toys to significant productive use. In many respects cyber technology has advanced only to the stage of toys.

[23]. Bunker has outlined several possible uses of electromagnetism that go far beyond the Internet itself.

[24]. For a case study of Stuxnet, see "Attacking Iranian Nuclear Facilities: Stuxnet" in Shakarian, Shakarian, and Ruef, *Introduction*

to Cyber-Warfare: A multidisciplinary Approach (Boston: Elsevier, 2013), pp. 224-239.

[25]. We need look only as far as contemporary popular music to see the significance of the electromagnetic spectrum for change in the modern world. Like fencing, archery, and dressage much of pre-1960 popular music is a folk art; contemporary popular music is virtually entirely electronic.

[26]. Lukas Kello, "The Meaning of the Cyber Revolution: Perils to Theory and Statecraft," *International Security* 30:2 (Fall 2013), pp. 7-40; Jeffry Carr, *Cyber Warfare: Mapping the Cyber Underworld* (2nd Ed.) (Sebastopol, Canada: O'Reilly Media, Inc. 2012; Richard A. Clarke & Robert K. Knake, *Cyber War: The Next Threat to National Security and What to Do About It* (New York: HarperCollins, 2010).

[27]. Erik Gartzke, "The Myth of Cyberwar: Bringing War in Cyberspace Back Down to Earth," *International Security* 30:2 (Fall 2013), pp. 41-73; Thomas Rid, *Cyber War Will Not take Place* (Oxford: Oxford University Press, 2013).

[28]. Get examples. Orange revolution in Ukraine; Green revolution in Iran; he "Arab Spring."

[29]. Will Clausewitz, Sun Tzu, Mahan, Douhet, and Mitchell suffice for an analytical framework?

[30]. War databases all define war as involving so many deaths. See, for example, J. David Singer's Correlates of War project at the University of Michigan.

[31]. Be careful to avoid thinking of only the Internet; the electromagnetic pulse can have the same effect—only more so.

[32]. Consider the current debate over the legality and wisdom of drone attacks carried out by the United States in several foreign nations.

[33]. Diplomatic negotiations, treaties, economic inducements and restrictions are examples of preventive action. The Israeli attack on the Iraqi reactor prior to the production of a nuclear weapon is also a preventive action. Nation-building grounded in the belief that "democracies do not make war on other democracies" is a preventive strategy.

[34]. The attack by Japan on the United States at Pearl Harbor was a preemptive attack. It was designed to prevent interference by the United States with Japan's actions in South Asia.

[35]. For a discussion of the range of issues involved, see Harold Kwalwasser "Internet Governance" in Kramer, Starr, and Wentz *Cyberpower and National Security* (Washington, DC: National Defense University Press, 2009) pp. 491-524.

[36]. Some argue that the use of cyber weapons will be preceded by a spike in probing activities. But this need not necessarily be the case. Attacks could be launched without prior probing immediately preceding the attack and there could be a significant delay between probing and attacking.

[37]. Carter, Steinbruner, and Zraker, *Managing Nuclear Operations* (Washington, DC: Brookings Institute, 1987).

[38]. The doctrine warned Europe to stay out of the affairs of the Western Hemisphere.

[39]. *Treaty on the Limitations of Anti-Ballistic Missile System*, 23 U.S.T. 3435 (July 1968).

[40]. Jeremy Rifkin, *The Zero Marginal Cost Society: The Internet of Things, the Collaborative Commons, and the Eclipse of Capitalism* (New York: Palgrave/MacMillan, 2014).

Appendix II:
Evolving Definitions of Modern Military Dimensionality

Compiled by Khirin A. Bunker

Definitions of modern military dimensionality have evolved from the later 20th century into the early 21st century based on the following evolutionary sequence:

a. 3 Dimensional (battlespace; $x+y+z$)
b. 4 Dimensional (battlespace; $x+y+z+t$)
c. 4 Dimensional+ (battlespace; $x+y+z+t+some\ mention\ of\ the\ electromagnetic\ spectrum$)
d. 5 Dimensional 'Primitive' (battlespace; $x+y+z+t+cyberspace\ as\ a\ domain\ such\ as\ air\ or\ sea\ but\ no\ dimensionality$)
e. 5 Dimensional 'Mature' (battlespace; $x+y+z+t+cyberspace\ dimensionality$)

Based on the frequency and use of military definitions in doctrinal and strategic futures publications it is evident that this evolutionary sequence represents a haphazard and incremental process within the US services and the joint force rather than a systematic linear progression. A sampling of definitional examples of this evolutionary sequence is as follows. Also listed is f. Rejection of the Battlespace Construct that presently appears to dominate some military thinking. In place of dimensionality a relativistic concept of the operational environment has been proposed that mentions ambiguous physical, cyberspace, and electromagnetic mediums.

3 Dimensional (battlespace; $x+y+z$)

Land Environment

Land forces are organized, trained, and equipped for sustained combat operations in the land environment. This environment consists of the earth's land surfaces and the contiguous water boundaries and layers of air...The land is a surface of infinite variety that is complicated by vegetation, by climatic extremes, and by the presence of man...

1-16. General, p, 1-5 to 1-6
FM 100-5 *Operations of the Army Forces in the Field*
Headquarters, Department of the Army
September 1968

Battlefield Framework

The battlefield framework consists of four interrelated components: area of operations (AO), area of interest (AI), battle space, and a specific battlefield organization. As a result of the battlefield visualization process, the commander can translate his vision into this framework.

(2-3)
FM 100-15 *Corps Operations*
Department of the Army
October 1996

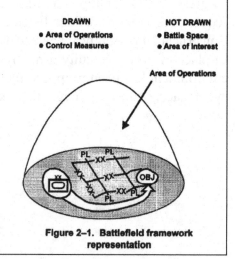

Figure 2-1. Battlefield framework representation

> **Battlespace**
>
> Battlespace includes the higher commander's area of operation and the command's areas of interest, influence, and operations described by physical area and forces of concern.
>
> (K-4)
> MCWP 5-1 *Marine Corps Planning Process*
> Department of the Navy. Headquarters United States Marine Corps
> August 2010

4 Dimensional (battlespace; $x+y+z+t$)

> **Battle Space**
>
> Battle space is a physical volume that expands or contracts in relation to the ability to acquire and engage the enemy.
>
> components determined by the maximum capabilities of a unit to acquire and dominate the enemy; includes areas beyond the AO; it varies over time according to how the commander positions his assets.
>
> Glossary-1
> FM 100-5 *Operations*
> Headquarters, Department of the Army
> June 1993
>
> Glossary-4
> FM 34-130 *Intelligence Preparation of the Battlefield*
> Department of the Army
> July 1994

Battle Space

Battle space is the volume of area in which the commander seeks to dominate the enemy. It is through battlefield visualization that he decides where, when, and how he will dominate the enemy within his battle space. A commander's battle space expands and contracts in relation to the ability to acquire and engage the enemy with joint or multinational forces. It can change as the commander's vision of the battlefield changes. It is influenced by time, tempo, depth, and synchronization.

(2-4)
FM 100-15 *Corps Operations*
Headquarters, Department of the Army
October 1996

Battlespace

battlespace. The commander's conceptual view of the area and factors which he must understand to successfully apply combat power, protect the force, and complete the mission. It encompasses all applicable aspects of air, sea, space, and land operations that the commander must consider in planning and executing military operations. The battlespace dimensions can change over time as the mission expands or contracts, according to operational objectives and force composition. Battlespace provides the commander a mental forum for analyzing and selecting courses of action for employing military forces in relationship to time, tempo, and depth.

(79)
Air Force Doctrine Document 1 *Air Force Basic Doctrine*
By Order of the Secretary of the Air Force
September 1997

Operational framework

4-69. The *operational framework* consists of the arrangement of friendly forces and resources in time, space, and purpose with respect to each other and the enemy or situation. It consists of the area of operations, battlespace, and the battlefield organization.

(4-2)
FM 3-0 *Operations*
Headquarters, Department of the Army
June 2001

Conceptually Organizing Operations

47. Army leaders are responsible for clearly articulating their concept of operations in time, space, purpose, and resources. An established framework and associated vocabulary assist greatly in this task. Army leaders are not bound by any specific framework for conceptually organizing operations, but three have proven valuable in the past. Leaders often use these conceptual frameworks in combination. For example, a commander may use the deep-close-security framework to describe the operation in time and space, the decisive-shaping-sustaining framework to articulate the operation in terms of purpose, and the main and supporting efforts framework to designate the shifting prioritization of resources. These operational frameworks apply equally to tactical actions in the area of operations.

(11)
ADP 3-0 *Unified Land Operations*
Headquarters, Department of the Army
October 2011

Modern Battlefield *(non-linear)*

By historical standards, the modern battlefield is particularly disorderly. While past battlefields could be described by linear formations and uninterrupted linear fronts, we cannot think of today's battlefield in linear terms. The range and lethality of modern weapons has increased dispersion between units. In spite of communications technology, this dispersion strains the limits of positive control. The natural result of dispersion is unoccupied areas, gaps, and exposed flanks which can and will be exploited, blurring the distinction between front and rear and friendly- and enemy-controlled areas.

(9)
FMFM 1 *Warfighting*
Department of the Navy. Headquarters United States Marine Corps
March 1989

Battlespace Dominance

Modern battlespace is multidimensional. Navy and Marine Corps operations encompass air, surface, subsurface, land, space, and time. Dominance of these dimensions continues to be an important factor in the survival and combat effectiveness of our force. Command and control integrates ships, submarines, aircraft, and ground forces, so their full range of capabilities can be extended effectively throughout our battlespace. The battlespace in which naval forces operate is neither fixed in size nor stationary. We can visualize it as zones of superiority, surrounding one or more units or even the entire force, that are shifted as the situation requires. The zones are regions in which we maintain superiority during the full period of our operations by detecting, identifying, targeting, and neutralizing anything hostile that enters or passes through. The battlespace is our base of operations that we position over any area of concern and from which we can project power. We can establish multiple zones of superiority as specific task forces are separated from the main force. All these zones are regions into which we receive information and support from outside sources, and from which we project

---

power. Theater commanders may direct naval forces to conduct a mission independently if the size of the battlespace they can dominate adequately covers the region of concern. By combining complementary capabilities of units working together including the U.S. Army and Air Force, allied, or coalition capabilities in joint or multinational operations we effectively extend the range and geographic influence of our battlespace. What distinguishes naval forces among armed forces is the combination of operational readiness and agility that creates these zones of superiority. These zones, based on the capabilities of our sensor and weapon systems, can reach out for hundreds of nautical miles and protect other entities such as convoys, amphibious groups, and land masses. We maintain our protective zones of superiority around us, establishing them not just upon arrival, but enroute to our objective area. The battlespace moves with the force. By extending zones of superiority over landing forces, naval commanders protect those forces while they are accomplishing their missions and establishing their own defensive zones. This concept applies both in war and in operations other than war.

(63)
Naval Doctrine Publication (NDP) 1 *Naval Warfare*
March 1994

Battlespace

battlespace. The commander's conceptual view of the area and factors that he must understand to successfully apply combat power, protect the force, and complete the mission. It encompasses all applicable aspects of air, sea, space, and land operations that the commander must consider in planning and executing military operations. The battlespace dimensions can change over time as the mission expands or contracts according to operational objectives and force composition. Battlespace provides the commander a mental forum for analyzing and selecting courses of action for employing military forces in relationship to time, tempo, and depth. (AFDD 1)

(p. 126)
U.S. Air Force Doctrine Document 2 (AFDD-2) *Organization and Employment of Aerospace Power*
By Order of the Secretary of the Air Force
September 1998

4 Dimensional+ (battlespace; *x+y+z+t+some mention of the electromagnetic spectrum*)

Battlespace

Components of this space are determined by the maximum capabilities of friendly and enemy forces to acquire and dominate each other by fires and maneuver and in the electromagnetic spectrum.

Glossary 1
Pamphlet 525-5 *Force XXI Operations*
US Army Training and Doctrine Command
1 August 1994

Battlespace

Battlespace: All aspects of air, surface, and subsurface, land, space, and the electromagnetic spectrum that encompass the area of influence and area of interest.

(NWP 1-02) (Glossary)
Naval Doctrine Publication (NDP) 2 *Naval Intelligence*
DEPARTMENT OF THE NAVY OFFICE OF THE CHIEF OF NAVAL OPERATIONS and HEADQUARTERS UNITED STATES MARINE CORPS
September 1994

Battlespace

4-77. Battlespace is the environment, factors, and conditions commanders must understand to successfully apply combat power, protect the force, or complete the mission. This includes the air, land, sea, space, and the included enemy and friendly forces, facilities, weather, terrain, the electromagnetic spectrum, and the information environment within the operational areas and areas of interest (see Figure 4-5).

4-20
Operations FM 3-0.
Headquarters,
June 2001
Department of the Army

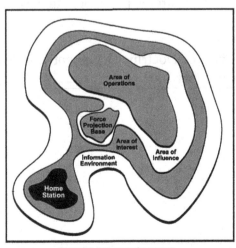

Figure 4-5. Battlespace Components

Battlespace

battlespace. The environment, factors, and conditions which must be understood to successfully apply combat power, protect the force, or complete the mission. This includes the air, land, sea, space and the included enemy and friendly forces, facilities, weather, terrain, the electromagnetic spectrum, and information environment within the operational areas and areas of interest. (JP 1-02)

GL-5
Joint Publication 3-0 *Doctrine for Joint Operations*
Joint Chiefs of Staff
September 2001

Electromagnetic battlespace

Electronic warfare operations are those military actions involving the use of electromagnetic and directed energy to control the electromagnetic spectrum or to attack the enemy across the electromagnetic battlespace. Control of the electromagnetic spectrum is gained by protecting friendly systems and countering adversary systems. The electronic warfare spectrum is not limited to radio frequencies; it also includes optical and infrared regions. The operational elements of electronic warfare operations are electronic attack, electronic protection, and electronic warfare support.

(p. 45)
Air Force Doctrine Document 1 *Air Force Basic Doctrine*
November 2003

Analog and digital portion of the battlespace

network warfare operations. Network warfare operations are the integrated planning and employment of military capabilities to achieve desired effects across the interconnected analog and digital portion of the battlespace. Network warfare operations are conducted in the information domain through the dynamic combination of hardware, software, data, and human interaction. Also called **NW Ops**. (AFDD 2-5)

(p. 110)
Air Force Doctrine Document 2-8 *Command and Control*
June 2007

Multidimensional Application

Dominant maneuver will be the multidimensional application of information, engagement, and mobility capabilities to position and employ widely dispersed joint air, land, sea, and space forces to accomplish the assigned operational tasks. Dominant maneuver will allow our forces to gain a decisive advantage by controlling the breadth, depth, and height of the battlespace.

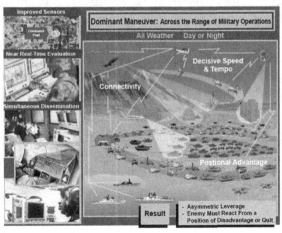

(20)
Joint Vision 2010
Joint Chief of Staffs

Battlespace

battlespace—1. All aspects of air, surface, subsurface, land, space, and electromagnetic spectrum which encompass the area of influence and area of interest.

(MCRP 5-12C part 1 of a 2- part definition)" (Glossary-3)
MCWP 5-1 *Marine Corps Planning Process*
Department of the Navy. Headquarters United States Marine Corps
August 2010

5 Dimensional 'Primitive' (battlespace;
x+y+z+t+cyberspace as a domain such as air or sea but no dimensionality)

The Cyberspace Domain

(U) *The Cyberspace Domain.* Recognizing that the understanding of cyberspace has evolved, for the purpose of this strategy, cyberspace is defined as:

(U) *"A domain characterized by the use of electronics and the electromagnetic spectrum to store, modify, and exchange data via networked systems and associated physical infrastructures."*

ix
National Military Strategy for Cyberspace Operations (NMS-CO)
Chairman of the Joints Chiefs of Staff
December 2006
~~SECRET~~ Unclassified

Cyberspace

Cyberspace. Cyberspace is "a global domain within the information environment consisting of the interdependent network of information technology infrastructures, including the Internet, telecommunications networks, computer systems, and embedded processors and controllers."

P. 1

Cyberspace is a domain. Cyberspace operations are not synonymous with information operations (IO). IO is a set of operations that can be performed in cyberspace and other domains. Operations in cyberspace can directly support IO and non-cyber based IO can affect cyberspace operations.

Cyberspace is a man-made domain, and is therefore unlike the natural domains of air, land, maritime, and space. It requires continued attention from humans to persist and encompass the features of specificity, global scope, and emphasis on the electromagnetic spectrum. Cyberspace nodes physically reside in all domains. Activities in cyberspace can enable freedom of action for activities in the other domains, and activities in the other domains can create effects in and through cyberspace.

P. 2

Air Force Doctrine Document 3-12 *Cyberspace Operations*
Secretary of the Air Force
15 July 2010 (Incorporating Change 1, 30 November 2011)

5 Dimensional 'Mature' (battlespace;
x+y+z+t+cyberspace dimensionality)

Advanced Battlespace *(devoid of t; time)*

I propose that it [advanced battlespace] should be based upon two spatial concepts—humanspace and cyberspace—and two spatial transcendents—stealth and data fusion (see Figure 1).[14]

Criteria	Definition
Humanspace	That aspect of battlespace composed of the traditional physical dimension of the human senses in which humans and their machines move and fight; the killing ground of future war.
Cyberspace	That aspect of battlespace composed of the electromagnetic spectrum and the non-human sensing dimension in which stealth-masked forces seek refuge from attack.
Stealth	The application of sensory defeating procedures and technologies which allow military forces to enter cyberspace.
Data fusion	The application of adaptive information processes to stealth-masked forces for target detection, identification, and location.

Figure 1. Advanced Battlespace Concepts

Humanspace represents the traditional physical dimension of the human senses within which military forces operate. This spatial concept has already been defined in *Force XXI Operations*, omitting the electromagnetic aspect. Cyberspace, on the other hand, represents not only the electromagnetic spectrum, but also that dimension in which military forces seek refuge for defensive purposes. Forces that enter this dimension are removed from the human-sensing based battlefield and are thus invulnerable to attack; at the same time, they retain the capacity to attack military forces that exist in humanspace. Any military force that has the capability of entering this non human-sensing dimension, be it Western or non-Western, must now be considered, respectively, either a highly advanced asset or a direct threat.

Based upon this tension between stealth and data fusion, the "human-sensing dimensional barrier" separating humanspace and cyberspace will represent a dynamic and contested frontier, a transdimensional forward edge of the battle area (FEBA) between opposing forces. [23]... The two concepts can be expressed as follows:

Defensive Premise: Stealth **>** Data Fusion **=** Cyberspace
Offensive Premise: Stealth **≤** Data Fusion **=** Humanspace

These spatial premises of advanced battlespace can be viewed in Figure 2, which portrays a threedimensional volume of battlespace bisected by a human-sensing fourth dimensional barrier. (Were time to be included in this concept of battlespace, it would represent a fifth dimensional attribute.) The figure is misleading— humanspace and cyberspace actually coexist in a given volume of battlespac—but it will have to suffice until conventions for expressing these concepts have become commonplace. Because stealth masked forces are inherently "invisible" to normal military forces, they can maneuver with relative impunity in cyberspace. Hence, the "battlefield" addressed in this essay, and portrayed crudely in Figure 2, appears to have twice the potential volume of the battlespace currently defined in FM 1005 and being applied to develop Force XXI theory.

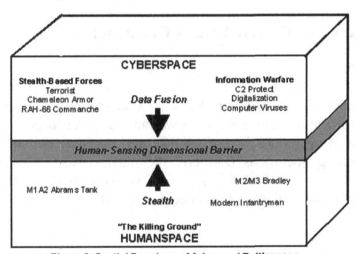

Figure 2. Spatial Premises of Advanced Battlespace

pp. 108-120.
"Advanced Battlespace and Cybermaneuver Concepts: Implications for Force XXI."
Parameters
Robert J. Bunker
Autumn 1996

Five-Dimensional Battlespace *(includes t: time)*

The basic theoretical outline of advanced, or five-dimensional, battlespace was provided in a BlueFor War College journal article.[23] It will suffice to say that it fuses the traditional three-dimensional battlespace cube (i.e., humanspace) and time (a fourth dimensional attribute) with the addition of a fifth-dimensional battlespace overlay which exists beyond the range of human senses (i.e., cyberspace).

pp. 7-8.
Five-Dimensional (Cyber) Warfighting: Can the Army After Next Be Defeated Through Complex Concepts and Technologies?
Carlisle Barracks, PA: Strategic Studies Institute, US Army War College
Robert J. Bunker
10 March 1998

Rejection of the Battlespace Construct

Battlespace

Rescinds the *operational framework* construct, including its subordinate constructs of *battlespace* and *battlefield organization*. (Area of operations is retained.) Retains decisive, shaping, and sustaining operations (formerly the purpose-based *battlefield organization*) and main effort as ways commanders describe subordinates' actions in the concept of operations.

Appendix D
FM 3-0 *Operations*
Headquarters, Department of the Army
February 2008

Appendix D
FM 3-0 *Operations*
Headquarters, Department of the Army
February 2011

Operational Environment *(relativistic concept; ambiguous physical, cyberspace, and electromagnetic mediums)*

1-2. An operational environment is a composite of the conditions, circumstances, and influences that affect the employment of capabilities and bear on the decisions of the commander (JP 3-0). Commanders at all levels have their own operational environments for their particular operations.

1-4. Modern information technology makes cyberspace and the electromagnetic spectrum indispensable for human interaction, including military operations and political competition. These two mediums inherently impact the influence of an operational environment and will be simultaneously congested and contested during operations. All actors—enemy, friendly, or neutral—remain potentially vulnerable to attack by physical means, cyberspace means, electronic means, or a combination thereof. Actions in and through cyberspace and the electromagnetic spectrum can affect the others.

1-1
ADRP 3-0 *Unified Land Operations*
Headquarters, Department of the Army
16 May 2012

Appendix III:
Selected Cyberspace and Dimensionality References

Compiled by Greta H. Andrusyszyn,
Robert J. Bunker, and Daniel Musa

This selected reference listing is principally drawn from the following resources along with some updated information specifically included for this book project. It does not contain the previously published works reprinted in sections of this new book:

Andrusyszyn, Greta. "The Fifth Domain." *Cyberspace: A Selected Bibliography.* Carlisle Barracks: U.S. Army War College Library, May 2013, http://www.carlisle.army.mil/library/bibs/Cyberspace2013.pdf

Bunker, Robert J. and Daniel Musa, *5ᵗʰ Dimensional Law Enforcement Operations.* FBI Library: Bibliographies and Subject Guides. 12 December 2012, http://fbilibrary.libguides.com/content.php?pid=330445

Books, Documents, and Internet Resources

Abbot, Edwin Abbott. *Flatland: A Romance of Many Dimensions.* London: Seeley, 1884. Reprint: Oxford: Oxford University Press, 2006. 124 pp. (QA699 .A13 2006)

Bunker, Robert J. "Chapter 10, "Technology in a Neo-Clausewitzian Setting," in Gert de Nooy, ed., *The Clausewitzian Dictum and the Future of Western Military Strategy*, Boston, MA: Kluwer Law International, 1997, pp. 137-165. (U162 .C57 1997)

Bunker, Robert J. "Reverse Engineering Asymmetric Warfare: Applying Space-Time, Matter-Energy and Organizational-Doctrinal Analysis to Al Qaeda Operations," in Tessaleno C. Devezas, ed., NATO Security through Science Series – E. Human and Societal

Dynamics, Volume 5: *Kondratieff Waves, Warfare and World Security.* Amsterdam: IOS Press, 2006, pp. 228-235.

Eassa, Charles N. *Enabling Combatant Commander's Ability to Conduct Operations in the Cyber Domain.* Strategy Research Project. Carlisle Barracks: U.S. Army War College, March 3, 2012. 22pp. (AD-A560-774) http://handle.dtic.mil/100.2/ADA560774

Gibson, William. *Neuromancer.* New York: Ace Book, 1984. 271 pp. (PS3557.I2264 N48 1984)

Gibson, William. *Burning Chrome.* New York: Ace Books, 1987. 200 pp. PS3557.I2264 B86 1986)

Gompert, David C., and Phillip C. Saunders. "Mutual Restraint in Cyberspace." In *The Paradox of Power: Sino-American Strategic Restraint in an Age of Vulnerability,* 115-151. Washington, DC: U.S. National Defense University, Institute for National Strategic Studies, Center for the Study of Chinese Military Affairs, 2011. (JZ1480 .A57C63 2011) http://www.ndu.edu/inss/docUploaded/Paradox%20 of%20Power.pdf

Gray, Colin S. *Making Strategic Sense of Cyber Power: Why the Sky Is Not Falling.* Carlisle Barracks: U.S. Army War College Press and Strategic Studies Institute, April 2013. 67pp. (U413 .A66G7292 2013) http://www.strategicstudiesinstitute.army.mil/pubs/download. cfm?q=1147

Henderson, Linda D. *The Fourth Dimension and Non-Euclidean Geometry in Modern Art.* Cambridge: The MIT Press, 2013. 729 pp. (N6490 .H44 2013)

Kaku, Michio. *Hyperspace. A Scientific Odyssey Through Parallel Universes, Time Warps, and the 10th Dimension.* New York: Anchor Books, 1994. 359 pp. (530.142 K13 1994)

Kaku, Michio. *Physics of the Impossible: A Scientific Exploration into the World of Phasers, Force Fields, Teleportation, and Time Travel.* New York: Doubleday, 2008. 329 pp. (QC75 .K18 2008)

Lanier, Jaron. *You Are Not a Gadget: A Manifesto.* New York: Vintage Books, 2011. 223pp. (HM851 .L36 2011)

May, Jeffrey A. *A Model for Command and Control of Cyberspace.* Strategy Research Project. Carlisle Barracks: U.S. Army War College, February 14, 2012. 23pp. (AD-A561-493) http://handle.dtic.mil/100.2/ADA561493

Mesic, Richard, et al. *Air Force Cyber Command (Provisional) Decision Support.* Santa Monica: RAND, 2010. 23pp. (UG633 .A47 2010) http://www.rand.org/pubs/monographs/2010/RAND_MG935.1.pdf

Morgan, Dwight R. *Defending the New Domain: Cyberspace.* Strategy Research Project. Carlisle Barracks: U.S. Army War College, March 21, 2011. 23pp. (AD-A560-175) http://handle.dtic.mil/100.2/ADA560175

Porche, Isaac R., III, et al. *Redefining Information Warfare Boundaries for an Army in a Wireless World.* Santa Monica: RAND, 2013. 142pp. (U163 .P67 2013) http://www.rand.org/content/dam/rand/pubs/monographs/MG1100/MG1113/RAND_MG1113.pdf

Reid, Desmond A., Jr. *Cyber Sentries: Preparing Defenders to Win in a Contested Domain.* Strategy Research Project. Carlisle Barracks: U.S. Army War College, February 7, 2012. 29pp. (AD-A561-779) http://handle.dtic.mil/100.2/ADA561779

Reister, Brett. *Cyberspace: Regional and Global Perspectives.* Strategy Research Project. Carlisle Barracks: U.S. Army War College, February 22, 2012. 25pp. (AD-A561-780) http://handle.dtic.mil/100.2/ADA561780

Rucker, Rudy. *Geometry, Relativity, and the Fourth Dimension.* New York: Dover, 1977. 133 pp. (QA699 .R8 1977)

Rucker, Rudy. *The Fourth Dimension: A Guided Tour of the Higher Universe.* Boston: Houghton Mifflin, 1984. 228 pp. (QA699 .R795 1984)

Schilling, Jeffery R. *Defining Our National Cyberspace Boundaries.* Strategy Research Project. Carlisle Barracks: U.S. Army War College, February 17, 2010. 26pp. (AD-A518-322) http://handle.dtic.mil/100.2/ADA518322

Schosek, Kurt. *Military Cyberspace: From Evolution to Revolution.* Strategy Research Project. Carlisle Barracks: U.S. Army War College, February 8, 2012. 26pp. (AD-A561-509) http://handle.dtic.mil/100.2/ADA561509

Shaul, Frank A. *Command and Control of the Department of Defense in Cyberspace.* Strategy Research Project. Carlisle Barracks: U.S. Army War College, March 24, 2011. 26pp. (AD- A560-146) http://handle.dtic.mil/100.2/ADA560146

Simpson, Michael S. *Cyber Domain Evolving in Concept, but Stymied by Slow Implementation.* Strategy Research Project. Carlisle Barracks: U.S. Army War College, March 19, 2010. 25pp. (AD-A520-145) http://handle.dtic.mil/100.2/ADA520145

Smith, Alan G.R. *Science and Society in the Sixteenth and Seventeenth Centuries,* History of European Civilization Library, in Geoffrey Barraclough, ed., New York: Harcourt Brace Jovanovich, Inc., 1972. pp. 9-27. (Q 125 S68 1972)

Stephenson, Neal. *Snow Crash.* New York: Bantam Books, 1992. 470 pp. (PS3569.T3868 S65 1993)

Tyrell, Marc W.D. 'Broad typologies of battlespaces.' Section of "The Use of Evolutionary Theory in Modeling Culture and Cultural Conflict," in Thomas H. Johnson and Barry Scott Zellen, eds.,

Culture, Conflict, and Counterinsurgency. Palo Alto: Stanford University Press, 2014. 46-76 pp.

Wertheim, Margaret. *The Pearly Gates of Cyberspace: A History of Space from Dante to the Internet.* New York: W.W. Norton & Company, 2000. 336 pp. (QA76.9.C66 W48 1999).

Articles

Adams, Thomas K. "Future Warfare and the Decline of Human Decisionmaking." *Parameters* 51, no. 4 (Winter 2001-2002): 57-71. http://strategicstudiesinstitute.army.mil/pubs/parameters/articles/01winter/adams.htm

Ahmed, Murad. "Muggle Scientist Unveils 'Invisibility Cloak." *The Times.* (1 March 2013): 3.

Alexander, Keith B. "Building a New Command in Cyberspace." *Strategic Studies Quarterly* 5, no. 2 (Summer 2011): 3-12. http://www.au.af.mil/au/ssq/2011/summer/alexander.pdf

Andrues, Wesley R. "What U.S. Cyber Command Must Do." *Joint Force Quarterly,* no. 59 (4th Quarter 2010): 115-120.

Associated Foreign Press. "New device invisible to magnetic fields." *ABC Science.* (23 March 2012). http://www.abc.net.au/science/articles/2012/03/23/3461975.htm

Associated Press. "Downloadable Gun Parts Trigger Worries." *Los Angeles Times.* (22 December 2012): B3.

Barcott, Bruce. "Invisible, Inc." *The Atlantic.* (July/August 2011): 80-82, 84.

Batson, Mickey, and Matthew Labert. "Expanding the Non-Kinetic Warfare Arsenal." *Proceedings: United States Naval Institute* 138, no. 1 (January 2012): 40-44.

Bhushan, Navneet. "Preparing Indian Soldiers for a 7-Dimensional war." *Frontier India*, January 6, 2013, http://frontierindia.net/preparing-indian-soldiers-for-a-7-dimensional-war#axzz2Zjrb5eg3

Bond, Nelson. "The Monster from Nowhere." *Science Fiction Adventure Classics*. (January 1974): 122-132. (Reprint of 1939 story)

Bunker, Robert J. "Weapons of Mass Disruption and Terrorism." *Terrorism and Political Violence* 12, no, 1. (Spring 2000): 37-46.

Butler, Sean C. "Refocusing Cyber Warfare Thought." *Air & Space Power Journal* 27, no. 1 (January-February 2013): 44-57.

Cameron, Charles. "Alice's Wonderland Battlespace." *Zenpundit Blog*. (23 August 2011). http://zenpundit.com/?p=4280

Card, Kendall L., and Michael S. Rogers. "The Navy's Newest Warfighting Imperative." *Proceedings: United States Naval Institute* 138, no. 10 (October 2012): 22-26.

Creedon, Madelyn R. "Space and Cyber: Shared Challenges, Shared Opportunities." *Strategic Studies Quarterly* 6, no. 1 (Spring 2012): 3-8. http://www.au.af.mil/au/ssq/2012/spring/creedon.pdf

Dawley, Shawn M. "A Case for a Cyberspace Combatant Command." *Air & Space Power Journal* 27, no. 1 (January-February 2013): 130-142.

Deibert, Ronald. "Tracking the Emerging Arms Race in Cyberspace." Interview. *Bulletin of the Atomic Scientists* 67, no. 1 (January/ February 2011): 1-8.

Deibert, Ronald, and Rafal Rohozinski. "Liberation vs. Control: The Future of Cyberspace." *Journal of Democracy* 21, no. 4 (October 2010): 43-57.

Dvorsky, George. "Scientists 'Freeze' Light for an Entire Minute." *io9*. (25 July 2013). http://io9.com/scientists-freeze-light-for-an-entire-minute-912634479

Economist Online. "Arms Control in the Fifth Domain: Cybersecurity." (6 October 2011). http://www.economist.com/blogs/clausewitz/2011/10/cybersecurity

Emspak, Jesse. "'Invisibility' cloak may hide things from sonar." *CBS News*. (24 March 2014). http://www.cbsnews.com/news/invisibility-cloak-may-hide-things-from-sonar/

Frystacki, Henryk. "Discovery of the Fifth Dimension." *Huffpost Tech: UK*. (12 March 2013). http://www.huffingtonpost.co.uk/henryk-frystacki-phd/discovery-of-the-fifth-dimension_b_2858709.html

Gjelten, Tom. "Internet Peace vs. Internet Freedom: Behind the Cyber 'Disarmament' Debate." *Army* 61, no. 3 (March 2011): 30-32, 34, 36.

Gompert, David C., and Michael Kofman. "Raising Our Sights: Russian-American Strategic Restraint in an Age of Vulnerability." *Institute for Strategic Studies Forum,* January 2012. http://www.ndu.edu/inss/docUploaded/SF%20274%20Gompert%20and%20Koffman.pdf

Granstedt, Ed, and Troy Nolan. "Securing the Info Advantage." *Armed Forces Journal* 147, no. 10 (June 2010): 28-30. http://www.armedforcesjournal.com/2010/06/4614742

Gray, Richard. "Star Trek-style force-field armour being developed by military scientists." *The Telegraph*. (20 March 2010). http://www.telegraph.co.uk/technology/news/7487740/Star-Trek-style-force-field-armour-being-developed-by-military-scientists.html

Greenert, Jonathan W. "Imminent Domain." [Future of warfighting will be in the electromagnetic-cyber arena] *Proceedings: United States Naval Institute* 138, no. 12 (December 2012): 16-21.

Hammes, T. X. "Offshore Control: A Proposed Strategy for an Unlikely Conflict." *Institute for National Strategic Studies,* June 2012. http://www.ndu.edu/inss/docUploaded/SF%20278%20Hammes.pdf

Hernandez, Rhett A. "Transforming Cyber Operations while at War." *Army* 61, no. 10 (October 2011): 195-197.

Hernandez, Rhett A. "U.S. Army Cyber Command: Cyberspace for America's Force of Decisive Action." *Army* 62, no. 10 (October 2012): 205-206, 208.

Hollis, David M. "USCYBERCOM [United States Cyber Command]: The Need for a Combatant Command versus a Subunified Command." *Joint Force Quarterly,* no. 58 (3rd Quarter 2010): 48-53.

Hurley, Matthew M. "For and From Cyberspace: Conceptualizing Cyber Intelligence, Surveillance, and Reconnaissance." *Air & Space Power Journal* 26, no. 6 (November- December 2012): 12-33.

Inkster, Nigel. "China in Cyberspace." *Survival* 52, no. 4 (August-September 2010): 55-66.

Jabbour, Kamal. "Cyber Vision and Cyber Force Development." *Strategic Studies Quarterly* 4, no. 1 (Spring 2010): 63-73. http://www.au.af.mil/au/ssq/2010/spring/jabbour.pdf

Klimburg, Alexander. "Mobilising Cyber Power." *Survival* 53, no. 1 (February-March 2011): 41- 60.

Lee, Robert M. "The Interim Years of Cyberspace." *Air & Space Power Journal* 27, no. 1 (January-February 2013): 58-79.

Leigber, William E. "Learning to Operate in Cyberspace." *Proceedings: United States Naval Institute* 137, no. 2 (February 2011): 32-37.

Li, Shan. "Putting 'real' in virtual reality." *Los Angeles Times.* (14 October 2011): A1, A12.

Lin, Herbert. "Escalation Dynamics and Conflict Termination in Cyberspace." *Strategic Studies Quarterly* 6, no. 3 (Fall 2012): 46-70. http://www.au.af.mil/au/ssq/2012/fall/lin.pdf

Lynn, William J., III. "Defending a New Domain: The Pentagon's Cyberstrategy." *Foreign Affairs* 89, no. 5 (September/October 2010): 97-108.

Manzo, Vincent. "Deterrence and Escalation in Cross-Domain Operations: Where Do Space and Cyberspace Fit?" *Joint Force Quarterly*, no. 66 (3rd Quarter 2012): 8-14.

Mick, Jason. "Scientists Simplify Cloaking Tech, Can Cloak Bigger Objects." *Daily Tech.* (21 May 2009). http://www.dailytech.com/Scientists+Simplify+Cloaking+Tech+Can+Cloak+Bigger+Objects/article15200.htm

Mowchan, John A. "Don't Draw the (Red) Line." *Proceedings: United States Naval Institute* 137, no. 10 (October 2011): 16-20.

Ozolek, David J. "The Rapid, Decisive Operation: A Construct for an American Way of War in the 21st Century." *Australian Defence Force Journal*, no. 144 (September-October 2000): 12-20.

Parascandola, Rocco. "NYPD Commissioner says department will begin testing a new high-tech device that scans for concealed weapons." *New York Daily News.* (23 January 2013). http://www.nydailynews.com/new-york/nypd-readies-scan-and-frisk-article-1.1245663

Porche, Isaac R., III, Jerry M. Sollinger, and Shawn McKay. "An Enemy without Boundaries." *Proceedings: United States Naval Institute* 138, no. 10 (October 2012): 34-39.

Redden, Mark E., and Michael P. Hughes. "Defense Planning Paradigms and the Global Commons." *Joint Force Quarterly*, no. 60 (1st Quarter 2011): 61-66.

Rustici, Ross M. "Cyberweapons: Leveling the International Playing Field." *Parameters* 41, no. 3 (Autumn 2011): 32-42.

Schmid, Randolph E. "Cloak of Invisibility Takes a Step Forward." *3 News*. (19 March 2010). http://www.3news.co.nz/Cloak-of-invisibility-takes-a-step-forward/tabid/1160/articleID/147165/Default.aspx

Science Daily. "Invisibility Undone: Chinese Scientists Demonstrate How To Uncloak An Invisible Object." (4 September 2008). http://www.sciencedaily.com/releases/2008/09/080903073016.htm

Science Daily. "'Invisibility Cloak' Successfully Hides Objects Placed Under It." (2 May 2009). http://www.sciencedaily.com/releases/2009/05/090501154143.htm

Science Daily. "New invisibility cloak hides objects from human view." (28 July 2011). http://www.sciencedaily.com/releases/2011/07/110727121651.htm

Serna, Joseph. "Scientists infuse 'life' into tiny particles." *Los Angeles Times*. (2 February 2013): AA2.

Shachtman, Noah. "'Invisible' Material Can Now Fool Your Eyes." *Wired*. (4 November 2010). http://www.wired.com/dangerroom/2010/11/invisibile-material-can-now-fool-your-eyes/

Shay, Christopher. "China's Great (Quantum) Leap Forward." *Time*. (9 September 2010). http://content.time.com/time/world/article/0,8599,2016687,00.html

Singh, Ajay. "Time: The New Dimension in War." *Joint Forces Quarterly*, no. 10 (Winter 1995-96): 56-61.

Stavridis, James G., and Elton C. Parker, III. "Sailing the Cyber Sea." *Joint Force Quarterly*, no. 65 (2nd Quarter 2012): 61-67.

Steenhuysen, Julie. "U.S. scientists learn how to levitate tiny objects." *Reuters.* (7 January 2009). http://www.reuters.com/article/2009/01/07/us-nanotech-levitation-idUSTRE50672320090107

Technology Review. "Invisibility Tiles Can Cloak Any Shape." (27 October 2011). http://www.technologyreview.com/view/425944/invisibility-tiles-can-cloak-any-shape/

Trias, Eric D., and Bryan M. Bell. "Cyber This, Cyber That... So What?" *Air & Space Power Journal* 24, no. 1 (Spring 2010): 90-100.

Vacca, W. Alexander. "Military Culture and Cyber Security." *Survival* 53, no. 6 (December 2011-January 2012): 159-176.

"War in the Fifth Domain; Cyberwar." *Economist* 396, no. 8689 (July 3, 2010): 25-28.

Wass de Czege, Huba. "Warfare by Internet: The Logic of Strategic Deterrence, Defense, and Attack." *Military Review* 90, no. 4 (July-August 2010): 85-96.

Weiss, Rick. "Their Deepest, Darkest Discovery: Scientists Create a Black That Erases Virtually All Light." *Washington Post* (20 February 2008): 1. http://www.washingtonpost.com/wp-dyn/content/article/2008/02/19/AR2008021902617.html

Wiezman, Eyal. "Lethal Theory." *2030: War Zone Amsterdam* (2009): 81-99. http://www.skor.nl/_files/Files/OPEN18_P80-99(1).pdf. See also http://roundtable.klein.org/files/roundtable/ weizman_lethal%20theory.pdf (2006 document).

Williams, Brett T. "Ten Propositions Regarding Cyberspace Operations." *Joint Force Quarterly,* no. 61 (2nd Quarter 2011): 10-17.

Zand, Bernhard. "Finding the Right Mix: German Invents Radar Camouflaging Paint." *Spiegel Online International.* (2 May 2008). http://www.spiegel.de/international/business/finding-the-right-mix-german-invents-radar-camouflaging-paint-a-551152.html

Biographies

Editors

Robert J. Bunker is a Distinguished Visiting Professor and Minerva Chair at the Strategic Studies Institute, U.S. Army War College. He is also Adjunct Faculty, Department of Politics and Economics, Claremont Graduate University. Past positions include Futurist in Residence, Training and Development Division, Behavioral Science Unit, Federal Bureau of Investigation Academy; Director of Research (Contract) Counter-OPFOR Program, National Law Enforcement and Corrections Technology Center-West; and Fellow, Institute of Land Warfare, Association of the U.S. Army. He holds a Doctorate in Political Science from Claremont Graduate University, degrees in Government, Behavioral Science, Social Science, Anthropology-Geography and History, and has undertaken hundreds of hours of counter-terrorism and counter-cartel training. Dr. Bunker has hundreds of publications including the edited works *Criminal Insurgencies in Mexico and the Americas* (Routledge, 2012), *Narcos Over the Border* (Routledge, 2011); *Criminal-States and Criminal-Soldiers* (Routledge, 2008), *Networks, Terrorism and Global Insurgency* (Routledge, 2005); and *Non-State Threats and Future Wars* (Routledge, 2002).

Charles "Sid" Heal retired as a Commander from the Los Angeles Sheriff's Department in 2008 after nearly 33 years of service, more than half of which was spent in units charged with handling law enforcement special and emergency operations. In addition, he retired from the Marine Corps Reserve after 35 years and four tours of combat in four different wars. He is the author of *Sound Doctrine* (Lantern, 2000) and *Field Command* (Lantern, 2012), as well as more than 160 articles on law enforcement subjects. He holds a Bachelor's degree in Police Science from California State University, Los Angeles; a Masters degree in Public Administration from the University of Southern California and a Masters degree in Management from California Polytechnic University, Pomona. He is also a graduate of the FBI's National Academy and the California

Command College. He continues to teach and consult throughout the United States and other countries and is a frequent presenter at the U.S. war colleges.

Contributors

Greta H. Andrusyszyn has a Masters of Library Science from Syracuse University and a B.A. in Creative Writing & Literature, with a minor in Anthropology, from LeMoyne College. She has been employed by the U.S. Army since August 2006, starting at Fort Knox Library and coming to the U.S. Army War College Library in 2008 as a Research Librarian. Since arriving at the U.S. Army War College, Mrs. Andrusyszyn has compiled several bibliographies on subjects including Terrorism, Officership, Civil-Military Relations, and Conflict Termination.

Khirin A. Bunker is in the political science honors program at the University of California Riverside and is a co-founder and a Director of the Political Science Society. He has interned at the Claremont Institute for the Study of Statesmanship and Political Philosophy, *Small Wars Journal—El Centro*, and at a law firm. He holds an International Baccalaureate (IB) degree, is a member of Phi Beta Kappa, and has co-written works on the Mexican cartels.

Adam Elkus is a PhD student in Computational Social Science at George Mason University. He studies computational models of strategy and evolution. He has published on technology, strategy, and security at *Foreign Policy*, the *Small Wars Journal, Red Team Journal*, and other publications. Adam holds a BA in Diplomacy and World Affairs from Occidental College, and an MA in Security Studies from Georgetown. He currently blogs at CTOVision, AnalystOne, and other technology publications.

Christopher Flaherty has been based in London since 2008 and is a Senior Research Associate of the Terrorism Research Center. He is an active contributor on security, terrorism early warning, and related international intelligence issues. He was involved in the development of a 'Scripted Agent Based Microsimulation Project', at the University of Wollongong (NSW, Australia). Dr. Flaherty specializes in the area of Mass Gathering Vulnerability analysis, and risk analysis projects for building facilities in the U.K. and U.S. His work covers a broad spectrum of risk-related endeavors including resilience, counter-terrorism, critical infrastructure protection, 3D tactics, fragmentation and vulnerability analysis. He has a Ph.D. in Economic Relations from the University of Melbourne with a focus on networking and, following this, he pursued a career in defence and security research initially in the Australian Department of Defence. He is co-primary author of *Body Cavity Bombers: The New Martyrs* (iUniverse, 2013) and the author of *Australian Manoeuvrist Strategy* (Seaview Press, 1996) and numerous security and terrorism focused articles.

Lois (Pilant) Grossman has been a contributing editor and writer for *TechBeat,* the award winning magazine for the National Institute of Justice (NIJ), National Law Enforcement and Corrections Technology Center (NLECTC) system, and many other law enforcement publications.

Lois Clark McCoy has been a life-long advocate for professionalism in disaster responses. She is the founder and former President of the National Institute for Urban Search and Rescue (NIUSR), a non-profit organization dedicated to finding improved ways of saving lives in times of disaster, both caused by Mother Nature and by man. She excels in forming cooperative efforts and gaining support from diverse groups, stakeholders and decision makers in both the private and public sectors.

T. Lindsay Moore is Adjunct Professor in the Center for Peace and Security Studies Program at The Edmund A. Walsh School of Foreign Service, Georgetown University. Past positions include Program Director at the Claremont Graduate University, Assistant Professorships at the Naval War College, the National Defense University, the United States Marine Corps Command and Staff College, the United States Military Academy (West Point), and the University of Miami. He holds a Masters degree in Government and a Doctorate in International Relations from the Claremont Graduate

School and a law degree from the University of Miami. Dr. Moore has spoken to various governmental, professional, and academic audiences including at the Association of the United States Army national meeting and the American Bar Association. Publications include book chapters, reports, papers, and encyclopedia essays. He was the principal writer and analyst contributing to *Comprehensive Report of the Special Advisor to the President on Iraq's WMD* (Washington: USGPO, 2005).

Daniel Musa is a student at the University of Southern California who will graduate in May 2015 with a B.A. in International Relations. Born in Nigeria, he is a dual citizen of both Nigeria and the United States. While at USC, he has served as a Resident Assistant for the Department of Residential Education, spent a summer in Washington D.C. doing a management consulting internship with Plexus Consulting Group, and did a business sales internship for Google in Mountain View. Mr. Musa is a co-contributor to multiple Subject Bibliographies for the FBI Academy Library, Quantico, VA.

John P. Sullivan is a career police officer. He currently serves as a lieutenant with the Los Angeles County Sheriff's Department. He is also an adjunct researcher at the Vortex Foundation in Bogotá, Colombia; a senior research fellow at the Center for Advanced Studies on Terrorism (CAST); and a senior fellow at *Small Wars Journal—El Centro*. He is co-editor of *Countering Terrorism and WMD: Creating a Global Counter-Terrorism Network* (Routledge, 2006) and *Global Biosecurity: Threats and Responses* (Routledge, 2010) and co-author of *Mexico's Criminal Insurgency: A Small Wars Journal-El Centro Anthology* (iUniverse, 2011) and *Studies in Gangs and Cartels* (Routledge, 2013). He completed the CREATE Executive Program in Counter-Terrorism at the University of Southern California and holds a BA in Government form the College of William and Mary, a MA in Urban Affairs and Policy Analysis from the New School for Social Research, and a PhD, Information and Knowledge Society, from the Internet Interdisciplinary Institute (IN3) at the Open University of Catalonia.

Back Images: (1) Photo of the Active Denial System (ADS) mounted on U.S. Military Humvee. ADS generates an invisible pain barrier which human beings are unable to penetrate. (2) Photo from policing magazine showing infrared attachment allowing for cyberspace imagery. Sources: U.S. DOD Photo (For Public Release) and Lois Pilant, "The Fifth Element." *Police Magazine*, August 2002.